M000043204

Professor Risley

and the

IMPERIAL JAPANESE TROUPE

Other Books by Frederik L. Schodt

ORIGINAL WORKS

Manga! Manga! The World of Japanese Comics

Inside the Robot Kingdom: Japan, Mechatronics, and the Coming Robotopia

America and the Four Japans: Friend, Foe, Model, Mirror

Dreamland Japan: Writings on Modern Manga

Native American in the Land of the Shogun: Ranald MacDonald and the Opening of Japan

The Astro Boy Essays: Osamu Tezuka, Mighty Atom, and the Manga/Anime Revolution

TRANSLATIONS

Mobile Suit Gundam: Awakening, Escalation, Confrontation, by Yoshiyuki Tomino

Gaku Stories, by Makoto Shiina (U.S. title: *My Boy: A Father's Memories*)

Jack and Betty Stories, by Yoshinori Shimizu

The Four Immigrants Manga: A Japanese Experience in San Francisco, 1904–1924, by Henry Yoshitaka Kiyama

Starting Point: 1979–1996, by Hayao Miyazaki (translated with Beth Cary)

Professor Risley
and the
IMPERIAL JAPANESE TROUPE

How an American Acrobat
Introduced Circus to Japan—
and Japan to the West

Frederik L. Schodt

Stone Bridge Press • Berkeley, California

Published by
Stone Bridge Press
P.O. Box 8208
Berkeley CA 94707
510-524-8732 • sbp@stonebridge.com • www.stonebridge.com

The author and publisher are grateful to The Japan Foundation and The Suntory Foundation for their generous support in difficult economic times.

Text ©2012 Frederik L. Schodt, www.jai2.com.

Book design and layout by Linda Ronan.

FRONTISPIECE: Detail of an illustration showing The Imperials at work. From *The Mask*, vol. 1, February–December 1868.

All rights reserved.

No part of this book may be reproduced in any form without permission from the publisher.

Printed in the United States of America.

10 9 8 7 6 5 4 3 2 1   2016 2015 2014 2013 2012

LIBRARY OF CONGRESS CATALOGING-IN-PUBLICATION DATA
Schodt, Frederik L., 1950–.
  Professor Risley & the imperial Japanese troupe : how an American acrobat introduced circus to Japan—and Japan to the West / Frederik L. Schodt.
    p. cm.
  Includes bibliographical references and index.
  ISBN 978-1-61172-009-9
1. Risley, Richard, 1814–1874. 2. Acrobats—United States. 3. Circus performers—United States. 4. Circus—United States—History. 5. Circus—Japan—History. 6. Circus—Japan—Western influences. 7. United States—Relations—Japan. 8. Japan—Relations—United States. 9. Popular culture—United States. 10. Popular culture—Japan. I. Title.
  GV550.2.R57S45 2012
  791.3'4092—dc23
  [B]
                        2012031056

This book is dedicated, with love, to Fiammetta Hsu

CONTENTS

PREFACE

On my desk I have a reproduction of an 1887 children's pop-up book by Lothar Meggendorfer called *International Circus*. It's one of my prized possessions, for it shows not only how cosmopolitan the circus world was in the nineteenth century, but also how popular Japanese acts were. It's a masterpiece of six scenes that unfold in three-dimensions and spectacular color, revealing Europeans, Africans, and Asians in a variety of acts. A Mr. Funtolo performs stunts atop his horse while it jumps over a flaming gate. Clara Springel leaps and somersaults through a hoop from atop her pony. And a man dressed in a Turkish outfit performs the "Sultan's Courier," straddling and standing on the backs of a quartet of galloping horses.

The fifth scene, the only nonequestrian one, is the most exotic. With the caption of "The clever acrobats of the Oriental Company perform amazing tricks," it unfolds to show two pairs of kimono-clad Japanese acrobats, executing exciting feats of balance in front of an adoring European crowd of top-hatted men and bonnet-wearing women. One pair is doing a "perch" act. A man stands, balancing a soaring bamboo pole vertically from his hips, while a boy, skillfully holding on to the top of the pole, carries out a variety of gymnastic gyrations. Despite the herculean effort required, the man holding the pole is shown nonchalantly fanning himself with a Japanese folding fan. The other pair is performing the "transformation fox scene." In this stunt, an adult Japanese man lies on his back on a mat on the ground, the top of his tonsured head facing us. His arms are free and he, too, is using one of his hands to fan himself, seemingly without a care in the world, but his legs are pointed straight up at the ceiling. On the soles of his feet he vertically balances a giant *shoji* screen, on top of which is poised a boy dressed up like a fox. This mischievous fox-boy has smashed many of the rice-paper panels of the screen while cavorting in and out of the frame, and he is making funny gestures at the amazed audience.

Both of these acts were regularly performed by Japanese acrobatic groups that toured the United States and Europe in the latter part of the nineteenth century. And no Japanese acrobatic group drew more attention than "Professor" Risley's Imperial Japanese Troupe, for it was one of the first, arguably the best, and certainly the most influential. Indeed, the fox character in Meggendorfer's pop-up book could well be a depiction of Hamaikari Umekichi, a young troupe member affectionately known as "Little All Right," who in 1867 became a global celebrity, his name a metaphor for agility and panache.

★

I have spent much of my adult life writing about Japanese popular culture, technology, and history, and about the flow of information and people between Japan and the rest of the world. My circus connections are tenuous. As a boy I never seriously considered running away to join the Big Top, nor did I have any particular acrobatic talent. But I grew up on four different continents, and since my mother always liked the circus, we often went to see local shows and magic or juggling acts. For the last fifteen years or so, moreover, I have lived and worked only a few steps away from San Francisco's Circus Center and with fascination watched aspiring young acrobats and jugglers and clowns train in its facilities. That, in addition to my interest in nineteenth-century cross-cultural events, is probably a big reason my curiosity was stimulated a few years back when I came across mentions in Japan of Professor Risley and his Imperial Japanese Troupe.

For me, this discovery of Risley and his troupe was quite an eye-opener. There are other well-documented examples of Japanese popular culture greatly influencing the outside world. The late nineteenth-century *Japonisme* art movement—when Japan's "low culture" woodblock prints became the rage among "high culture" European and American artists—is one. The end-of-the-millennium "Cool Japan" movement—which includes modern Japanese *manga, anime,* fashion, and J-pop music and continues today—is another. Yet despite having studied and written about Japanese culture for decades, I had somehow been unaware of the late-nineteenth-century, short-lived global boom in the popularity of Japanese performers, especially acrobats. This other boom began right after the opening of Japan, after it had been secluded from the outside world for nearly two and a half centuries. It coexisted in time with the *Japonisme* art movement, yet had little in common with that movement except for its "Japanese-ness." It involved not things, but people—Japanese commoners who were traveling overseas and viewing the West for the first time, and ordinary Europeans and Americans who were ogling the exotic performers from the East. And it was triggered by the work of Professor Risley.

It was inevitable, perhaps, that Risley and the Imperial Japanese Troupe, and even the global boom in Japanese performers that he helped spawn, would later be largely forgotten. Risley was literate. He straddled the worlds of both theatre and circus, and he could socialize with both the high and the low. But as far as is known, he never authored a book or diary or left any letters in his own hand that survive. There are numerous illustrations of him. Yet despite living a life that depended on self-promotion and publicity and extended well into the age of daguerreotypes, tintypes, and even modern photographs, the few photographs usually attributed to him—that might make him seem more modern—are difficult to authenticate. And despite his notoriety, he failed to inspire any writers of his era to write at length about him. The reasons for this include timing, his absence from the United States at critical periods, and the ultimate failure of many of his enterprises.

Another factor, however, is that, in both Japan and the West, circus and theatre performers existed on the fringes of normal society. Acrobats and jugglers, especially, were often only semiliterate and sometimes treated almost as social outcasts who inhabited a transient, ephemeral, and mysterious world. When generations turned over, when the twentieth century began, with all its revolutions and convulsions and new technology and slaughter, and when Japan forgot its own past in its pell-mell rush to modernize, many wonderful performers from earlier years faded from sight.

In doing the research for this book, the story of Professor Risley became as interesting to me as that of his Imperial Japanese Troupe. Risley was born in New Jersey around 1814 and died in a lunatic asylum in 1874. In an era of many larger-than-life figures, he was without doubt one of its more colorful characters. An acrobat who became an impresario, he was certainly one of the most widely traveled, for he went back and forth among multiple continents at a time when the average person was probably born, lived, and died within a fifty-mile radius. As an individual in the mid-nineteenth century who lived in the demimonde of the theatre and circus and left few records of his own, Risley's movements are remarkably well-documented. Yet he remains a mysterious figure who fades in and out of the mist of history, sometimes coming into clear focus and then sometimes vanishing completely from view. While doing research on him, I constantly found myself consumed by burning questions. How did he decide to go to Japan? In 1866, how did he come up with the idea of forming a troupe of Japanese acrobats and jugglers and taking them overseas? How did he succeed, when so many others did not? What, in his background, made him such a pioneer in the globalization of popular culture?

This book will not answer every question about Risley and his Troupe, but I hope it will contribute to a greater awareness of them and will stimulate curiosity about the spread of popular culture and the performing arts around the world. If I can shed light on a little-known but fascinating story, and show how individuals—who may not have high social status or official connections—can transcend vast cultural differences and do extraordinary things, I will be happy.

★

Wherever possible I have relied on primary source information, rather than what others have written, and kept speculation to a minimum. Even thirty years ago, a project like this would have been next to impossible, because there was either not enough information available or it was too fragmented and difficult to access. Since then, however, several big changes have occurred.

In 1975, the diary of Takano Hirohachi—the overseer or manager of the Imperial Japanese Troupe—was rediscovered by some of his descendants in Iinomachi, his village in Japan. In the poorly documented world of semi-literate nineteenth-century popular entertainers, this diary is an extraordinary document. It is first and foremost a day-to-day, detailed record of the troupe's movements in the United States and Europe, showing where they went and what they did. But it also represents the written impression of one of the first Japanese commoners—other than a few poor shipwrecked castaways—to see the West, after Japan's nearly two hundred and fifty years of official seclusion from the outside world.

The discovery of the diary subsequently set in place a movement among Japanese writers and scholars to confirm the movements of the troupe, and to correlate them with global events. And without their formidable efforts my book would have been impossible. The original diary, in hard-to-read and fading, free flowing mid-nineteenth-century Japanese calligraphy—rendered by a social outsider who spoke a north-eastern dialect and probably taught himself how to read and write—is exceedingly difficult to read today.

Luckily, in 1977 the Iinomachi historical society painstakingly transcribed Hirohachi's handwritten diary and published it as a small, limited-edition book. This generated much media interest. In 1983 the well-known writer Yasuoka Shōtarō began serializing a story titled *Daiseikimatsu saakasu* ("The grand fin-de-siècle circus") in the prestigious *Asahi Journal* magazine, and five years later it was compiled into what became a popular book. It was one of the first attempts to put the diary into a historical context, and it greatly helped raise awareness of Hirohachi's story. In 1999, another book based on the diary appeared, titled *Umi wo watatta bakumatsu no kyokugeidan* ("The *bakumatsu* acrobatic troupe that crossed the seas"), by popular historian Miyanaga Takashi. In this case, Miyanaga undertook the physically daunting task of traveling to most of the sites mentioned in the diary and attempting to confirm them. During this period there was also considerable research done by other scholars, writing articles in journals and magazines. Of the academic researchers in Japan, no one has done as much work on the story of the Imperials as Mihara Aya, a specialist in nineteenth-century Japanese performing arts history, especially that of the multiple Japanese troupes that then toured the United States and Europe. Working with the local historians of Iinomachi, she painstakingly went back over the original diary, checked for errors, correlated it with her knowledge of the nineteenth-century entertainment world, and added new annotations. In 2005 her work was included in a multi-volume history of the Iinomachi area, and it is this transcription of the diary that has been most useful for me. Mihara's other work on early Japanese troupes—in academic papers and articles and especially in a 2009 book that summarizes much of her research, titled *Nihonjin tōjō: Seiyo gekijō de enjirareta Edo no misemono* (*"Enter Japanese: A Night in Japan at the Opera House"*)—has also proved invaluable in unlocking many of the secrets of the Imperials and of Risley's association with them.

The second thing that has made this book possible is new technology. The story of Risley and the Imperial Japanese Troupe is particularly complicated. It encompasses many languages and geographic regions, and it requires correlating a vast number of disparate shards of information. The travel expenses and the time required for a project like this would normally have been prohibitive. Research would have involved traveling to four continents, spending weeks if not months in libraries around the world, and poring over dusty original documents and viewing scratchy, blurred microfilm and fiche. I still spent considerable time in libraries in America, Europe, Asia, and Australia, but I was greatly aided by the development of online databases of scanned nineteenth-century newspapers and magazines that have recently become available to researchers. Each country has begun to implement these historical databases in different ways. Japan, alas, lags far behind the rest of the advanced world. The American databases are disparate, diverse, specialized, sometimes hard to use, and largely commercial. The French system is beautiful and broad and free and sometimes quirky. In an attempt to preserve their national heritage, many smaller countries now also often offer remote access to their historical files, and do so with remarkable clarity and quality. The newspaper files of New Zealand, for example, are so immaculate and easy to search that reading them remotely from nearly seven thousand miles away often feels like taking the paper pages in hand.

When considering a character like Professor Risley and his Imperial Japanese Troupe, this technological revolution is enormously useful. It helps cut through decades of accumulated misinformation and myths. It allows me to rely mainly on primary sources, instead of what other people have written, and to quote extensively from Risley's contemporaries, in their wonderfully colorful nineteenth-century voices. And it creates an almost voyeuristic thrill. Because Risley survived by generating publicity and running advertisements in newspapers, it becomes suddenly possible to track his movements at an extraordinarily granular level, on multiple continents and through the fourth dimension of time. In a sense, online databases are rather like the new satellite, sonar, and undersea robotic technologies that have made the world's oceans increasingly transparent, allowing discovery of more and more valuable treasures and old wrecks hitherto hidden beneath the sea. By searching through vast seas of newspapers and magazines on multiple continents, through multiple languages, the movements and actions of people over a century ago become visible in ways they never imagined, to degrees they might even have found embarrassing. In the nineteenth century, after a failure or scandal, simply changing towns was often enough to allow one to start anew; not so any more. We can now view the past movements of people almost as if we are omniscient gods, looking down on humans from outer space.

★

Many people have aided me in the production of this book, and they deserve more thanks than I can adequately provide in this preface.

For agreeing to read part or all of my manuscript and provide valuable comments, many thanks to Ricard Bru i Turull, Jonathan Clements, Fiammetta Hsu, John Kovach, Aya Mihara, Leonard Rifas, and Mark St. Leon. Aya Mihara performed the especially arduous task of meticulously checking detailed references in such a complicated story and making many valuable suggestions; she also helped in the identification of CDVs ("carte de visites," or a type of card-mounted photograph), and I am particularly grateful to her. For much other useful assistance in research and assorted favors, thanks and a special tip of the hat to: Nobuko Aoki, Norihiko Aoki, Vivien Burgess, Yen Mei Chen, Mimi Colligan, Peter Field, Bernard Gory, Jacques Gordot, Andrea V. Grimes, Allister Hardiman, Yin-chiu Hsu, Nanae Inoue, Yuki Ishimatsu, Dominique Jando, Yumiko Kawamoto, Lytfa Kujawski, Raymond Larrett, Raymond Lum, Mitsunobu Matsuyama, Motoka Murakami, Judith Olsen, Daniele Rossdeutcher, Robert Sayers, David W. Schodt, Laurence Senelick, Mikey Sullivan, Kiyoyuki Tsuta, Jane Walsh, and Matthew W. Wittmann. My mother, Margaret Birk Schodt, was a constant inspiration. Also, many thanks to the employees of the following libraries and organizations: the Bibliothèque Nationale de France; the British Library Newspapers; the California Historical Society; the East Asian and Bancroft Libraries of the University of California, Berkeley; the Fukushima Prefectural Library; the Harvard Theatre Collection of the Houghton Library; Hong Kong University's Hong Kong Newspapers and Special Collections Department; The John and Mable Ringling Museum of Art; the Mitchell Collection, State Library of New South Wales; the Oregon Historical Society; the Philadelphia Library Company; the San Francisco Performing Arts Library and Museum; the San Francisco Public Library (especially the Inter-Library Loan folks and the History Center and the Schmulowitz Collection of Wit and Humor); the Society of California Pioneers, the Yokohama Archives of History; and the Winterthur Museum, Garden & Library.

Except for the names in this credit list, which are listed in Western order for alphabetical consistency, Japanese names in the main text are listed in Japanese order of surname first and given name last. All maps and translations are the responsibility of the author, unless otherwise noted. Bruce Rutledge, of Chin Music Press, kindly served as the text editor and was so gentle and skillful that it was entirely painless. Finally, without the support of my good friends at the intrepid Stone Bridge Press—including the wonderful designer Linda Ronan and especially Peter Goodman, the founder and publisher—this book would never have been possible.

FREDERIK L. SCHODT
San Francisco, 2012

Professor Risley
and the
IMPERIAL JAPANESE TROUPE

ACT 1
Setting the Stage

"The trade of the United States with Japan must pass
through the Golden Gate, and San Francisco will be the
American depot of all importations from the Japanese
empire."

—*The Sacramento Daily*, January 27, 1867

The rainy season was about to begin in San Francisco, but the weather
was still mild and the skies clear. On November 19, 1866, for readers
hungry for news from the far-away East Coast and the larger world, the
local *Daily Alta California* highlighted articles about President Andrew
Johnson's troubles, Negro suffrage, and soon-to-be deposed Emperor
Maximilian I in Mexico. Entertainment was always a big topic in the
city, so for front page local news there was an article about the awful
fall the previous day of a popular tightrope walker. And in the "Amusements" column, there was a cryptic announcement:

> A Japanese Troupe.—A private letter from Yokohama,
> Japan, October 18th, states that Prof. Risley had effected
> an engagement with a full troupe of Japanese athletes
> and actors and with the permission of the Government
> would leave for this city in a short time, intending to
> give exhibitions in the United States and Europe.[1]

View of San Francisco and its waterfront, from Vallejo and Battery, circa 1867. SAN FRANCISCO HISTORY CENTER, SAN FRANCISCO PUBLIC LIBRARY.

Three days later a full advertisement appeared, providing more detail. "THE GREATEST NOVELTY YET," it dramatically announced, would arrive imminently and consist of "The First Japanese Artistes Who Have Left Their Native Land." They would be both male and female performers, "acrobats, balancers, top-spinners, etc., etc., etc." and they would perform tricks only found in the Japanese Empire. It was all possible, according to the ad, because Professor Risley had gone to "infinite trouble" and "prodigious expense" to get the Japanese government to allow them to leave Japan "after a prohibition of three hundred years." It stressed that they had already appeared before numerous of the elite of Japan and various foreign dignitaries in the foreign settlement of Yokohama. Scheduled to leave Japan "on or about" November 1 on the *Archibald*, they would appear before the citizens of San Francisco in their native costume, "in their own manner," accompanied by "competent interpreters," just in time for the holidays.[2]

This was a remarkable advertisement in 1866, even for a city as cosmopolitan as San Francisco. Mentions of Professor Risley also elicited extra interest because he was world-famous in his own right and well-known in the city, as both an acrobat and a showman. The same ad appeared not only in the *Alta*, but in several of the young city's already-numerous papers, and would continue to do so throughout most of December.

On December 1, the *Alta* announced that Risley and his troupe had arrived in San Francisco on a British bark from Yokohama, the *Alert*. In reality, however, that ship carried an entirely different troupe of Japanese performers, and four days later the *Alta* was forced to print a retraction. It said that yet another letter had subsequently been received from Risley, still in Yokohama, dated October 28. He had reportedly chartered a ship—not the *Alert*, but the British *Archibald*—expressly to convey his troupe to America, and he would sail the following week. The last sentence hinted at Risley's painful awareness of his situation and his competition, for it specifically stated that he "desired it to be understood by the public that the company under his management is the only legitimate one, having the endorsement of British and American Ministers, and of the foreign officers in Yokohama, and permits of their government to undertake the journey."[3]

Where Is Risley?

In an era before any trans-Pacific telegraph, radios, telephones, and instant messaging, it could take weeks, if not months, to receive news from overseas, and people were used to a certain fuzziness in their information. But if the citizens of San Francisco were extra confused this time, they had every right to be. On December 6 an advertisement appeared in local newspapers for the Japanese entertainers who had arrived on the *Alert*. Placed there by Tom Maguire—known locally as the "Napoleon of the Stage" for his ability as a theatrical manager and impresario—it trumpeted in typically showman fashion that on December 10 twelve Japanese jugglers, brought from Japan "at enormous expense," would perform "THE MOST MARVELOUS FEATS OF LEGERDEMAIN ever witnessed in the civilized world, together with the MOST STARTLING AND EXCITING ACROBATIC PERFORMANCES." Just like Risley's group, these Japanese were the only troupe "ever allowed to leave their native country," and they would be appearing for "a few nights only."[4] Also like Risley's group, they were on their way to an international exhibition in Paris, and San Francisco was merely one stop along the way.

As if symbolizing the interest suddenly building in Japanese acrobats, a parody show opened elsewhere in the city two days later titled "Catching a Japanese," with local white actors imitating Japanese. In what was clearly a subtle dig at the still-yet-to-arrive Professor Risley and troupe, the show featured a "Professor Ichaboo," who performed his wonderful "Japanese Tricks, accompanied by the TOM-TOM and JAPANESE FIDDLE ('Cremona Japanica')."[5]

On the tenth, after a brief press preview two nights earlier, real, live Japanese acrobats and jugglers from the *Alert* opened to acclaim at Maguire's own Opera House in San Francisco. They followed, on the same program, a burletta by Lady Don of "The Water Witches." They faced considerable competition elsewhere in the city; that same night a young Mark Twain was nearby giving a popular lecture on the Sandwich Islands, as Hawaii was then known, after his recent trip there. Nonetheless, the Opera House was jammed with excited locals assembled to watch the Japanese perform a variety of feats and tricks, and the event was covered by local reporters who wrote about it in glowing terms. As the *Daily Evening Bulletin* described it:

> The mere appearance of the Japanese, in their robes and flowing sleeves; their shaven crowns, almond eyes and copper color; their strange speech; their oriental prostrations; their barbarous music; were alone an entertainment, even in a community which is so familiar as San Francisco with their congeners the Chinese.[6]

The acrobatic feats, the reporter continued, were "among the most wonderful we have ever seen." They consisted, among other things, of a man lying on his back, balancing a twenty-foot-long bamboo pole on his feet, while a small boy climbed to the top and performed various maneuvers; a similar act that involved balancing a large tub with the feet and having the boy perform in it; and two men tossing a large keg back and forth, also with their feet. Some of the acts required more space, so it was announced that the following night the show would reopen in the nearby Academy of Music, which had a proscenium that was twenty feet higher and would allow for even more spectacular feats. Like the Opera House, it was owned by Tom Maguire, the highly successful owner-manager of the city's best entertainment venues.

San Francisco that year was buffeted by unusually harsh winter storms, dense fogs, and—on December 19—even a mild earthquake. Yet save for a few shows that were rained out, the citizens kept going to see the Japanese acrobats and jugglers from the *Alert*. Advertisements for them continued to appear regularly in the newspapers, along with those of the still-absent Risley group, and from them one could learn that the company on the *Alert* had been brought from Yokohama by Americans named Thomas T. Smith and G. W. Burgess, and also learn the names of each of the twelve performers, awkwardly spelled "FOO-KEE-MATS," "KEE-SA-BORO," and so on. These names sounded completely alien to the audience, and probably to the Japanese as well, because in 1866 there was still no standard system of rendering Japanese in the Roman alphabet, and the results tended to be haphazard.[7]

Local newspapers vied to run daily reports on the performances. Among the routines performed by the jugglers and acrobats, one of the most popular was a ladder and slackrope trick performed by a young boy named Rinkichi. On December 16, the *Daily Morning Call* noted that "'Sing-Kee-Chee,' whom the 'outside barbarians' have christened 'Little Tommy' has grown into quite a favorite. He is a bright, intelligent, eight years old, and makes a central point of interest in the group." The *Call* reporter further marveled over the tricks performed by magicians, which included "seeming impossibilities with ribbons, mock butter-flies, fire, fans, and compartmented cabinets." Contrary to the "hitherto received opinions of the effeminacy and weakness of the race," he was also impressed by the strength of the men who held the ladders and supported the lighter acrobats such as Tommy:

> The contractor who makes his living by house-raising, would do well to import a few of these iron-legged Asiatics, and dispense with his hydraulic pumps. One thing is certain . . . the lucky hombre who first conceived of the idea of bringing them to America and Europe, and

who now has them in charge, will make his fortune,
unless the cholera strikes them in New York.[8]

Tom Maguire was so impressed with his receipts that he purchased
a controlling interest in the company for ten-thousand dollars (buying
out Burgess's share) and extended its stay in San Francisco. But while
the show remained popular throughout the month and the all-impor-
tant Christmas holidays, toward the end of December voices of discon-
tent began to be heard. On December 22, the *Daily Dramatic Chronicle*
reported that, at the Academy of Music, "The Japanese jugglers have
experienced a sad falling off in the attendance. The public went at first
out of curiosity, but the novelty is now paling. The jugglers do some
very good gymnastic feats, but their juggling tricks are abominable."[9]

Even if Professor Risley could not yet be in San Francisco, he had
his local allies who could guarantee him favorable advance publicity and
support. On December 30, the *Morning Call* ran an article on the Japanese troupe still in town, noting that it was going to move to Sacramento
before heading to New York, adding, "What, by the way, has become
of Risley's troupe? Compared with which the lot at the Academy are,
according to report, 'mere rubbish.' It is time the *Archibald* was here with
these daimos. Hurry up, Risley; there is a good feeling in favor of your
protégés. It won't do to allow a Japan lack here."[10]

For the first Japanese entertainers, San Francisco would be only
one stop along a long journey. They would receive an enthusiastic local
welcome there, but it would be unlike what they would experience
elsewhere, for the citizens of San Francisco were already far more connected to Asia, and Japan, than their counterparts on the East Coast or
in Europe. And in that sense, San Francisco also becomes a good vantage
point from which to introduce the complicated and global story of Risley and the Imperial Japanese Troupe.

The Context

San Francisco is perched on top of a narrow peninsula. It faces the Marin headlands across the Golden Gate, through which the waters of the Pacific surge into one of the world's best natural harbors. Settled by Spain in 1776, taken over by Mexico in 1821, and then by the United States in 1846, until the Gold Rush of 1848-49 San Francisco was a sleepy town of only a few hundred people. By 1866, however, the population had exploded to over 120,000 and the city had become the commercial and intellectual hub of the entire, brand-new state of California. On the western edge of a now vastly expanded United States, fueled by the notion and vast ambition of "Manifest Destiny," San Franciscans tended to look even further west, directly across the Pacific Ocean to Asia and Japan.

Outwardly, the city affected a cosmopolitan pose, with tall buildings on its dusty main street and multiple places of entertainment, but it could not yet hide its rough edges and origins as a frontier outpost. One contemporary writer called San Francisco "a monument to California's march from barbarity to vulgarism."[11] In 1866, aspiring novelist Bret Harte—consoling nervous residents after cholera scares, heavy rains, and another recent earthquake—stated "we have passed through ordeals more serious. . . . Ruffianism, brigandage, chivalry, gambling, scandalous legislation, lynch law and extravagant speculation have in turn retarded our progress. The pistol and the knife, drunkenness and debauchery, have claimed more victims than ever pestilence, flood or volcanic throe."[12] Part of San Francisco's rawness came from the fact that it was a young city, with young inhabitants, and although an influx of women had improved the gender odds in recent years, the majority was still male, and ravenous in the pursuit of wealth and entertainment.

Gold had also made San Francisco one of the most culturally and racially diverse cities in North America, because it drew hordes of fortune-seekers from all parts of the globe. European Americans of every stripe, Latin Americans, African Americans, Native Americans, and Chinese; Protestants, Catholics, Jews, Buddhists, and ancestor-worshippers; all coexisted, but not in harmony. The bloody American Civil War had ended only a year earlier, but the city had its faction of "Copperheads" who had sympathized with the Confederacy, and in the 1866 Fourth of July celebrations, the Irish refused to march with the free Negros. There were also thousands of Chinese already living in San Francisco, highly valued as inexpensive good workers but increasingly resented and persecuted by working-class whites, who felt threatened. Still, in 1866 opposition to Asians in general had not yet fully coalesced. A year earlier, a troupe of Chinese jugglers had delighted a San Francisco audience. In December, after the arrival of the first group of Japanese, the *Alta* even editorialized on the need to instruct young San Franciscans in both Chinese and Japanese in public schools, because the day would surely come when "a knowledge of these Asiatic languages will soon be required, especially by merchants in San Francisco."[13]

In 1866, San Francisco was in some ways closer to Asia than New York. With the transcontinental railroad still under construction, rather than risk starvation, attacks by Indians, and being stranded in the wilderness, most people traveling to the East Coast took steamers down to the Isthmus of Panama, crossed overland (there being no canal yet), and then caught other steamers on the other side to travel up the Atlantic seaboard. It could take over a month, and the inconvenience encouraged one writer in 1870, in describing the older residents of San Francisco, to say that they had lived until recently "in a condition of isolation, with respect to the rest of the world, which was almost Japanese in its exclusion."[14]

He was referring to the fact that Japan was still famous for its isolation. At the beginning of the 1600s, in reaction to encroachment by the Spanish and Portuguese, the shogun (whom Westerners also called the "Tycoon") had expelled almost all foreigners, banned Christianity, exterminated recalcitrant believers, and prohibited almost all trade and communication with the outside world. It was a draconian social experiment that lasted nearly 250 years. At its most extreme, it meant that foreigners landing in Japan could potentially be executed, and that Japanese were prohibited from leaving (or if they left, of ever returning, on penalty of death). It also meant that, up until the middle of the nineteenth century, to most Europeans and Americans, Japan remained one of the last great unknown places in the world—a distant, isolated, mysterious island nation, once exoticized by Marco Polo for its presumed riches and sought after by Christopher Columbus.

Yet even in the early nineteenth century, San Francisco had a special connection to Japan. Information on Japan flowed into San Francisco via Hawaii, and from sailing ships returning from Japan's coast. In the 1840s, after the American whaling fleet began fishing in the Sea of Japan, more and more stories of Japan began to trickle back home, from shipwrecked sailors and from failed official or unofficial attempts made to communicate with the Japanese. In addition, since the Japanese government had banned construction of ocean-going ships, more and more hapless Japanese vessels were being blown off course and disabled. Sometimes they were intercepted and helped by American ships. And sometimes Japanese crews—in ships dismasted and made rudderless by violent storms—drifted helplessly, borne by the winds and tides of the Pacific, all the way to the shores of Hawaii, North America, and Mexico.

In 1850, in the midst of the Gold Rush, the city was visited by the most famous Japanese castaway of all—Nakahama Manjirō. Marooned in 1839 as a fifteen-year-old fisherman on a Pacific island, Manjirō had been rescued by an American ship, taken by the captain to Massachusetts, and given a modern education. An adult by 1850 and fluent in English, he had joined in the California Gold Rush. Only one of tens of thousands of people from over the globe who then swarmed through San Francisco, he attracted little local notice, possibly because he went by the name of John Mung and most people assumed he was Chinese. He later made it back to Japan and contributed to Japan's eventual modernization.

On March 4, 1851, seventeen Japanese castaways arrived directly in San Francisco. Their ship, the *Eiriki-maru*, had foundered at sea, and the lucky men had been rescued by an American ship. The men, regarded as visitors from one of the world's most exotic and mysterious civilizations, were wined and dined at a fancy ball at the California Exchange, which was then controlled by a local impresario named Edward Cole (and showcased a "celebrated fire eater, necromancer, and optic magician" named "Professor Courtier"). They stimulated a flurry of articles in the local press on Japan and stayed in San Francisco over a year. Locals were particularly taken with a young man of around thirteen named Hamada Hikozō who, like Manjirō, was eventually educated in the United States. He later became the first naturalized Japanese American, took the name of Joseph Heco, met Abraham Lincoln, and eventually returned to live in Yokohama where he certainly knew Professor Risley. In San Francisco, where he sojourned twice in 1850 and 1858, he was a well-known figure.

On March 25, 1851, the impresario Cole wrote to the *Alta*, offering to arrange a ship and captain to take the Japanese back to Japan, providing the local merchants could donate enough money. "Everyone is satisfied of the immense advantage," he concluded, "that must accrue to the government who shall first open a trade with Japan." Unfortunately, the next day the *Alta* paper slapped down his San Francisco–centered proposal with its own editorial, suggesting that it would be better to have the national government take the lead, using military force. China, the *Alta* pointed out, had recently been intimidated into opening her ports, and so would Japan.[15]

Around this same time, American interest in Japan began to reach a fever pitch. Newspapers ran more and more articles on the isolated nation, vociferously advocating its opening, if not by diplomacy, then by force. And the result was exactly as the *Alta* had advocated. In 1853 and 1854 Commodore Matthew Perry and a group of United States warships sailed to Japan and—without firing a shot—managed to force Japan to finally end its isolation policy and to sign a treaty of friendship; this paved the way in 1858 for a treaty allowing rudimentary trade and the openings of ports such as Yokohama. California had been granted statehood in 1849, making United States a Pacific nation. Perry's visit to Japan in 1853–54 marked his country as a new power to be dealt with, in a region until then dominated by the colonial empires of Europe. It was a source of enormous pride to Americans at the time, and especially to San Franciscans.

As a result of Perry's mission, in 1860 San Francisco had already been graced by a visit from the first official Japanese embassy to the United States, en route to Washington, D.C. After a nearly disastrous voyage, the group of elite samurai officials arrived in the *Kanrin-maru*, the first Japanese-owned ship to cross the Pacific. Accompanied by former castaway Manjirō, who helped them with navigation and interpretation, they wore two swords and top-knots, and stayed for an entire month. They were of course feted far more than the shipwrecked sailors had been in San Francisco, and by the time they arrived on the East Coast of America they were a national sensation—celebrated with parades down Broadway and a poem by Walt Whitman, swooned over by women, and treated like royalty at the highest levels of government, including at the White House. Compared to the rest of the nation, San Franciscans were thus already a bit jaded. As Bret Harte wrote of the city on November 3, 1866, only two months before Risley's Imperial Japanese would arrive:

> Men and women pass for what they are worth from a California standard, which I need not say is remarkably elevated. Our conceit consequently is more apt to make us patronizing than obsequious. Recall the difference between the reception of the Japanese quasi-mercantile ambassadors in New York and San Francisco. Here, these two-sworded, brocade-legged, amber tinted dip-lomats . . . passed and repassed through the streets hardly eliciting more remark than well dressed Chinamen. We have had lords and bishops, Indian Chiefs and foreign dignitaries among us.[16]

The Imperials at Last

On New Year's Eve, 1866, Professor Risley and the Imperial Japanese Troupe finally arrived in San Francisco harbor on the British sailing bark *Archibald*. A nearby Sacramento newspaper reported that it was a record crossing of the Pacific, lasting only nineteen days, and that the captain got so drunk in a disreputable bar after his victory that he was impris-oned and then ejected in the morning, "minus his money, watch, jew-elry, and everything but his undershirt and drawers." Some less generous San Francisco newspapers put the crossing at twenty-five days.[17]

Today we know with considerable precision how long the *Archibald* actually took, and that the first reports were indeed a bit of an exaggeration. Fairly good information comes from a member of Risley's Imperial Troupe named Takano Hirohachi. Although he could play the banjo-like Japanese *samisen*, Hirohachi was not a performer. Probably a man with a gambling instinct, who lived on the fringes of respectable society, for the Imperials Hirohachi served as a type of overseer, or supervisor, of the troupe's jugglers and acrobats. He kept a simple diary, or daily record, a copy of which survives in Japan today. Written in a highly informal and cryptic style, it is sprinkled with the unique dialect of the semi-literate author and his now-archaic language. Rough, often disappointingly skeletal, with dates that are sometimes off, in this case the diary shows a voyage of around twenty-seven days. Allowing for the international dateline, and different ways of recording departure and arrival times, it appears quite accurate, for "Shipping Intelligence" columns in newspapers in both Japan and San Francisco show that the 393-ton *Archibald* left Yokohama on December 5, 1866, and arrived in San Francisco on December 31.

The *Archibald* docked on the evening of what had been a fine sunny day, but the voyage had hardly been pleasant. For the Japanese, who had not been allowed beyond their immediate coastal waters for over two centuries (and who had been raised to believe that they might be executed if caught leaving the homeland), it was terrifying. They of course immediately experienced the then-usual bouts of violent seasickness in heavy swells. On December 13, a dog on the trip began biting people, so the American interpreter on board, Edward Banks, shot and threw it overboard. There is no mention of what Risley thought of this, but he must have been heartbroken, because he loved animals. In the first part of the journey, the ship sailed through huge westerly gales and sleet and rocked violently, the passengers sometimes unable to stand. The sails were torn, and one of the masts, another troupe member would later recall, was also struck by lightning and had to be repaired. The Japanese feared they were doomed, but they were reassured by seeing that the captain was unfazed, and that the ship was well made.[18]

On arrival in San Francisco, Hirohachi mentions that three

"foreigners" went ashore and the troupe stayed on board. Throughout his diary, he never mentions Risley by name, instead occasionally alluding to him with the now archaic word, *ijin*, or "foreigner."[19] Most of his interactions were probably with the interpreter Banks, who was a former U.S. Marshal in Yokohama and himself an investor in the troupe. Banks is an intriguing character about whom little is known, but in those days there were almost no Europeans capable of speaking Japanese, let alone interpreting, so he possessed a rare talent. In Hirohachi's diary Banks is referred to as *henkutsu*, and it was only after many years that Japanese researchers established his identity. The third person in the group to which Hirohachi refers was William F. Schiedt, who is listed under "Passengers" in the January 1 edition of the *Alta*, along with Risley, Banks, and "eighteen Japanese jugglers." Like Banks, he was an investor in the group, and in charge of managing the finances, and he too may have known some Japanese and acted as an interpreter. We know from his 1867 U.S. passport application that he was remarkably young, only twenty-eight, and that he was 5'8" tall, with a high forehead, blue eyes, prominent nose, round chin, light brown hair, fair complexion, long oval face, and tattoos on both arms and chest, including one of the "American Shield." There may also have been a fourth "foreigner" with the group, for a quarter of a century later one troupe member would recall that a Chinese lad named "Lee" served as Risley's personal interpreter and helper. He reportedly spoke wretched Japanese, and his name never appears in Hirohachi's diaries or any surviving reports of the time.[20]

Risley had some serious negotiations to do in San Francisco before his Imperial Troupe and all their accompanying stage paraphernalia could be properly landed. They had arrived nearly a month later than planned, and while at sea there had been no way to communicate with San Francisco. There was first and foremost the basic logistical problem of where to lodge the troupe, and where and how to put on the long-delayed show that had already been advertised in the local papers since November. And it was surely a crushing blow to learn that a competing troupe had already stolen much of their planned thunder. Making matters more complicated for Risley was the fact that he had been out of the country for nearly ten years.

From recent research, we now know that the first troupe of Japanese that arrived in the United States was comprised of the Tetsuwari family of performers. Risley's "Imperials," on the other hand, was an amalgam of eighteen members from primarily three performing families—the Hamaikari, Sumidagawa, and Matsui families of jugglers and acrobats—presumably selected by Hirohachi and Banks for Risley. For reasons impossible to say today, the Imperials were often advertised and described as having twenty members, instead of eighteen. Although only Risley's group would make it, both companies were headed for the Exposition Universelle, which was held by Emperor Napoleon III in Paris in 1867. One of the first true world fairs, this exposition attracted great attention from entertainers around the globe, and entrepreneurial foreigners in Yokohama saw it as the perfect opportunity to exploit curiosity in Japan, showcase the unique talents of Japanese performing artists, and make a galomping fortune. At least five Japanese troupes left Japan around this time, some traveling west and some—like the Imperials and the Tetsuwari faction—traveling east. Some made it to Europe but not the Exposition, and some stayed in the United States, but it meant that nearly everywhere the Imperials went, they faced competition from fellow countrymen.

The departure of Risley's Imperials from Yokohama had been delayed for many reasons. First, the members were all lucky to leave with their lives, because Yokohama had erupted in flames on November 26 and most of the settlement, including the American consulate, had been destroyed. Second, their departure was also delayed because Risley went to the trouble of applying for passports from the Japanese government while the other groups apparently did not bother. The Japanese government was still a feudal one—soon to collapse in a semirevolution and be replaced by a modern system—so in 1866 considerable bureaucratic confusion was the norm. One result of Risley's efforts, however, was that Sumidagawa Namigorō, a prominent troupe member in the Imperials, received the first passport ever issued by the Japanese government to an ordinary citizen.[21]

Risley wasted no time on arrival in generating publicity and in setting up performances. On January 1 and 2, he arranged mentions in the *Alta* proclaiming the superiority of his troupe "over all other of their profession, either in or outside the Empire of the Tycoon."[22] And in multiple local papers he also arranged for detailed, official announcements of upcoming performances, which hinted at some of the reasons for his delay:

> Months after the contract was made with these artists to proceed to foreign countries on a professional trip, the Japanese Government finally issued the passports and necessary permits for them to depart from their native country, when it was made known to the Government that Mr. Edward Banks, late U.S. Marshal at Kanagawa, Japan, after his resignation of office, after his sojourn of seven years in the country, was to accompany the artists on their professional trip, to secure their safe return to their native country, the difficulties and obstacles were all the greater, as the applications demanded passports for female artists to depart from Japan, which was entirely new to the Japanese government.[23]

The local correspondent for the *New York Times* later elaborated on Risley's situation. After describing how the newspapers had all advertised Risley's coming and how a ship with different Japanese performers had actually arrived in San Francisco earlier in December, he wrote:

> But behold! Another vessel came in a few days since, bringing the original Jacobs, and we discovered that we had been sold. Some smart Yankee, taking advantage of the idea originated by RISLEY, had gathered a company together, slipped off in advance, and had had a "run" and the advantage of all RISLEY'S prestige and advertising. Discovering this, RISLEY determined to open for three nights only . . .[24]

Up against a professional like Risley, the other troupe—the Tetsuwari family—never really had a chance, even if equally skilled. With his competitors out of town, in Sacramento, Risley quickly made arrangements with Maguire for his group to appear at the Academy of Music on January 7. As another paper put it, "'Tis whispered in the house, and muttered on the street, that they are wonderful fellows; that it is a good thing for the other company that Smith took them to Sacramento. Had they seen Risley's performers in some of their feats, they certainly would have committed, out of pure envy, the *hari karii*, on the spot."[25]

The Imperials left their ship on January 1, after Risley had procured lodging for them. And Risley knew how to show his troupe off, for according to Hirohachi they traveled through crowds of spectators to their hotel in five horse-drawn carriages decorated with gold and silver inlay, "a sight that even a *daimyō* in Japan would have a hard time matching."[26] Hirohachi's simple words, referring to a Japanese feudal lord, hid the scale of his true sentiments as a commoner in Japan's feudal system, for back home he could have had his head lopped off for the slightest offense by nearly any member of the samurai class.

For the Japanese performers, who had never set foot abroad or been surrounded by different races of people, San Francisco was a dizzying experience. They normally ate fish but never the meat of four-legged animals. They had rarely seen wheeled vehicles or even large mirrors or so many houses with glass windows. Nor had they any familiarity with the modern scientific advances of mid-nineteenth-century America or Europe. During their stay in San Francisco, when not resting, checking their equipment, or performing or rehearsing, they would see much of the city. They would ride in carriages through the sand dunes of western San Francisco to Cliff House and Seal Rock, and marvel at California sea lions. They would visit the United States Mint in San Francisco (where Bret Harte then worked) and see huge piles of gold coins being minted. They would visit the Olympic Club and observe American gymnasts at work. They were enchanted with photographs and would have theirs taken at the studio of the pioneering portraitists, Bradley & Rulofson, to use as promotional calling cards known as *cartes de visite* (those by Bradley & Rulofson are lost, but others, and from other cities, survive). They would marvel at cobblestone roads and buildings as tall as five and seven stories high and be astounded at the sight of a steam train. In their hotel, they were amazed by faucets and drains, and even more so by gas lights in the room. They were sternly warned to be careful with the latter, since gas-related explosions and conflagrations were then frighteningly common (as they would later discover). But there was humor, too. As the group's magician/juggler, Sumidagawa Namigorō, recalled years later, when served rice on flat plates with knives and forks they did not know how to go about eating, so they put the rice in a chamber pot they found, only to be told that it was for urinating at night.

Opening at the *Academy of Music*

On the seventh, the Imperials finally opened at Maguire's Academy of Music for what was billed as a limited, three-day run. It was a huge success and made the performances of the previous troupe, the Tetsuwari family, look tame. But the Imperials were aided by a spike in interest in Japan that occurred in the city; that same week the first regular steamship line between San Francisco and Japan had been inaugurated with much fanfare in the media. And the Imperials also had the professional production and choreography of Professor Risley. Indeed, they had more of everything. As the *Alta* noted right before they opened, "They are said to excel the first troupe in the variety of their feats—besides having more ladders, more tubs, more bamboo poles, more juvenile prodigies, and more female rope-walkers." The females alone might have been enough to draw a crowd, but it was a jammed and suffocating house, so much so that, as Hirohachi marveled in his diary, the doors had to be shut to prevent any more people from entering.[27]

The curtain at the Academy rose to reveal all "twenty" members of the troupe, including two adult females, a little girl, and three boys, all salaaming deeply in Japanese style to the audience. The show unfolded with astonishing exhibitions of flexibility and balance, spinning of tops on the edge of a sword, and the female juggler doing a lantern trick. One other woman accompanied the performances by playing the Japanese samisen, with its percussive and, to Americans, grating sound. It gave reporters another reason to rank the Imperials over the Tetsuwari troupe.

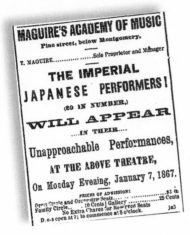

MAGUIRE'S ACADEMY OF MUSIC
Pine street, below Montgomery.

T. MAGUIRE..............Sole Proprietor and Manager

THE IMPERIAL
JAPANESE PERFORMERS!
(20 IN NUMBER,)
WILL APPEAR
....IN THEIR....
Unapproachable Performances,
AT THE ABOVE THEATRE,
On Monday Evening, January 7, 1867.

PRICES OF ADMISSION:
Dress Circle and Orchestre Seats.............$1 00
Family Circle.....10 Cents | Gallery.............25 Cents
No Extra Charge for Reserved Seats
D.o.s open at 7; to commence at 8 o'clock.   ja3

Announcement for the Imperials at Maguire's Academy of Music. *SAN FRANCISCO DAILY
EVENING BULLETIN,* JANUARY 3, 1868.

"This troupe, by the way," wrote one, "give very little of their own style
of music, and that little is quite sufficient for the untutored ears of San
Franciscans."[28]

Another huge hit of the show was a young boy acrobat named Umekichi. Usually described in Western press as the son of the troupe's elder,
Hamaikari Sadakichi, he was really the man's nephew. But his panache
and charisma would eventually win all of America's hearts. Because he
also finished his spectacular stunts with a fractured English "You bet!"
and "All Right!" he would also become known as "Little All Right." He
was regarded as superior in every way to Tommy, of the rival Tetsuwari
Company, except perhaps in his daring, but he more than made up for
that with charm and skills. The local correspondent from the *New York
Times* later wrote his audience back home what to expect:

> The ladies will faint and the men go crazy over a juve-
> nile performer whom we have called "All-right." The
> people [here] have a custom of testifying their apprecia-
> tion of a performer in a substantial manner—throwing
> money upon the stage. After the termination last night
> of little "All Right's" perilous ladder feat, the audience
> nearly covered the stage with half dollars, five, ten and
> twenty-dollar gold pieces, at which the cunning little
> juvenile shouted, "All right—you bet!" and down came

Maguire's Academy of Music, Pine Street, between Montgomery and Sansome. SAN FRANCISCO HISTORY CENTER, SAN FRANCISCO PUBLIC LIBRARY.

another shower of gold and silver! "You bet" is the most popular and fashionable vulgar ejaculation here I have ever heard. Everybody uses it, and all travelers have reported it.[29]

But not all went well. Perhaps the long sea voyage—and the stress of a foreign country, alien diet, new technology, languages, and the excitement of the moment—had been too much for some of the company's members. Denkichi, a young man described as the older son and pupil of the troupe's lead performer, Hamaikari (but also believed to be the adopted son of Hirohachi), lost his balance in a critical maneuver on a high ladder. It broke under his weight, causing him to plummet to the

1.

CARTES DE VISITE, 1–10

All photographs taken at the Numa Blanc Studio, Paris, except CDV 3, taken at the J. Gurney Studio. New York.

1. From left to right in back: Sumidagawa Namigorō, unidentified Caucasian male, and Hamaikari Sadakichi. In front, probably Sumidagawa Matsugorō and Denkichi. There is some reason to believe that the Caucasian male may be Edward Banks, but the facial shape also bears a striking resemblance to hand-drawn portraits of the younger Risley.

2. Matsui Kikujirō, the top-spinner.

3. Hamaikari Umekichi, or "Little All Right," photographed as a proud samurai with two swords.

4. Sumidagawa Namigorō, the butterfly artist and magician.

5. The ever-handsome Denkichi.

2.

3.

4.

5.

8.

7.

9.

6.

6. Hamaikari Sadakichi.

7. Sumidagawa Namigorō.

8. Probably Kanekichi.

9. Probably Sumidagawa Matsugorō.

10. Sumidagawa Koman, the wife of Namigorō.

CREDITS. CDV 1, 5, 7, 8, 9: F MS THR 828, HARVARD THEATRE COLLECTION, HOUGHTON LIBRARY, HARVARD UNIVERSITY. CDV 2, 4, 6, 10: COURTESY LAURENCE SENELICK COLLECTION. CDV 3: TCS 20 HARVARD THEATRE COLLECTION, HOUGHTON LIBRARY, HARVARD UNIVERSITY.

10.

11.

CARTES DE VISITE, 11–20

All photographs taken at the Numa Blanc Studio, Paris.

11. Yonekichi and Sentarō.

12. Probably Takano Hirohachi.

13. Sumidagawa Koman and Tsune.

14. Yonekichi and Sentarō.

15. Denkichi, Chōkichi, and Matsugorō.

14.

13.

12.

15.

17.

18.

19.

16.

16. Rinzō and son, Yonekichi.

17. Chōkichi (top) and Denkichi (bottom).

18. Hamaikari Umekichi, or "Little All Right," seated with fan.

19. Hamaikari Umekichi, or "Little All Right," standing.

20. Unidentified Caucasian male, Umekichi (Little All Right), and Hamaikari Sadakichi. The unidentified Caucasian is certainly an American and probably either Professor Risley, Edward Banks, or William F. Schiedt.

CREDITS. CDV 11, 20: COURTESY, LAURENCE SENELICK COLLECTION. CDV 12–19: F MS THR 828, HARVARD THEATRE COLLECTION, HOUGHTON LIBRARY, HARVARD UNIVERSITY.

20.

stage, striking his face and cutting open his lip. The shocked audience feared for his life. But after the curtain briefly came down the show went on and, as a reporter recalled later with relief, "the surgeons are not apprehensive of fatal result."[30] As sometimes happens with such accidents, the drama and excitement created seemed to endear the troupe to the citizens of San Francisco even more.

A Deal with Maguire

Thomas Maguire was quick to notice the extraordinary popularity of the new troupe and the potential to make even more money. He was turning hundreds away each night at the Academy and people were begging him to extend their booking. The Imperials were originally scheduled to leave San Francisco on January 10 for the east coast of America on a steamer named the *Golden City* (and they would appear on the passenger lists published in the papers as having actually left then), but Maguire was able to persuade them to stay longer. First it was announced that they would continue to perform until the steamer of January 19, at "the enormous nightly expense of $1,000."[31] Then the stay was extended until the steamer of the thirtieth.

As he had with the Smith and Burgess Tetsuwari group, Maguire decided to invest in Risley's Imperials, too, and in this case to follow them to the East Coast and on to Paris. Maguire was called the "Napoleon of the theatre" for good reason. He was aggressive, ambitious, and already had a near monopoly on professional entertainment in northern California and even Nevada, and he regularly sent performers on touring circuits he created through the gold country, even to Australia and Asia. He also had dreams of transcontinental theatre management, with operations in New York, too.

On one level, Maguire and Risley were quite similar. Maguire was around forty-two years old, and younger than the nearly fifty-three year old Risley. Both men were flamboyant, charismatic, larger than life personalities, and good looking. Maguire, said to be one of the handsomest men in San Francisco, dressed like the typical California gambler that

The ever-dapper Thomas Maguire. *CALIFORNIA HISTORICAL SOCIETY QUARTERLY*, VOL. 21, NO. 1 (MARCH 1942).

he was, with an enormous diamond in his scarf, jeweled rings on his fingers, and a heavy gold watch chain hanging from his waistcoat. But he was also moody, opportunistic, arrogant, and nearly illiterate. Like many impresarios in the mid-nineteenth century, he was also constantly involved in lawsuits and feuds, including one with the *Daily Dramatic Chronicle*, one of the few San Francisco newspapers that regularly dared to criticize him. Even that paper, however, conceded that Maguire might be able to make the $200,000 fortune that he bragged he would make by investing $100,000 in both acrobat companies. Under this scheme, he would leave Risley in charge of the Imperials, and the combined companies could be his "left and right wings." With the additional performers, there would be backups in case more injuries occurred and sudden substitutes were needed. The Imperials, thenceforth, could be referred to as the "Risley-Maguire Imperial Japanese Troupe."[32]

Risley was well aware of potential problems in a union with Maguire. He had already known Maguire for over a decade, and he knew the turbulent mid-nineteenth-century entertainment world—with its shifting fortunes, jealousies, alliances, struggles, and potential riches—better than anyone. But the added capital investment could not hurt, for the Imperials were paid the then-huge sum of twenty dollars per person per day (at a time when skilled carpenters earned less than five dollars for ten hours of work), and had to be housed and fed. Maguire's connections would help too, for—unlike Risley—he was still well connected to the East Coast and even Europe. Risley also had several reasons to want to postpone his departure for the East Coast. Denkichi, the star acrobat injured in the first San Francisco show, needed time to heal (and in fact would not appear on stage again until January 28, just before the Imperials finally departed). As it happened, Risley himself was involved in one of his many lawsuits, this time with a woman named Louisa Gordon and her daughter, who claimed that Risley owed them $5,200 plus interest for services performed a decade earlier when they had been in his employ (it would eventually be settled in her favor). Furthermore, Risley, along with Maguire and three members of the Imperials, had been arrested and was on trial for having violated the "Anti-Sunday Amusement Law," which prohibited most amusements on Sunday (they would be given the minimum fine). And finally, Risley, the well-known lover of animals, had lost his favorite dog, which had run away, and he wanted him back. For the remainder of January, advertisements ran in the San Francisco papers, offering a thirty dollar reward for the return of a black spaniel, with a gray nose, that answered to the name of Prince and had been stolen or strayed from the *Archibald*. Prince was never found.[33]

In the midst of all this, the performances went on, almost daily. The weather was terrible, with heavy rain and buffeting winds. Nonetheless, both Hirohachi's diary and the local newspapers confirm that at nearly every performance audiences clamored for more, and people had to be turned away at the doors of the Academy of Music. Given that the Imperials followed in the wake of the Tetsuwari Company's long December run in San Francisco, and that they themselves appeared for a total of three weeks, this was quite an accomplishment. It required not only an extraordinarily high level of skill from the Imperial troupe members, but an ability to vary their performances every night to sustain interest, for San Franciscans were hardly an uncritical audience. Six months later, after the arrival of yet another Japanese acrobatic troupe headed for Paris, one newspaper would grumble about having been completely "Japanned" and state: "Being the probably extreme rear of the Jap army that the Tycoon has kindly permitted us the honor of passing in review, we thank the Tycoon, and don't care a raccoon whether we look upon their like again or not."[34]

But this was not the case with the Imperials. The troupe stood out not only for the skill of its performers, but for the quality of the overall production, and for the way it was packaged and promoted for American audiences, who loved it. Ultimately, the troupe's success was a testimony to the skills of Professor Risley. As a January 20 article in the *Daily Morning Call* put it,

> . . . Risley's previous triumphs, brilliant as they were, have culminated in his recent splendid Japanese *coup*. If he don't make a fortune out of those sad-looking, but iron-muscled Asiatics, it will be because the spirit of curiosity has died out, and the appreciation of the wonderful has been lost.[35]

At eleven o'clock on the morning of January 30, after a suffocatingly crowded final performance the night before, the Imperials finally left San Francisco, headed for the East Coast on a steamer named the *Constitution*. They were accompanied by Risley and Edward Banks, Thomas Maguire and wife, and Smith and his company of performers. A brass band played at their farewell, and the papers predicted their resounding success in New York and eventually Paris. The passenger list included the names of prominent citizens who traveled in better-class cabins, and "175 whites and 30 Japanese in the steerage."[36]

Meanwhile, San Franciscans, knowing Maguire's personality and ambition, soon began speculating on his ultimate intentions vis-à-vis Risley and the Imperials. Maguire had decided to later send a Japanese man from the Tetsuwari faction, nicknamed Yo Shid, back to Japan to

The Imperial Japanese Troupe Members, Listed by
Stage Family Affiliation, in Order of Age

STAGE NAME	GENDER	AGE	ROLE
Sumidagawa Namigorō	M	37	Listed as "Conjurer, Magician, and Charmer of Butterflies."
Sumidagawa Namishichi (also Umekichi or Mikichi)	M	36	Namigorō apprentice. Listed as "Costumier and Designer."
Sumidagawa Koman	F	35	Top-spinner, listed as "Top Charmer."
Sumidagawa Tō	F	20	Shamisen player, listed as "Musical Directress."
Sumidagawa Matsugorō	M	17	Rope walker, acrobat, listed as "Cord Dancer, &c."
Matsui Shinjirō or Matsugorō	M	37	Props and assistant. Listed as "Second Chief Assistant and Master of Toilette."
Matsui Kikujirō	M	30	Top-spinner.
Matsui Tsune	F	9	Listed as "Aged Nine years, the Little Wonder from the World of Tops."
Hamaikari Iwakichi (Hirohachi)	M	45	Overseer, diarist, and "recording secretary."
Hamaikari Sadakichi	M	35	"Bottom" in balancing act, listed as "Chief of the Troupe."
Hamaikari Shigematsu	M	38	Drums, stage management, scenic artist.
Hamaikari Rinzō	M	30	Flute, listed as "Master of Training."
Hamaikari Kanekichi	M	27	Interlocutor/narrator, chief assistant and stage manager.
Hamaikari Denkichi	M	19	Acrobat/foot juggler, Sadakichi's pupil.
Hamaikari Yonekichi	M	13	Listed as "Hamaikari Tanekichi, The Juvenile Acrobat."
Hamaikari Sentarō	M	13	Acrobat, listed as brother of Yonekichi.
Hamaikari Umekichi / Mikichi /a.k.a "Little All Right"	M	12	"Upper" in act, and young star, the real "Little All Right."
Hamaikari Chōkichi	M	11	"Upper" in balancing act, listed as "Brother of All Right."

Sources: Iinomachi, *Iino chōshi, vol. 3 (2)* (Iinomachi, Fukushima Prefecture: Iinomachi, 2005), pp. 18-19; "Autographs of the Members of the Imperial Japanese Troupe" (listed on poster in possession of National Museum of Japanese History).

look for even more Japanese jugglers and acrobats and especially child stars like "Little All Right." According to the *Call*, it was to make the Tetsuwari Company better than Risley's Imperials, at which point Maguire would "probably cut his connection with that gentleman." And Maguire's nemesis, the *Daily Dramatic Chronicle*, ran an even more provocative but suggestive article. It described a scene witnessed on the quarter deck of the *Constitution* just before the ship's departure. A constable from San Francisco Judge Barstow's court (possibly where Louisa Gordon had sued Risley) approached Risley with some business, whereupon Risley turned to Maguire, said something unintelligible, and Maguire reached into his pockets and withdrew some money, which Risley then handed to the constable. "This was indeed a noble act," the paper editorialized, sarcastically, "for if the Professor had been left in the clutches of the law, we suspect that the great Napoleon would scarcely have regretted to find the *entire* management thrown upon his shoulders."[37]

The Risley Act

"The story of professor Risley Carlisle . . . is full of curious changes."
—*Hartford Daily Courant*, May 30, 1874

Who was Professor Risley? In 1866, when he arrived in San Francisco as the manager of the Imperial Japanese Troupe, he was already well known, in an age that produced many legendary and colorful impresarios. As a writer for the San Francisco *Daily Morning Call* put it in 1867, just as Risley left that city,

> Everybody has heard of this famous man, and his life and varied experiences will form a conspicuous chapter in some history of "American Showmen," to be written in the future. He has in the pursuit of his profession travelled over nearly the whole of the globe, and is as well known in Paris as he is in New York; his name is as familiar in Yokohama as it is in San Francisco. . . .[1]

"Professor Risley" was the stage name of Richard Risley Carlisle, who used it for most of his adult life. Born around 1814, newspaper obituaries at the time of his death in 1874 generally gave his birthplace as Salem, New Jersey. For most of his life, he called nearby Philadelphia,

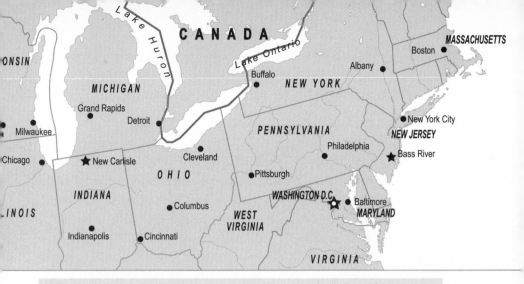

Map of northeastern United States.

Pennsylvania, his hometown. Recent research pinpoints the place of his birth in Bass River, Burlington County, New Jersey, near the coast. Noted circus historian Stuart Thayer, who wrote one of the best summaries of Risley's life, aptly refers to him as "A Man in Motion," but until the beginning of the twenty-first century, when it became easier to search disparate sources of information, it was not clear how early Risley developed his extraordinary velocity. At times, he appears to us almost as someone who appeared on earth fully developed, with muscles tensed, ready to spring into action. [2]

As an adult, Risley was described as "proficient in athletic sports and a man of great personal strength and endurance." Solidly built, he was also "a fine wrestler, skater and swimmer, with a fine musical voice, and performed with taste on the flute." From an 1849 passport application, we also know he was 5' 8", had gray eyes, brown hair, fair complexion, high forehead, oval face, an average mouth, round chin, and a Roman nose. One detailed obituary in 1874, apparently written by someone who knew him, describes him as "a man of wit, a rapid talker . . . , and of a most jovial disposition." He was also said to have had a speech impediment that, combined with his speed of talking, sometimes made him hard to understand. But it did not stop him from being highly entertaining.[3]

Nothing in Risley's origins immediately suggested that he would become the first person to introduce American-style circus into Japan, or to stage some of the first presentations of Japanese acrobats in the West. In 1814, Japan was about as far away from the shores of New Jersey, figuratively speaking, as the moon is from Earth today. The United States was a brand-new nation, having declared its independence from Britain only thirty-eight years earlier. It was a fraction of its current size, consisting of only eighteen small states hugging the Atlantic coast, and its focus was entirely on expanding its own western frontier, and on Europe. In the year of Risley's birth the so-called "War of 1812"—America's second war with Britain—was ending, and that summer the White House was burned by British troops. Japan, meanwhile, was isolated from the outside world and had been so for two hundred years, so whatever Americans knew about it usually came indirectly, via China or Holland, which had limited interaction with the Japanese. If ordinary Americans referred to anything remotely Japanese, it was usually with the adjective *japanned*, which meant "lacquered" items.

A Restless Spirit

In an era when most people lived and died in the same area, Risley was born into a traveling tradition. His father was John Carlisle, a sea captain at a time when the ports of southern New Jersey were bustling with commerce and ships from distant lands. In 1821, in preparation for his retirement from the sea, the captain built a house overlooking the Mullican River in New Jersey, where young Risley presumably lived with his sister, Elizabeth. In 1945 the house still survived, and a faded photograph from that period shows it to have been quite substantial, with at least two stories. One of four giant sycamore trees planted by the "jolly sea captain" was still standing, and the owner of the house had one of the captain's original ledgers—written in a neat, looping hand, with copious notes.[4]

At the beginning of the twenty-first century, skillful sleuthing by John Kovach, the official historian for St. Joseph's County, Indiana, helped fill in some of the missing details in Professor Risley's early life.

An article appeared in the local *South Bend Tribune* about a man who, when cleaning out a former old church, had discovered an iron cross with a note that said, "This cross marks the graves of the two children of Richard Carlisle, founder of New Carlisle." The next day, Kovach was deluged with questions from readers, and he began unearthing old, forgotten records, revealing the astounding gyrations of Risley's early years, before he became a professional acrobat. As Kovach reflected in 2011, "Little did I know what roads I would be traveling down!"[5]

On October 15, 1833, following his father's death in 1828, Risley married Rebecca C. Willits of Philadelphia. He was not yet twenty-one, and it must have been an awkward union since (for reasons that are not entirely clear) the next year Risley's new father-in-law named him as a defendant in a lawsuit, establishing a trend that would last throughout his life of being involved in legal actions. The year after that, in 1835, Risley's first son, John, was born, and that spring the new family moved to St. Joseph County in the then-new state of Indiana. The area had been rapidly opened up to settlers in the wake of an 1827 treaty with the Potawatomi Indians. Perhaps hoping to make his fortune, in 1835, for two-thousand dollars, the twenty-one-year-old Risley purchased 160 acres of land from Lazarus Bourissa, a French fur trader in the area, and in the same year he submitted a "plat," or plan, for a town he called (after himself) "New Carlisle." Risley's original "dedication" shows his meticulous attention to detail and linearity in design, for he specified that the main boulevard, Michigan Street, should be made one hundred feet wide, with alleys parallel to it sixteen and a half feet, while those perpendicular to it were to be eight feet in width.[6]

New Carlisle survives today, but Risley did not live long in the town that he established. In 1836, his second son, Henry, was born, but all did not go well. As Kovach has discovered, in 1837 the twenty-three-year-old Risley was sued by his brother-in-law, John Egbert. And while the lawsuit was going on, a campaign advertisement in the April 17, 1837, edition of the *South Bend Free Press* newspaper shows that Risley apparently decided to run for the Indiana State Legislature, as a representative of the County of St. Joseph. In 1838, a daughter was born and died, and that same year Risley sold his land and declared bankruptcy. He was briefly hired by St. Joseph County to be a bounty hunter, and in 1839 he purchased 160 acres in Michigan. The certificate of purchase survives, made out to a "Richard R. Carlisle, of St. Joseph County Indiana," and testified to by then-President Martin Van Buren. It seems to have been one of the last times Risley used his real name.[7]

Much information about Risley's movements in this period is still murky. In addition to being a bounty hunter and investing in real estate, he also was at one point a postmaster and a shopkeeper or merchant. One man who knew Risley later claimed that he lived in Philadelphia and was in the glass-cutting business with a shop and a warehouse "in Third Street near Arch," but where this fits into an already complicated timeline is unclear.[8] At any rate, by 1840 Risley had left Indiana, and he had also left some deep impressions on its people. Two decades later, the *Ohio Repository* in Canton ran a long, humorous article titled "How Prof. Risley Went in on His Muscle," about his Indiana days. It gave a rare glimpse of his early character, and fits the classic pattern of several recorded Risley stories, which have drama and humor and an interesting emphasis on vernacular language. It described him as then being a South Bend, Indiana, merchant, who

> . . . was quite a favorite with the ladies and the best part of "Young America" [. . .]—but a perfect terrifier to the rowdies. . . . [He] was the best natured fellow in town, but he was known to be as quick as a cat, and as muscular as a horse, and the rowdies seemed to have an instinctive knowledge that he was bad stock for them to invest in.[9]

In this story, a group of rowdies disrupted a local ball but were dispelled by Risley, who took one of the men by the heels and swung him around like a battle axe, scattering the others. Chastened, they then hired the biggest thug they could find, who days later appeared in Risley's store. Ever the gentleman, Risley agreed to a fight on the local green, as long as the loser paid any fines for disturbing the peace. He encouraged the bully to have a friendly drink before the combat began, and then managed to "spread him out like a wet rag." He thereafter nursed the bloodied giant, taking his pulse and talking to him kindly, as though to an old woman, saying, "You needn't have any fears of being sued for breach of peace. . . . Nobody around here would call this a fight. . . . We're only playing. . . . Shall we play anymore?" The two men reportedly resumed drinking and remained fast friends ever after, the bully later becoming a baggage handler in a circus.[10]

The role of ordinary businessman did not suit Risley well. According to some sources who knew him, around 1838 he also began appearing in "Welsh's circus" on the East Coast, "playing the flute."[11] Exact dates aside, when Risley's name does start to appear regularly in newspaper advertisements in 1841, he clearly already has considerable name recognition as an acrobat and entertainer.

On November 24, 1841, the *New York Evening Post* ran an advertisement for Welsh's circus at the Bowery Ampitheatre in New York. It boldly announced upcoming evening performances, commencing with a grand Waltz and Gallopade and some equestrian performances, followed by Mr. Cole and "his singing Dog Billy, who will walk on two feet." Another main attraction was to be "Mr. Risley and his little son only five years old who will go through their astonishing performances in imitation of the Polish Brothers." There would also be vaulting by Mr. McFarland, a "Negro Extravaganza" by Messrs. "Risley and Williams" and, following a fifteen-minute break, some arena entertainment by the whole company and a comic afterpiece of "Poor Snip!" Box seats were fifty cents, but seating in the pit was a quarter. The Polish Brothers were a popular acrobatic act in the Northeast, and exactly what aspect of them Risley and son imitated is not clear. The "Negro Extravaganza" that Risley performed was presumably an early type of minstrelsy, a soon-to-be hugely popular form of musical, dancing, and comic entertainment in which White performers imitated Blacks, and especially Black slaves.[12]

Beyond Circus

Circuses were already popular entertainment in 1840s America. Introduced from England, they had not yet evolved into giant multi-ringed extravaganzas, but they were already well organized and populated with exotic wild animals, thrilling equestrian stunts, acrobats, jugglers, magicians, and musical and comedy acts, the last often taking the form of black-faced minstrel skits. In an era when people had few entertainments and a great curiosity for the unknown, the foreign, the exciting, and the risqué, circuses were hugely popular among the masses and could draw enormous crowds. Still, they were often scorned by the elites and the more puritanical members of local communities. An article titled "Circus" in the *Freeman and Messenger* newspaper in Lodi, New York, put it this way in 1840:

> Our village is soon to be paid a visit by a gang of strolling mountebanks, jugglers, rope-dancers, equestrians and loafers, accompanied by their pimps and abandoned wretches. Music, excentricities [*sic*], negro songs and vulgar slang will be the principle feats to procure the patronage and attract the gaze of all who may be so sensually disposed as to give their money to so worthless a set of beings. We would ask, what are the benefits to be derived from visiting the circus? No one is benefitted thereby; but on the contrary thousands are corrupted in their morals, and hundreds ruined.[13]

In nineteenth-century America, the circus had far less social status than even the theatre, which was itself regarded as dubious entertainment at best. As the greatest impresario of the nineteenth century, P. T. Barnum (who elevated American hucksterism to an art form and helped create the modern circus) noted in 1841, "Actors maintain a profound disgust for the sawdust, and the circus people have a supreme dislike to the legitimate business, which they regard with supreme contempt. Yet it is the ambition of the circus folks to play in a regular theatre."[14]

Partly because the circus belonged to a subculture and demimonde that catered to the cravings of the American public for novelty and exoticism, it was from the beginning also extremely multicultural. It was one of the few places in nineteenth-century America where performers of so many different backgrounds and utterly unrelated talents could mingle with relative freedom. And the names of the acts presented in early advertisements reveal the public's curiosity and hunger for the foreign. When the previously mentioned "Polish Brothers" performed in Baltimore in January 1838, they also appeared in a piece called "Bedouins of the Desert." They were followed by "Chinese and Grecian Exercises" and a then-popular equestrian number titled "The Courier of St. Petersburgh."[15]

Risley may have found one potential role model for the future in General Rufus Welch, the well-known impresario and owner of Welsh's Circus, where Risley first made his name as an acrobat. In the 1840s, no one better represented the international aspects of circus than Welch, or Welsh, as he was sometimes called.

The portly Welch lived from 1800 to 1856 and was no more a real "general" than Risley was a "professor." Yet he had a general's view of organization and of the world, for his scope and his ambition seemed boundless. A much beloved man, he formed a variety of menageries and (often with associates) some of the most famous circuses of the mid-nineteenth century. He worked especially in the northeast of the United States, in the area of New York, Baltimore, and Philadelphia, staging increasingly spectacular events. But he was also an early world traveler. As later obituaries noted, Welch "traveled in nearly every quarter of the globe," through North and South America and Europe. He is also said to have visited Africa to collect lions and elephants and other exotic fauna, reportedly introducing the first giraffes into North America.[16]

Whether Welch directly triggered Risley's interest in the outside world, and eventually in Asia, is unclear. But Welch's circuses did help Risley make the acquaintance of other artists and performers who would later help him in his international career. And Welch's international ambitions foreshadowed those of Risley. In 1843, New York newspapers were reporting that Welch would, "with his troop coast up the Mediterranean, visit Cairo, and crossing the Isthmus of Suez, descend the Red

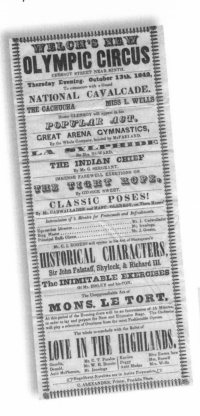

Playbill for an October 13, 1842, performance of Welch's New Olympic Circus, showing "The Inimitable Exercises of Mr. Risley and Son" in Philadelphia, Pennsylvania. COURTESY, THE LIBRARY COMPANY OF PHILADELPHIA.

Sea, visit Western and Eastern India, and push his way to China, and ere the lapse of eighteen months, exhibit an American equestrian troop to his majesty the brother of the Sun and Moon, at the Royal *Chon Chon* amphitheatre at Pekin." There is no evidence that Welch ever made it to Beijing, but he was nonetheless awe-inspiring for his time, "astonishing the semi-barbaric hordes of the East," and "edifying the Christians, Jews and Mahometans of Algiers." By the spring of 1844, he was said to have toured "Gibraltar, Cadiz, Algiers, Genoa, Marseilles, Palermo, Mahon, and crossed the Atlantic for South America, and at the last advices was performing in Rio with success."[17]

In 1842 Risley appeared with his young son on the playbills of several Welch-associated circuses and events in the Northeast, and the pair quickly began to attract attention as something that straddled the line between circus and a more refined type of entertainment. In March, they were featured at Welch & Delavan's Front St. Theater in Baltimore,

Maryland, performing what was billed as "The Magnificent Italian Scena of Gymnastics." This involved not only acrobatic feats, including perch acts, but posturing in classical styles, which became a trademark Risley feature, and it hinted at what Risley would come to promote as a kind of "drawing room entertainment." Little John, in particular, completely charmed the heart of audiences. In July the Baltimore *Sun* proclaimed that the "gymnastics of Mr. Risley and his son, are universally admitted to be of the most extraordinary in character; these can be only understood and appreciated by sight itself."[18]

By the end of 1842, Risley and son had become something of a sensation. Writing about the local highlights, the editor of the *Boston Gazette* boldly stated:

> The performances of Risley and his son have since been imitated, but never equalled. He was Magnus Apollo in comeliness, a Hercules in strength, and the son a Cupid in beauty. Of all exhibitions of physical grace in classical posturing they surpassed any we have ever seen. The throwing of the boy into the air, who turned a somerset and alighted safely on his father's feet, invariably drew forth the loudest applause.[19]

This would be only one of the many superlative reviews with which the Risley family would be showered, and it is one of the first clear references to what would become known as "The Risley Act." The expression "Risley Act" is one of the few still in use in gymnastics today that takes its name from a real person. Loosely speaking, it generally consists of one person lying on the ground on his or her back, juggling someone else using the feet. In Risley's time, however, it referred to his juggling of his own small children. It is highly unlikely that he was the first person in the world to perform this act, as some have claimed, but he raised it to a new level of perfection and style, to the point where it was always associated with him. At least one writer claimed that Risley could toss his son twenty-five feet in the air. Even allowing for exaggeration, the sight must have been awe-inspiring, if not terrifying.

The Pointe-à-Pitre, Guadeloupe, earthquake of February 8, 1843. COURTESY, NATION-AL INFORMATION SERVICE FOR EARTHQUAKE ENGINEERING, UNIVERSITY OF CALIFORNIA, BERKELEY.

At the beginning of 1843 Risley became famous not only for his stage performances, but for a long article he wrote that was widely reprinted in American newspapers and even (six months later) as far away as Sydney, Australia. There is no solid evidence that Risley ever had much formal education, but this story is an example of how he learned to use events to promote himself, leading one American wag to comment, "it has done as much for his present fame as the graceful performances of his 'truly astonishing Ellslerian boy.'"[20] It is also around the same time that Risley appropriated the title of "Professor" for himself.

Early in February 1843, Risley was visiting French-controlled Pointe-à-Pitre, Guadeloupe, as part of a tour of the Caribbean, probably with a troupe from the Welch & Mann Circus. At ten-thirty in the morning of February 8, just when he finished breakfast at a local coffee shop, one of the worst earthquakes ever recorded in the area struck.[21] In his account, in a dramatic fashion fit for an adventure novel, Risley tells how he felt the jar and saw the building he was in start to collapse. As a quick-witted, professional acrobat, he was able to jump out the window just in the nick of time, smashing through the glass and landing some ten or twelve feet below in the yard. Later, during an aftershock, he was knocked completely unconscious and awoke to find his clothes in tatters. He also miraculously found himself holding his son, John, who had been separated from him—the only two survivors in a building said to have held seventy-one at the time. The city was ruined, with collapsed buildings bursting into flames and what Risley estimated as fifteen thousand people dead. His printed account is one of the rare times that we can read his own words and hear his unique voice.

> I scarcely knew what had happened, and whether it were not all a dream.—I then began to look about me, and saw various individuals, men, women, and children, of all classes and individuals, wandering about half frantic, like myself. . . . All weeping, or in the utmost conceivable agony, pitching and falling about among the ruins and dead bodies. They would go from one dead body to another, overhauling them to see if they could find the person sought for—and if not successful, pass on to another.[22]

Risley was able to escape, although he claims he lost six thousand dollars, including four thousand dollars in gold, which in those days was a grand sum, since general admission to a circus in America then cost around twenty-five cents. It would be just one of many times when he amassed, and lost, a fortune. To North American audiences, most of whom had never experienced anything as terrifying as a major earthquake, his story was nearly as fascinating and thrilling as one of his performances, and it only helped to further cement his reputation as an extraordinary individual.

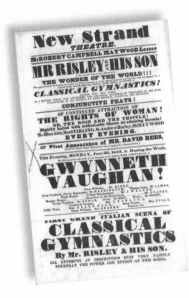

June 26, 1843, playbill from the New Strand
Theatre, London. BPF TCS 63, HARVARD
THEATRE COLLECTION, HOUGHTON LIBRARY,
HARVARD UNIVERSITY.

Off to Europe

By the summer of 1843, Risley was in London, and his movements subsequently become a near blur of constant travel. On June 26, he appeared
with son John at the New Strand Theatre, performing what was billed
as his "Italian Scena of CLASSICAL GYMNASTICS." A newspaper ad
in *The Age* for the performance announced, "all attempts at description
must very faintly portray the power and effect of this scena." Then after
a Burletta,

> Mr. Risley and his Wonderful Son will give their second
> grand Italian Scena, in which feats will be performed by
> this incomparable Boy, aided by his father, unequalled
> by any other artists in the known world, incredible as it
> may appear to even beholders, this infant prodigy will
> conclude his unparalleled classical feats, by turning cir-
> cles, high in air, and alight into his father's hands![23]

Thereafter, Risley and son John would perform throughout England, Scotland, and Ireland, their reputation growing ever greater. In

the media, John would be called, variously, the "infant prodigy," "the wonder of the age," and "le petit Mercure." Audiences simply could not get enough of the family act, and what was sometimes called "Aerial Dancing."

On September 24, *The Age* ran an even more detailed and laudatory review of one of their performances at the Surrey Theatre.

> We, on Wednesday evening last, again witnessed the extraordinary evolutions of Mr. Risley and his son, and were far more than ever delighted. It is decidedly the most finished, the most classical performance of the kind we ever beheld. Mr. Risley himself is a finely-formed person, with every muscle beautifully developed; he is, in short, a most perfect model of a man, while his son is one of the sweetest little fellows we ever saw. It is pecu-liarly pleasing to see the mutual confidence displayed, and it is that very confidence which renders the exhibi-tion so admirable, seeing that no alarm is created, no fear is inspired. Every movement is natural, graceful, and elegant, and while our wonder is excited, we are filled with admiration. They who imagine that these performances are but a series of gymnastic exercises, are deceived. The exhibition is not a mere display of *phy-sique*. Intellect is perceptible in every motion, while the performance, as a whole, indicates strongly the exer-cise of mind. We, therefore, cannot marvel at the sensa-tion created. It is, in reality, a beautiful display, and one which affords a striking example of what nerve, when coupled with physical power, and guided by intellect, can, without danger, achieve.[24]

In Edinburgh, Scotland, the locals awarded John a special medal. In Belfast, Ireland, the *Dublin University Magazine* took a slightly cyn-ical view of Risley's use of the title, "Professor," noting that "almost everybody now-a-days dubs himself a professor, doctor, or member of something scientific, expressed by many mysterious hieroglyphics and capitals." But it also noted that what Risley called "classical gymnasia" were indeed "applauded by the celestials," and their booking had been extended. Risley and John played through the holiday season and closed out the year with more drawing room entertainment at London's renowned Theatre Royal, Haymarket, performing a piece called "Peter Parley's Gambols of Puck with the Elf King Oberon." Their "extraordinary performance" was described as "being executed with such perfect ease and elegance, that the most fastidious lady might have them in a drawing-room without the fear of censure."[25] Posters amplified this message, describing the performances as "The Most Extraordinary and Chaste Exhibition," countering whatever unsavory reputation such acts might normally have had.

In January 1844, London newspapers began to advertise that Risley would add his youngest son, Henry, to his act, and from that point on he usually did. While John and Henry were presumably at this point around nine and eight years old, respectively, even allowing for a slight fuzziness in documentation, they were billed as being considerably younger. The *Weekly Chronicle* of January 21, for example, advertised John as Risley's "infant son" and Henry as being "only four years old."[26] Nonetheless, the interplay between the father and the two boys only increased the overall popularity of the act. In June, the *Age and Argus* gushed:

> The theatre has literally been besieged every night. . . .
> To give the performances in detail is akin to impossible,
> for from the emerging by the trap-door of the King
> Sprite (Master John Risley), the *entree* of King Oberon
> (Mr. Risley), and the appearance, of little Puck (the
> infant Risley), their movements, evolutions, and scien-
> tific attitudes are so rapid, so varied, so everything that is
> classical and graceful, that it would take a greater space
> than we can afford to do them ample justice. Indeed we
> should be at a loss to signalise any one of the innumer-
> able features of this miraculous performance, which is

throughout a combination of every anatomical beauty
of which the human form is capable.²⁷

What really impressed the audiences, in addition to the artistry, was
the way Risley could juggle his children with his feet. Over a century
and a half later, Risley's name survives in the *Guiness Book of Records*
because in Edinburgh, in February 1844, he and one of his sons executed
the world's first back somersault, feet-to-feet.²⁸

England was in the midst of the long and prosperous Victorian Age,
and its citizens had an increasingly intense curiosity about the exotic
outside world (into which their empire was rapidly expanding). Circuses
and spectacles were an important type of entertainment, and although
the circus had first developed in England, performers from America were
particularly popular. Yet Risley was careful to position his act as something straddling circus and theatre. Calling it "Classical Gymnasia," his
act consisted of "aerial dancing, poses, groups, and studies of arts," and
incorporated elements of gymnastics, ballet, and spectacle.²⁹ He was also
particularly adept at exploiting the Victorian penchant for romanticizing
the innocence of young children.

The appeal that these performances had was extraordinary. As a
reporter for the *Age and Argus* wrote after witnessing one of the family's
performances in the Haymarket in 1844:

> It is a singular fact, that the usually quiet audiences of
> this theatre, seem to have undergone some talismanic
> revolution, by witnessing the elegant feats and evolu-
> tions they go through, as every night they have been
> called before the curtain to receive anew those testimo-
> nials of applause from every part of the house, which
> had been so liberally bestowed upon them throughout
> their performances; the waving of hats and handker-
> chiefs was as general as prolonged and hearty.
>
>   The Herculean symmetry of the parent, which
> the sweet children seem likely to inherit, was beauti-
> fully displayed by one of the most *recherché* and splendid

LE PROFESSEUR RISLEY ET SES DEUX FILS.

Lithograph portrait of Professor Risley and his two boys, around 1843–44, in Paris. Drawing by Jules Petit. F TS 939.5.3 (II/XI), HARVARD THEATRE COLLECTION, HOUGHTON LIBRARY, HARVARD UNIVERSITY.

Lithograph illustration of Ris-
ley performing with his two
boys, in Paris. Drawing by Jules
Petit. F TS 931.10, HARVARD THE-
ATRE COLLECTION, HOUGHTON
LIBRARY, HARVARD UNIVERSITY.

costumes we ever saw. A pretty little ballet of action has
been specially composed for them, interspersed with
well selected music, which certainly contributed much
towards the interest they always excite.[30]

This sweetness and innocence allowed an ever-wider audience to
enjoy the shows, including high-ranking members of society who might
normally not be expected to do so. In his diary for April 1844, James
Fraser, a high-ranking bishop in the Church of England, notes that on
the ninth he went to see "General Tom Thumb," the tiny American
midget being exhibited, as well as some Ojibewa Indians (both sponsored by P. T. Barnum), but he was not particularly impressed. On the
thirteenth, however, he stopped in at the Haymarket and writes that "I
never was more electrified in my life than by witnessing the gymnastic

performances and postures of a certain Mr. Risley and his son '*Le petit Mercure.*'[31]

For the next few years, Risley and his boys took Europe by storm. After touring England, Ireland, and Scotland, they moved to France, Belgium, Holland, Italy, Germany, Austria, Russia, playing the capitals of the continent, eliciting praise wherever they went. Their popularity was extraordinary, and they drew crowds that numbered in the thousands. In Paris, they debuted on June 15, 1844 at the prestigious Porte-Saint-Martin, with a performance titled "A Midsummer Night's Dream" (after Shakespeare's play). Several major papers soon ran ecstatic reviews, and from them and some lithograph illustrations of their performances that appeared, it is clear that Risley's success was partly in the presentation—in the aesthetics of his shows. He and his boys would wear classically themed silver-sequined and spangled costumes ("fleshings" or flesh-colored tights) and perform on top of a beautiful carpet. The staging was also elaborate, complete with artistic scenery (in Paris a pretty forest with flowers and stars) and a dreamy mood augmented by music. But more than anything else, it was the sheer athleticism of Risley and his boys that impressed people.

On June 20, a critic writing under the initials C. B. in the *Independent*, said: "These three characters are neither dancers, nor clowns, nor tightrope balancers; they are all of them, together, and their talent is universal. . . . [T]he father and both young sons surpass in agility and suppleness whatever amazing feats we can dream of in our imagination."[32] On June 24, a lengthy review appeared in *La Presse* by the famous French writer and arts critic, Théophile Gautier. He was so impressed that he thought the Risleys put professional ballet dancers to shame. His enthusiasm oozed from his flowery phrases. A century later, in 1948, dance historian Marian Hannah Winter would discover Gautier's article and translate much of it:

> The two adorable gamins, successively or together, climb
> to the assault of their father, who receives them on the
> palms of his hands, the soles of his feet, launches them,
> returns them, throws them, passes them from right to

left, holds them in the air, lets them go, and picks them up with as much ease as an Indian juggler manoeuvres his copper balls. . . .[N]ever was more grace united to more strength. These turns accomplished, they next execute them heads down on his feet, without being excited, or breathless, or sweaty. . . . While watching them catapulted so far, falling from so high, we thought to what degree the training of dancers of the opera is incomplete and backward.[33]

In 1948 Winter was motivated to include a detailed and well-researched section on Risley's early life in a piece titled "Theater of Marvels," in *Dance Index* magazine, and in the process, she helped to resurrect him from what was then near-complete obscurity. In her writing on Risley, however, she mentions multiple times that there never seemed to be any mention of a wife or of ever marrying. She clearly suspected—as have subsequent writers in both France and America—that John and Harry were not his real children.

There was good reason for this suspicion, for it was quite common in the early days of the Victorian era for entertainers to "adopt" young children and showcase them in their acts as their real progeny. It is a practice that at its worst evokes all sorts of nightmarish images of circus life, where small children were sometimes kidnapped, horribly abused, or at the minimum exploited. In Risley's case, however, we now know from census and other records in the United States that he was married to Rebecca, even if she rarely accompanied him in his adventures and stayed in Philadelphia. Today he probably would have been arrested for child abuse because he tossed his children about on stage, but the children were indeed his.

Risley was an extraordinarily powerful man, and gifted athletically, but there are clearly limits to working with growing children, and in 1845 John was presumably already ten years old. The year after Risley opened in Paris, some local wags had already wondered aloud whether, "when the boys grow too big to be knocked about like cricket balls, it is the father's intention to change places with them."[34]

With success, as would happen throughout his life, Risley quickly faced imitators. By December 1844, Gautier—the same illustrious French critic who had earlier written so glowingly about Risley—was calling him "surpassed," after seeing three tiny American children named Ohio, Missouri, and Arkansas tossed about by a youth of eighteen.[35]

Even more serious competition came from another American named Richard Sands. An equestrian, gymnast, and posturist, Sands would one day become famous, among other things, for walking on the ceiling using special shoes. With two beautiful golden-haired "children," he also appeared in Paris in June of 1845. Japan, still closed to the outside world, did not feature prominently in French consciousness at the time, but China did, for like the British Empire, Napoleonic France was starting to nibble at a weakened China's borders. In a ridiculously faux-Chinese-themed act called "The Juggler and the Mandarin," Sands juggled the children on stage with his feet, and the critically promiscuous Gautier fell in love with him, too, calling him Risley's "teacher" and writing that "the pupil was strong, but the teacher is astonishing."[36]

Luckily, Risley was generally acknowledged to be the leader in this new genre of entertainment, as well as its inventor, and other writers usually sprang to his defense. In August of 1845, when describing Risley's appearance at the Porte-Saint-Martin Theatre in Paris, the arts critic of the paper *Le Tintamarre* stressed that "he is the real Risley, not the fake one we have seen at the Variétés [theatre], named Sands. . . . "[37]

Going Global

Risley's reputation traveled fast, through published accounts and word of mouth. And he began performing in front of more and more exalted people, and also associating with them, for he was now a true celebrity. In the spring of 1845, he visited Russia, performing in St. Petersburg at the Grand Alexandrian Theatre, and in Moscow, meeting with Russian nobility and generals and being awarded multiple medals. Back in London, on January 27, Risley and his boys appeared before Queen Victoria and Prince Albert at the Old Drury Theatre and "had the honour of attracting the especial attention of the royal auditors and their marked approbation."[38] A month later, on February 27, Risley visited and break-fasted with Gansevoort Melville (the older brother of novelist Herman Melville and head of the U.S. legation in England, who would die of illness only months later). As Melville wrote in his diary for that day, clearly impressed:

> I was much pleased with the boys & on the whole with the father. He has been 3½ yrs abroad & mark-edly successful. He played 70 nights at the Haymarket, 110 in Paris, & brought out of Russia with him 65,000 rubles—65 cents to the rouble. He has bought a place near Phila for $33,000 to which he means to retire in about 2 yrs. He is 39 yrs old & a crack shot—5 ft 9 ½ inches high and most symmetrically built.[39]

Wherever possible, Risley collected autographs of important people in a little morocco-bound book, and in a conscious effort at self-promo-tion he would often display it to reporters, friends, and even, sometimes, to the general public. Twenty years later, a San Francisco reporter for the *Daily Morning Call* would marvel tongue-in-cheek:

> Hiram Powers testifies to the gratification the perfor-mances of Risley and his sons have afforded him, so does Fanny Ellsler, and C. Edwards Lester, and Lord Holland, and the Maharajah of Burdwan, and dozens more whom it would be interesting to publish, could we decipher the crooked chirography of their signs manual.[40]

Wherever Risley went, he had an extraordinary ability to create stories that tended, in today's parlance, to quickly "go viral" and to fur-ther enhance his fame. In Vienna, where public baths were very popular, it was normally necessary to first pass a swimming test before entering the deep end. Risley and his boys refused and created a sensation by doing cannonball somersaults into the water from the upstairs gallery, an audacious act described a few years later in the normally staid U.S. magazine *Ladies Repository*.[41]

Sometimes it was not just what Risley did, but what he said, that made the news. At the beginning of January 1847, Risley and sons made their first appearance at the Theatre Royal, St. Carlo, in Naples, Italy. When the performance ended the family was called out by the audience ten times to appear on stage, at a theatre that held four thousand people and where, according to the correspondent of the *New York Sun*, they were "reaping a golden harvest" of money. The brother of the King of Naples was so impressed that he called on Risley and, in the course of the conversation, asked him what he planned to do when the children got bigger. Risley, ever the wisecracker, rejoined by asking if the royal recalled the story of a Roman athlete, who "commenced by carrying a calf and continued, by practice, to carry it, after it got to be a cow."

At a party later held at the local U.S. minister's residence, Risley's words generated even more publicity. The young United States was at war with Mexico. While the war was highly controversial, many Americans were proud of their nation's performance on the battlefield and still sensitive about their relationship with England. Risley thus told a joke about a Yankee and an Englishman discussing the war wherein—after the Englishman questioned Americans' pluck because of reports of peace offers with Mexico—the Yankee retorted, "Well, I don't know what our folks have offered to do with Mexico; but, stranger, I'll jest tell you one thing—I'll be d___d if we ever offered to make peace with you!" While perhaps not particularly funny to modern readers, this joke so resonated with patriotic readers in the United States at the time that it was reprinted in scores of papers over and over again for the next several years, even in the *Manitowoc Tribune* in faraway Wisconsin, as late as September 20, 1855.[42]

Another aspect of Risley's character that always guaranteed notoriety was his extreme competitiveness and penchant for risk-taking. As noted before, Risley's trip to Russia in the spring of 1845 was a huge success. As one story goes, since he was known to be a crack shot with

the rifle, in Russia he was also asked to enter, and bet on, a competition with the best local marksman. He of course won spectacularly. A
gifted skater, he also undertook a competition with some top Russian
skaters which he won in an electrifying manner, skating at high speed,
leaping over twelve foot holes cut in the ice, and executing somersaults
as he did so, repeatedly. Later, when back in London, Risley boasted
at a fancy dinner party that he was the best shot, the toughest wrestler,
the longest jumper, the finest billiard player, and the farthest hammer-
tosser in all of London. Some of his dinner companions took him up
on his comments, and found the best men they could in the city. Yet
Risley easily won the rifle match and, to unnerve his opponent, "threw
up an orange and put a bullet through it, and nicked a piece cut of a
penny that was also tossed into the air." He also vanquished the English
wrestler, set a new record in the long jump, and won at the hammer
toss. But when it came to billiards—the skill of which Risley was most
proud—he was defeated by John Roberts, an English champion. Stung,
Risley later brought Andrew Stark, one of the best American billiard
players, to London and wagered on his beating Roberts. He lost up to
thirty-thousand dollars, an even greater fortune than he had lost in the
earthquake of Guadeloupe.[43]

Despite Risley's bravado about being able to juggle his sons as they
grew older and heavier, he clearly knew what the future held. In September 1847, he returned to the United States and put on successful
performances with his sons in New York and, in early February, in New
Orleans, possibly even moving on to Vera Cruz, Mexico. But then he
did something of a business somersault and went into partnership in the
United States with John Rowson Smith, the descendant of a long line
of professional painters, who had created a giant panorama of America's
Mississippi River. Leaving his sons behind in Philadelphia with their
mother and his in-laws to be educated, Risley started a new career as an
impresario and a showman.

John K. Chapman & Co. broadside for Risley's "Panorama of the Mississippi," when shown at the American Hall in Leicester Square, London, circa 1849. COURTESY, THE WINTERTHUR LIBRARY: JOSEPH DOWNS COLLECTION OF MANUSCRIPTS AND PRINTED EPHEMERA.

Panorama Man

In the mid-nineteenth century, before moving pictures had developed, giant moving panoramas were a popular form of entertainment. Consisting of colossal paintings on canvas that could be unrolled on a wooden framework and thus tell a story, they allowed people to experience exciting far-away places or events and often featured exotic locales or scenes of famous battles. With dramatic narration, some music, and clever lighting and effects, the panoramic experience came as close to a cinematic virtual reality show as was possible at the time.

One of the best-known panorama painters of the day was an American painter named John Banvard. He created, among other items, an enormous panorama with thirty-six scenes of the Mississippi River. After achieving huge success with it in the United States, he took it to Britain in 1848. The English then had a nearly boundless curiosity about wild and untamed America and its unimaginably huge open spaces, and they helped Banvard—whose painting purported to depict "three thousand miles" of scenery—temporarily become a rich man.

Risley knew John R. Smith from his days with the Rufus Welch circuses, for Smith prominently features in Welch's newspaper advertisements dating back to January 1843 as the decorator and painter of backdrop scenes. Exactly who first painted a giant moving panorama of the Mississippi is not clear, but Banvard's was first exhibited in London, and a scandal erupted when both the Smith-Risley and Banvard panoramas were displayed there in 1849.

Risley arrived in London from America around February 13, 1849, with Smith and a man called Henry S. Risley, who is not to be confused with Henry C. Risley, the professor's son. Henry S. presumably had some familial relationship with the professor, but what, exactly, is unclear. He was, however, some sort of specialist in panoramas and apparently critical to their set-up. Professor Risley and Smith's work appeared in London early March. It was billed as larger and grander and better in all ways than that of Banvard and advertised as a "Gigantic American Panorama" that required "four miles of canvass" and depicted—not three thousand miles—but "nearly four thousand miles of American scenery, being the largest and most perfect moving painting in the world." It took over two hours to view, seated in chairs in a theatre-like hall with fancy chandeliers.[44]

Many London newspapers acknowledged the charms of both productions, but some delighted in comparing the fidelity and skill of the respective painters, or in supporting either the Banvard or Risley-Smith versions, or in simply reporting on the dueling that occurred in the overheated advertising campaigns waged by the two camps. Banvard accused the pair of having plagiarized his idea and copied his painting. Risley, for his part, wrote the famous painter of American Indians, George Catlin, to have him vouch for the originality and wonderfulness of his production, and published the response. In broadsides, he filled nearly all available space with laudatory quotes from the many London papers who sided with him. Banvard, not to be outdone, collected the signatures of prominent Americans living in England who vouched for the superiority of his work, and published them in the newspapers. He also had glowing reviews from the popular novelist Charles Dickens. On November 14, one could find testimonials running by both Banvard and Smith on the same page of the *Manchester Guardian*, each proclaiming the superiority and originality of their works. Smith asserted that Banvard had stolen his idea way back in 1839, from an identical panorama that had subsequently been lost in a fire.[45]

Risley and Smith may have had more energy than Banvard, because Smith created a copy of his giant painting and thus made it possible for Risley to tour it even more widely, gaining ever more exposure. He appears to have subcontracted the panorama business to Henry S. Risley, but either way the panoramas were shown with the Risley name in other European countries, even as far away as Norway. In Oslo (then Kristiana) as late as 1852, it "touched the imagination of the Norwegian poet Vinje, who came away from the exhibition convinced that America was destined to conquer the world."[46] And, of course, it helped to spread Risley's fame.

The Sky Is the Limit

In 1849, Risley also had other business ventures going on in England. In London's Vauxhall Gardens he ran a bowling alley, or what was called a "bowling saloon," where he served an assortment of American drinks. Vauxhall Gardens was at the time one of the more popular London outdoor entertainment spots, where performances and spectacles were often staged, and it gave Risley a chance for even more publicity. Ballooning, still very much in its infancy, was then something of a public spectacle, and some of the most famous balloon ascents at the time took place at Vauxhall Gardens, performed by the legendary aeronaut of the day, Charles Green.

On August 1, 1849, at Vauxhall Gardens, Risley ascended with Green and a party of several other men and women, watched by a cheering crowd of thousands, with music playing and guns firing. As one of the few humans then ever privileged to fly, he later wrote about the experience in an article that resembled his account of the Guadeloupe earthquake of 1843, except that his language was even more colorful. Titled, "Professor Risley's Ascent in a Nassau Balloon," it was given wide circulation in newspapers throughout Europe and the United States (including *Scientific American*).

Because the article was in Risley's own "voice," some publications introduced it as an example of "slang literature," but it reveals much about Risley. He mentions several of the exotic locations he has visited, and he hints that he may have at one point had some formal, higher education. He mentions being accompanied by "Young Hernandez," whom he refers to as his "protégé," but who was actually a celebrity in his own right—an Irish-American boy who was a former member of Welch's Circus and a star equestrian, with whom Risley would have a long association.[47] Most of all, however, the article again reveals Risley's charismatic personality, for it was written with humor and mixed mid-nineteenth-century vernacular with flowery and classical allusions. Stylistically, it might be mistaken for something by Mark Twain.

The article starts out with Risley noting that he has been on mountain tops before, but never aloft, and that practical Americans usually have no interest in building castles in the sky.

> The milky way yields no butter, the moon don't furnish us with cheese; the dog-star don't follow game. . . . Venus is not half so bright as the dazzling eyes of Kentucky; the shooting stars never bring down anything worth having; the "golden rays of Sol ain't worth a clod of California earth; . . . the 'blanket of the night' is not a marketable commodity—don't keep one warm; while sheets of lightning are too hot for any climate."[48]

When the balloon actually begins to ascend, Risley describes being nearly rendered speechless by the thrill, until he has a sip from a flask of sherry provided by the pilot. "Talk of sensations! I felt as though my soul had slipped slick from its clay, and was going a holiday making with my heart in its hand." But amid the light-heartedness, he also sounds like a

SHAKSPEARE RESTORED.

The British satirical magazine *Punch* imagines Shakespeare's *Hamlet*, redone by Risley. *PUNCH*, VOL. II, 1846.

philosophical twentieth-century astronaut, viewing earth from space for the first time. He realizes that from his exhilarating and precarious new perspective, the normal worries and differences and squabbles of mankind soon pale in significance.

> Our lives hung on the chance of a moment, and the best thing we could do, while in the enjoyment of vitality and health, was to gild the pill of existence as brightly as possible. Had I read the Bible from Genesis to Revelations, I could not have learnt a better lesson; national animosities and human prejudices subsided before it.[49]

With such a flair for publicity, it should not be surprising that, during the 1840s and 1850s, Risley's name became a household word. His ability to juggle his sons with his feet became known as the "Risley Act," or the "Risley Business," but his name also became a metaphor for great agility and thus acquired an even wider usage, as in the expression "à la Risley." The British humor magazine *Punch* in 1846 delighted in using Risley as a way to measure British politics and politicians. One writer stated, "We should as soon as think of recommending Professor Risley, the posture master, to regulate the present posture of the nation, as dream of accepting Brougham in the capacity of a Prime Minister."

Another cracked: "Professor Risley and his Sons are positively stiff and inflexible when compared with the very supple state of the Marquis of Anglesea and his aide-de-camps. . . . "[50]

To keep his career going, Risley required a great deal of agility. After the success with his panorama of the Mississippi, he had a giant panorama of the River Thames created, which he took back to the United States for American audiences, and which Henry S. Risley later frequently toured. In 1853 he also imported a ballet troupe from Europe to America, and it proved a failure, so much so that he fell terribly in debt. At the end of the year, an expensive and expansive 114 acre property—that he had purchased in his glory days in Chester, Pennsylvania—was repossessed by the local sheriff. He toured cities on the Atlantic coast with his children and he developed a variety show, but the fates were not smiling on him. In the spring of 1854 someone abducted his beloved dog Pro, a purebred Newfoundland used in one of his acts. He was able to make the most of this misfortune and generate more newspaper articles when the dog miraculously returned alive, having apparently made his way home to New York from far away Pittsburgh, Pennsylvania.[51] But times were difficult.

The world was changing. At the end of 1854, Risley was performing in New York with one son and a contortionist, named D'Evani. By the spring of the following year, he was finally appearing with a new protégé he would call his "son," named Charles. It was time to try something new, and in 1855, for those seeking newness, the American West was a powerful magnet.

ACT 3
Going for Gold

"It is hard to yield the palm of mistress of the world's golden wealth, but at the rate at which discoveries are making in Australia, California will soon be stripped of her title to so proud a distinction."
                              —*Daily Alta California*, July 31, 1852

On June 18, 1855, Professor Risley made his first appearance at San Francisco's Metropolitan Theatre with his "son" Charles and the contortionist D'Evani. It was not a resounding success, at least for Risley. The audience was sparse, and the next day the *Daily Alta* lavished far more praise on D'Evani, also implying that the evening's entertainment was partly saved only by the inclusion of two theatrical pieces. Still, the paper did concede that, once word of the performances got around, the theatre would soon fill up. Oddly, for his first west coast appearance Risley had not arranged any advance publicity. And his performance may have been affected by fatigue, since the three performers had arrived from the east coast only days earlier, setting a record for speed of 21.5 days. But it had been an arduous trip, one that required sailing to Central America, crossing over to the Pacific by river boat and stagecoach at San Juan, Nicaragua, and then traveling up along the West Coast on a fast steamer named *The Uncle Sam*.[1]

In the mid-nineteenth century, people in the performing-arts

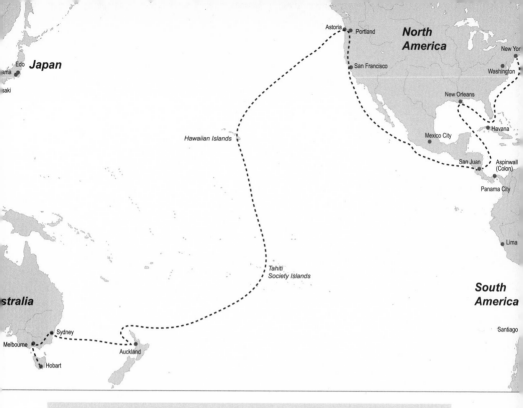

Astoria · Portland
North America
New Yor
Edo **Japan**
ama ·
San Francisco
saki ·
Washington
New Orleans
Hawaiian Islands
Mexico City
Havana
San Juan · Aspinwall (Colon)
Panama City
Lima
Tahiti Society Islands
South America
stralia
Santiago
Sydney
Melbourne
Auckland
Hobart

Map of Risley's route to the Pacific.

business often had to travel continuously. In the absence of television and video and radio, performers could only reach new audiences by physically going to them; staying in the same spot risked slow death for an act because repetition would eventually bore even the most devoted fans. For his time, Risley was an abnormally mobile entertainer, yet he was not the only one traveling to California. While he was in Europe, the territorial map of the United States had been redrawn, the young country now completely spanning the North American continent. With the discovery of gold nearby in 1848, San Francisco had been inundated by people from all over the world hoping to strike it rich, to the point where the shoreline was at one point littered with ships, abandoned by crews who had taken to the goldfields. And not all of the newcomers went mining for gold. With the sudden boom in the population of California, and in huge new wealth, optimistic entrepreneurs flocked to the state, and so did entertainers. In the beginning, a gold-rush town like San Francisco was an El Dorado for entertainers willing to travel, because audiences were flush with money, largely young, and single and male. They craved diversion and fun and rarely complained about the quality of the entertainment. But by 1855, things had already begun to change.

California Dreaming

In July, shortly after Risley's arrival, one local newspaper correspondent wrote that most of the entertainers then in the city (including Risley and his troupe, who he specifically mentioned)

> . . . were all doing nothing, *positively nothing*; most of them without the means of getting away, and "cursing" like mad the S.F. correspondents of Eastern papers, whose flaming accounts tempted them to tread the Pacific shores. We are a theatre-going community still, and a liberal one at that, but we have our wives now to spend our evenings with, which we had not in the palmy days of the San Francisco stage, when actors of fifth-rate talent were stars of the first magnitude with us.[2]

Risley worked mightily to overcome the challenges he faced. His new apprentice, Master Charles, could not be expected to perform at the same level as his own sons, and now over forty, Risley was himself hardly young. But as the opening night at the Metropolitan in San Francisco suggested, he was aided by the popularity of his contortionist colleague, D'Evani, who would perform and travel with him for the next five years. Born as John Evans, for the stage he went by "John Devani," "Mons. D'Evani," "Signor D'Evani," and sometimes just "Devani"; he was said to have "Frenchified" his name at the request of some admirers in England because "distance lends enchantment in the matter of a public performer's birthplace as well as in natural scenery." D'Evani was twenty-two years old and, like Risley, he had already achieved great fame throughout Europe, but not for the usual acrobatics. His skill was his ability to twist himself into the most inhuman of positions, like a pretzel, an eel, or a piece of India Rubber.[3] As the *New York Times* correspondent had delighted in describing him in Paris in 1853, comparing him to a famous French diplomat, he was,

> The Talleyrand of Clowns, being in physics what the cunning politician was in morals, utterly destitute of principles; standing indifferently on his head, hands or feet, swelling, collapsing, twisting, doubling and elongating himself in the most inexplicable, and sometimes, apparently in the most inextricable manner.[4]

In San Francisco, D'Evani's fame was enhanced after a group of local physicians examined his body at the Metropolitan. They carefully and scientifically measured his physical expansions and contractions, the statistics of which were published in the *Alta* by the local press (who were invited to the exclusive performance and later testified to his unrivaled prowess as a contortionist). Little information about D'Evani's background has survived, but when he appeared with Risley in San Francisco, he was billed as already having professionally traveled through Europe, Asia, and America. Given his age, it is hard to imagine that he had been to Asia, at least as we know it today, but in mid-nineteenth-century parlance the "Orient" and "Asia" could refer to Turkey and parts of the Middle East, even including Egypt. And D'Evani had definitely been to the Far East in spirit, at least, for London newspapers show him appearing in that city in 1852 with the always internationally minded Louis Soullier's "Cirque Oriental."[5]

During the summer of 1855, Risley, Master Charles, and D'Evani performed mainly at San Francisco's Metropolitan Theatre, but they also gave exhibitions to packed audiences at the popular Russ Gardens, where Risley lodged and there was an outdoor amphitheatre. On July 4 Risley appeared at the Metropolitan with other acts and personally performed a polka routine. For entertainers in San Francisco, it was common to start with a run in the city, and then begin touring towns in the California countryside and in the Gold Country on what was a fairly established

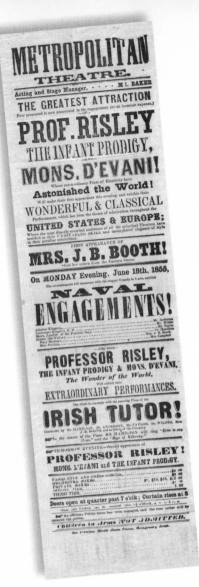

June 18, 1855, playbill for San Francisco's Metropolitan Theatre. BPF TCS 71, HARVARD THEATRE COLLECTION, HOUGHTON LIBRARY, HARVARD UNIVERSITY.

circuit. By July 19 the trio therefore moved to nearby Sacramento, the capital of California, and performed there in an outdoor pavilion where they were well received. While noting that their performance would be more correctly termed a series of "tableaux," the local paper praised them, saying, "The contrast between Mr. Risley—herculean in figure—and the infant prodigy, full of life and grace, was a marked feature of the entertainment. The performances of Mons. D'Evani—apparently contravening the laws of nature—may well non-plus the medical faculty and challenge the credulity of those who have not witnessed them."[6]

RISLEY'S VATICAN,
Old Sacramento Theater, Third street,
between I and J.
Lessees and Managers ....W. VENUA & M. B. MILLER
Prices Reduced to Suit the Times.
Will open THIS (Monday) EVENING, November 19th,
and continue EVERY NIGHT DURING THE WEEK.
The company at the VATICAN will embrace some of
the best talent in the world—commencing with
PROFESSOR RISLEY AND SON, the Classic Gymnasts.
MONS. D'EVANI, the Graceful Evolutionist, and the
WONDER OF THE WORLD,
THE CARONI FAMILY, composed of
SIG. and MADAME CARONI,
M'LLE CARONI,
M'LLE CELESTINE, and
MASTER GULIAN.
Sig. and Madame Caroni made the ascent from the
ground to the top of the International Hotel, in San
Francisco, lately, on a double rope, without balance
poles.
LA PETITE CERITO, the graceful Infant Danseuse.
MISS LIZZIE BURBANK, Chorist, Vocalist and Dan-
seuse.
MIKE MITCHELL, (late of Campbell's Minstrels,) the
greatest living Ethiopian dancer.
H. DONNELY, the far-famed Banjoist and delineator
of Negro eccentricities.
HERR LOTHAMER, the extraordinary Gymnast,
who will nightly ascend a pole 18 feet in hight, while it
is supported by Prof. Risley.
DAN CONNOVER, the "Pike County" Jester,
Edmunds' Brass Band
Will furnish free music for the million.
PRICES FOR ADMISSION:
Private Boxes $5 00
Dress Circle and Orchestra Seats. 1 00
Parquet. 50
Boxes for Colored Persons. 1 00
Box Office open from 10 A. M. to 4 P. M. daily.
An efficient police and polite ushers in attendance.
n10   J. W. WALSH, Agent.

Ad for Risley's Vatican in Sacramento. *SAC-RAMENTO DAILY UNION, NOVEMBER 22, 1855.*

By August, Risley was appearing with a "Vatican," or circus, in El Dorado County's Placerville—a tiny town today but then the center of gold mining and the third largest city in California. In September "Risley's Vatican" was in Amador and Calaveras counties, and in October it was back in San Francisco on Jackson Street across from the International Hotel, in a tented pavilion with a new tricolor marquee that could hold 1,300 people. Forming a circus allowed Risley to add more variety, expand his audience, and generate more profits. In addition to his own acrobatic acts with his "son," he sometimes sang and danced, and he of course had D'Evani's contortions and posings. But he also added the Caroni family, who could do pantomime "ballet" and the ever-exciting tightrope walking; Herr Latimer (or "Herr Lothamer"), the gymnast; La Petite Cerito, the "infant danseuse"; Mr. Caldwell and his trained pony; and a variety of other acts. Eventually he even hired a brass band. Women were always popular in the Gold Country, so in 1856 Risley went back east, and in June he returned with a troupe of fifteen people, including ten females, or what he called a "Ballet of Living Statuary" or a "Tableaux Troupe." In Sacramento the ballet performance fell flat, but it added more variety. As a later advertisement for one of Risley's productions announced, he had "equestrian performances, gymnastic performances, elegant ballet dancing, classical attitudes, sentimental and comic singing, aerial dancing, corde volante, perche and trapez performances."[7]

Pricing for Risley's shows varied wildly, depending on the season, the venue, and the popularity of event. On July 4, 1855, before forming his circus and while still at San Francisco's Metropolitan, proscenium box seats were going for fifteen dollars, while second- and third-tier seats were one dollar. Even in gold-crazed country, where prices were inflated, this was expensive. Later, with his circus and reduced pricing in effect, reserved cushioned seats went for two dollars, dress circle seats for one dollar, and pit seats for fifty cents. In November, after moving to Sacramento where his Vatican performed at a theatre indoors (and where he added comedians, minstrel artists, and a "delineator of Negro eccentricities"), he was charging five dollars for private boxes, one dollar for dress seats, one dollar for boxes for "Colored Persons," and fifty cents for floor seating. The bigger his circus got, the more overhead he had. Still, he was careful to participate in benefit performances, to stage performances with familiar and patriotic themes, and to be a good community member, even occasionally donating money to charity.

California was not an easy environment in which to operate a circus. San Francisco and the Gold Country were still rough and tumble places; crime and corruption were so out of control that in 1856 a Committee of Vigilance took matters into its own hands in the city, arresting and occasionally lynching people it deemed guilty of the most heinous offenses. But there were also the usual circus problems of financing, personnel management, accidents, and lawsuits. A fight broke out between patrons in Oroville over politics in September 1856. In San Juan, in October, a storm blew down the circus tent. In Oroville, in July, 1857, a circus member from Australia died. During the run of Risley's Tableaux troupe in San Francisco in 1856 there were mechanical problems with the staging, which resulted in bad reviews.

And there were always legal problems. In October 1855, Risley was accused of larceny in San Francisco by a man for having taken a few sofas; although the case was thrown out, it was a distraction. A month later the papers reported that he was scheduled to go on trial in Sacramento for another unspecified offense, brought by "the State of California." Of course, when Risley was successful, he also had to confront the risk of imitators. On December 18, 1855, he ran an ad in the *Sacramento Daily Union* warning readers not to mistake his Vatican circus for an inferior version—one that had usurped the name of his and was touring the Gold Country.[8]

Unlike in Europe or on the East Coast, in California it was not as easy for Risley to generate the viral type of publicity that he had in the past. In San Francisco, he showed the local reporter from the *Alta* his scrapbook, with playbills from "London, Glasgow, Liverpool, Belfast, Brussels, Paris, Hamburg, St. Petersburg, Amsterdam, Rotterdam, Dresden, Marseilles, Florence, Naples, Milan, Madrid, and about a dozen more of the great capitals of Europe." And he impressed the man with the "autographs of Eugene P. Bonaparte, a Turkish poem by Abdel Hager, the handwriting of Crobriand, Lord Holland, Gen. Mininakir, the Marquis de Negro of Genoa; Henry F. Lee, Albert R. Kemble, Hyram Powers, and Fanny Ellesler."[9] These staged viewings generated a newspaper article, but little more.

Even astonishing stunts generated only limited publicity. On October 16, 1855, in his Vatican circus in San Francisco, Risley personally balanced Mons. Lattimer (who weighed 165 pounds) on a twenty-five-foot-long pole and waltzed around the ring to the accompaniment of the band's horns and huge applause.[10] The most publicity he gained was in the same month, with Senor and Signora Caroni, the tightrope walkers in his circus. After stringing ropes from the ground to the top of the International Hotel on Jackson St., the pair ascended on them, about three feet apart, their arms locked around each other, for a distance of 150 feet. Dressed in flesh-colored tights, Indian-style muslin skirts, and ornamented with ostrich feathers, they were watched by a crowd reported as five thousand people. This feat was widely talked about and reported, even back East in the December 23 issue of *Scientific American*. But the magazine only mentioned the names of the tightrope walkers, and not Risley.[11]

Part of Risley's problem in California was the level of competition. It was another good reason to keep traveling. Despite the remote frontier nature of Northern California in the 1850s, dreams of riches had attracted many top-notch performers. As a result, local citizens already had access to a remarkable amount of fairly high-quality entertainment. In San Francisco, Risley's acts had to compete with musical acts, panorama demonstrations, regular theatre, and the appearance of famous professional actors, such as the young Edwin Booth, later one of the most famous Shakespearean actors of his time (and the brother of John Wilkes Booth, who would assassinate President Lincoln). California had been admitted to the Union as a "free" state, where slavery was prohibited, but minstrel troupes that burlesqued Southern and African American culture were all the rage. In the spring of 1856, when Risley's group was performing in the city, on the advertising pages it had to compete with a popular burlesque extravaganza titled "Niggerism in A.D. 2856."[12] And there were more direct rivals, too. There were traveling menageries of wild animals and multiple circuses, sometimes with bigger, even more spectacular acts. In the San Francisco area alone, between 1855 and 1857, other circuses besides Risley's Vatican and Circus included the following: Lee and Marshall's popular and big National Circus and Hippodrome, Joseph Rowe's Pioneer Circus, Bartholomew and Co.'s Pacific Circus, Lee and Bennett's Great North American Circus, and several variations of all of them. Sometimes owners cooperated with each other; sometimes they competed. There was also a certain amount of movement among the circuses by star performers making guest appearances, as well as attempts by managers and owners to poach the most popular figures for their own outfits; many of the performers knew each other from having worked together back East or even in Europe.

Joseph Rowe's Pioneer Circus was one of Risley's frequent competitors and, as the name implies, one of the veteran outfits in the area. As early as 1849, during the California Gold Rush, Rowe had brought his circus to the area, entertaining audiences in San Francisco and the burgeoning mining towns of Northern California. In 1856, his Pioneer Circus had William F. Wallet, the famous Shakespearian clown; Mons. Gillot, the strongman; a full complement of equestrian artists; and a brass and string band that traveled in its own gaudily painted wagon drawn by a team of eight decorated horses. By the time Risley arrived in California, Rowe was already an extremely popular figure and something of a legend. His itinerant nature rivaled that of Risley, and he had already pioneered an entirely different performing circuit, sailing to Hawaii in 1851 and then moving on to New Zealand and Australia, returning to San Francisco a wealthy man in 1855, reportedly with "$100,000 in cash and numerous chests of treasure."[13] One of Rowe's most famous performers was "Juan Hernandez," otherwise known as James Hernandez or even "Jimmy Robinson," formerly of Welch's circus and the same lad with whom Risley had ascended in a balloon in London in 1849. Hernandez was for a while under contract with the owner of the North American Circus, and in such demand in California that, in March 1857, he was slapped with a lawsuit to prevent him appearing at the San Francisco's Metropolitan Theatre with D'Evani and Risley. In May, moreover, he was performing with Rowe's Pioneer circus. Surviving letters from the Pioneer Circus show that at one point in 1857 Rowe even briefly employed D'Evani, but Risley was able to entice the contortionist back into his operation.[14]

With all the competition, and with a deteriorating California economy despite all the gold, by 1857 it was time for Risley to think up something new. Sailing back to the East Coast was a possibility but probably not a very attractive idea without some radically different acts to present there. Much of the rest of the American West was still unsettled. The Rocky Mountains were still extremely difficult to cross by land, there were still Indian troubles in the interior of the West, and in Utah there were conflicts with Mormons. To start with, Risley therefore took his group on a tour of the mining country, then Camptonville, and by September of that year he was way up north in Salem, Oregon, soon moving to The Dalles along the Columbia River. His production was described much later by a local pioneer, Elizabeth Lord, as having been "some acrobatic feats, some poor songs, and some attempts at a dramatic production of the 'Lady of Lyons.'" He had stars such as Rossetter, Lizzie Stewart, and Madame Louise, the mother of "El Cerito," or Cerito Gordon. El Cerito and her mother would later sue Risley for back wages in San Francisco. She is described by one source as "a little girl who had some talent, and was the only acrobat of any account."[15]

In Oregon—which was not yet even a state—Risley faced nearly as

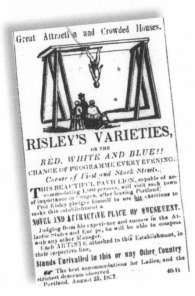

Risley's ad in the *Weekly Oregonian*, show-
ing a "walking on the ceiling" trick. WEEK-
LY OREGONIAN, COURTESY OF THE OREGON
HISTORICAL SOCIETY, AUGUST 29, 1857.

much competition as in California. In Portland he ran elaborate ads in
the papers, showed reporters his autograph book, and gave benefits for
the local fire department, but he was going up against the much-larger
Mammoth Circus, also from California. In Salem, as one reporter noted,
"The town is crowded with theatrical companies. . . . There is also Risley, D'Evani and Roesseter, performing under a tri-colored tent. They
all expect to reap golden luck, but this is very doubtful, as there is very
little money spent here. They are waiting . . . for some of the rich Cali-
fornians to come up here and distribute some of their change." Tellingly,
one of the companies in Portland was reported as planning to give up
and leave for the Sandwich Islands, or Hawaii.[16]

In San Francisco, when Risley and D'Evani had first arrived in 1855,
interest in the further reaches of the Pacific, and in Asia, had been at a
high level. The city had already hosted Japanese castaways for an extended
time in 1851. And only a year earlier, in 1854, the U.S. Navy's Commodore Matthew Perry, backed by an armed fleet, had forced Japan to sign
a treaty that would eventually lead to trade and full diplomatic relations.
Among San Franciscans this had created high hopes for trade with Japan
and for new riches. At the beginning of 1855, some bold Americans had
even privately sailed to Japan on a schooner named the *Caroline E. Foote*,

hoping to take advantage of the new treaty and set up shop in Japan as traders. Denied permission to stay, they had returned to San Francisco in the summer of that year, embittered by the obfuscation of Japanese officialdom and convinced Japan was not yet really serious about trading. To offset their failed attempt to set up shop in Japan, they proceeded to auction off what was billed as the first commercial cargo ever imported from Japan. In 1855, therefore, along with Risley's playbills, advertisements for the goods had therefore appeared in local San Francisco newspapers, generating extraordinary interest in Japan for months.

Did Risley fantasize about going to Asia, or even Japan in 1857? If he did, it probably would have been far too difficult to put such a plan into action. There was another option, however, and that was to head for Australasia, on the Pacific and Southern Hemisphere circuit already established by Joseph Rowe and his Pioneer Circus.

The Sandwich Islands

On November 23, 1857, Risley, his protégé Master Charles, and D'Evani arrived in Honolulu, in the Sandwich Islands, on the *Metropolis*, from Astoria, Oregon. According to the local newspapers, the voyage took twenty-seven days, but why it took so long is a mystery, as the trip normally required only around two weeks.[17]

In 1857, Hawaii was still an independent kingdom. American businessmen and missionaries had gradually started to whittle away at, and eventually would usurp, the authority of the native people, who were also starting to perish in high numbers from European diseases. Then as now, Honolulu was the main center of population and—along with Lahaina, on the island of Maui—the center of the entire whaling industry in the Pacific Ocean. The whaling industry was at its peak in the 1850s. Ships from all over the world, but especially from New England, wintered with their crews in Hawaii before going out to fish in the Northwest and the Sea of Japan, sometimes boosting the population of Honolulu to twelve thousand. Hawaii's links with Asia were already deep, for nearly all ships, whether whalers or cargo or military vessels that crossed the Pacific in those days, stopped at the islands for reprovi-sioning, rest, and repairs. By1857, ships regularly arrived from ports on the East Coast of the United States and Europe, from Canton, and even from newly opened Yokohama, making Hawaii one of the most cosmo-politan spots on earth.

With missionaries in increasing control of Hawaiian social life, the islands had a complicated attitude toward entertainment. Crews from sailing ships—especially whaling ships from the East Coast that had to sail round the southern tip of South America—often endured extraordi-nary hardships and death-defying hazards simply to get to Hawaii. Under the slogan of "No God West of the Horn," once on shore they wanted to enjoy the weather and indulge in the island's charms, including its beautiful women, often aided by some alcoholic libations. Businessmen were more than happy to indulge the sailors, but puritanical missionar-ies were trying mightily to Christianize the native population, and they frowned upon pleasure-seeking. This conflict was reflected in a variety of ways over time. In the 1820s, in Lahaina, whaling ship captains had lobbed cannon balls at missionary residences out of revenge, when the latter tried to prevent young Hawaiian women from swimming out to the ships. In the 1850s, in Honolulu, the conflict played out in the pages of two major English-language newspapers—the secular *Polynesian* and the more religious *Friend*.

The Friend was run by missionary-editor Samuel C. Damon (who had an abiding interest in Japan and had helped the most famous cast-away of all, Manjirō, return home in 1850-51). In the spring of 1857, Damon confronted what he considered a most scandalous charge, brought by an American newspaper, that missionaries in Hawaii had been attending local theatre performances. Although he had himself recently aided a stranded agent of an American circus in Honolulu and was normally a very progressive man, he was adamantly opposed to such entertainment and wrote indignantly to admonish his readers that " . . . church members should never venture within the precincts of the theater."[18] Because of the missionary influence, even non-church mem-bers found their entertainment severely proscribed. The same month Risley arrived, the *Friend* ran a public notice from the governor of

Oahu announcing new regulations on seamen. They were banned from "galloping horses carelessly, getting drunk, 'hallooing' or singing in a loud voice, and carrying bowie-knives, sword-canes, pistols, air-guns, sling-shots, or other deadly weapons." In what must have been the most painful restriction of all for sailors, they were also forbidden from being on shore after 9:30pm.[19]

As one might expect, one result of the suppression of entertainment was a huge, pent-up demand for it, which worked in Risley's favor. Shortly before he arrived, the *Polynesian* noted that it was the first season for many years that "Honolulu has not had a theatre, circus, or both, nor public dance houses, and as those things have been looked upon and cried down by many as unmitigated sources of evil and sinks of perdition, it would perhaps be instructive to learn what improvement, if any, has been effected in the morality of the town by their absence or suppression."[20] Throughout Risley's stay in Honolulu, the paper would strongly support him. On November 28, shortly after his arrival, it ran an announcement for "Risley's Varieties" and stated:

> . . . we have nearly lost all patience with those "steel-engines of the Devil's contrivance," as Hawthorn calls a certain class of philanthropists, who "never once seem to suspect that the false deity, in whose iron features, immitigable to all the rest of mankind, they see only benignity and love, is but a spectrum of the very priest himself, projected upon the surrounding darkness." To us, however,
> —it is joy
> To think the best we can of human kind.
> And we therefore hail with pleasure the arrival of Risley's Troupe to vary the monotony of the season.[21]

"With a tact and *savoir faire* that marks the gentleman, and an indefatigability of energy that marks the businessman," Risley performed in Hawaii to great success throughout December, billing his performances as "Risley's Varieties."[22] He had brought his tri-colored pavilion tent and

Silk playbill for Risley's Varieties in Honolulu, 1857. BPF TCS 68, HARVARD THEATRE COLLECTION, HOUGHTON LIBRARY, HARVARD UNIVERSITY.

equipment with him from Oregon, as well as a "Captain Wilber" and Philip Dickerson, who served as his treasurer and band leader, respectively. It was a stripped down configuration, featuring himself and Master Charles, as well as D'Evani doing contortions. On January 2, however, he performed in a benefit for himself at the Royal Hawaiian Theatre, where he was joined by ten local performers as well as the popular actress, Miss Anna Immel. Risley appeared as eight different characters, D'Evani performed various new features, Charles did "La Perche," and there was even an "incredible Disappearance Trick." The *Polynesian*, in addition to running an ad for the group, lauded their appearance as a "rare treat" and took another dig at the missionaries, saying, "Life is not all a dungeon with loop-holes pointing to the sky alone. There is untold beauty in earthly things as well; and he, who will not laugh when he may, is—well,—anything you like."[23]

Risley and his little band attracted interest at the highest levels in

Hawaii, and a surviving playbill printed on beautiful satin-silk also shows that they performed before King Kamehameha IV and Queen Emma at their palace. In addition to Risley and his protégé's aerial acts, as well as D'Evani's contortions, Mr. Dickerson performed a violin solo, and a Mr. Pickering gave a piano performance.

On January 2, 1858, the *Polynesian* lauded Risley's presence in Honolulu, contrasting the effect of churches, the circus, and a drinking establishment in Honolulu:

> Ah! Here is Smith's Church, Risley's Varieties and the Commercial in close confab, smiling on each other and their customers. One prays for you in the morning; the other plays for you in the evening, and with the kind belief that life is but a compromise you balance your mind with a nightcap at the third. . . . The one can be as little spared as the other to the healthful performance of man's mental functions.[24]

It was soon time to move again. In a few weeks, the American Circus, a new circus of which veteran showman Joseph Rowe was a co-proprietor, would take over entertainment in the town. It was much larger and had star equestrian performers such as Risley's old friend, the young Hernandez. With it, Rowe hoped to duplicate his earlier Pacific success, by visiting Hawaii and then Australia again.

Ahead of his competitor, Joseph Rowe, Risley would take the plunge and embark on the Pacific Circuit that Rowe had pioneered years earlier. He would travel to Tahiti, New Zealand, and Australia. And later he would enter Asia. All-in-all, he would effectively disappear from the pages of American newspapers for nearly a decade.

On January 8, 1858, Risley and his little band, with their tent and performing equipment, left Honolulu harbor for Tahiti on the schooner *Caroline E. Foote*, with the ultimate destination of New Zealand and Australia. Along the way, Risley had ample opportunity to learn about Asia and Japan, for this was the same vessel that had taken a group of American adventurer-businessmen to Japan two years earlier, on an abortive mission to set up shop in a newly opened Japanese port. But at this point Risley was clearly more interested in New Zealand and Australia, especially the latter. Ever since gold had been discovered in Australia in 1851, it had drawn adventurers from all over the world. They needed entertainment, and Risley intended to satisfy their needs.

On May 1, 1858, after a voyage of four months, the *Caroline E. Foote* finally reached Auckland, New Zealand, after stopping at Tahiti and the Society Islands and clearing "heavy and baffling gales." It was fall in the Southern Hemisphere, and it rained heavily that day, but when David Burn, a local newspaperman, boarded the ship in the harbor, he found that "she had a quantity of splendid oranges and brought more amusement in the form of Professor Risley and troupe."[25]

New Zealand

Why Risley chose to visit New Zealand rather than go directly to Australia is not clear, but it was often a stop along the way and he was guaranteed a warm welcome there. New Zealand, about 1,200 miles southeast of Australia, was a British Crown colony, and Auckland, on North Island, was its biggest European settlement. Geographically even more isolated than Australia, the citizens of Auckland relished visits by entertainers from the outside world. Despite leaving Hawaii after Risley, only a month earlier Rowe and Marshall's American Circus, with star equestrian James Hernandez, had stopped in at Auckland en route to Australia and held forth locally for two weeks.

Upon arriving, "Risley's Varieties" quickly set to work, staging their first performance at the Theatre Royal on May 10. The local *Southern Cross* the next day declared that they "completely took the house by storm," and lavished praise on Risley, D'Evani, the music, and "Master Charles," who showed himself to be a "chip off the old block" with his songs and a "stump speech." The writer of the review had previously seen Risley in England with the Queen present and noted that "Mr. Risley's reputation is too well established to need support from our journal."[26] Master Charles made such a local impression that two years later a

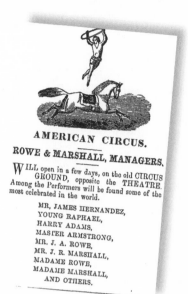

AMERICAN CIRCUS.

ROWE & MARSHALL, MANAGERS,

WILL open in a few days, on the old CIRCUS GROUND, opposite the THEATRE. Among the Performers will be found some of the most celebrated in the world.

MR. JAMES HERNANDEZ,
YOUNG RAPHAEL,
HARRY ADAMS,
MASTER ARMSTRONG,
MR. J. A. ROWE,
MR. J. R. MARSHALL,
MADAME ROWE,
MADAME MARSHALL,
AND OTHERS.

Ad for Rowe and Marshall's American Circus in Auckland, New Zealand. *DAILY SOUTHERN CROSS*, APRIL 9, 1858.

legislator in parliament would recall having seen him with Risley in the Exchange Hotel, where he,

> . . . in consideration of sixpences and shillings from the bystanders, got upon a tub and delivered a speech in true Yankee style. The boy spoke quite as fluently as the honourable member for Wanganui, and used about the same amount of argument. It was a kind of speech which he (Sir Curtis) believed was usually called "buncombe."[27]

Risley and his troupe stayed in Auckland for four months. During such a long run, it wasn't possible to win over everyone, every night. When David Burn stopped in to see Risley's entertainment on May 15, it was pouring "cats and dogs," and he found the show to be "a miserable house to a miserable show." But generally Risley did everything possible to ensure success. To add variety to the show, he added other local entertainers. He augmented his regular acrobatics and D'Evani's contortions with some of his own singing and acting. He announced in the newspapers that interested parties could stop by the Exchange Hotel, where he was staying, to see his book of autographs from notables in Europe. To generate further publicity, he offered the tidy sum of one-hundred pounds to anyone in all New Zealand who could perform the same feats as D'Evani or "Master Risley." In July, after a major conflagration in Auckland, he held benefits to raise money for the aid of those displaced and injured by the fire. In August, when the troupe decided to rest, Risley generated yet more publicity by using a special net to go fishing in a creative way in the Auckland harbor, at one point hauling up seven hundred fish at a time. This astonished onlookers and won a prominent description of the stunt in the local papers, as well as those in Australia and far away England.[28]

Australia

On September 11, the Risley Varieties arrived in Sydney, New South Wales, Australia, after a two-week voyage from Auckland in the *Caroline E. Foote*. After a short stint in Sydney, the troupe moved to Melbourne, in the state of Victoria, near the goldfields, and by October they were opening at the Royal Theatre. While also a British colony, Australia had an entirely different environment from that of New Zealand. Claimed for Britain by explorer Captain Cook in 1770, eastern Australia had at first been used as a giant penal colony for British convicts. With a land mass nearly the size of the continental United States and a tiny European population then of only around one million, Australia was a wide-open place. The discovery of large amounts of gold in Victoria in the early 1850s attracted adventurers from all over the world, including the United States and China. The result was a population boom, chances for overnight wealth, and the worst domestic armed conflict in all of Australian history when, less than four years before Risley's arrival, miners in the Ballarat goldfields revolted against the high taxes they were being forced to pay.

As with California, this potent mixture of money, single-male chaos, and the monotony of physical labor brought opportunity for entertainers, who flocked to the area. Often they were performers Risley already knew from Europe or the United States, such as Hernandez (who had

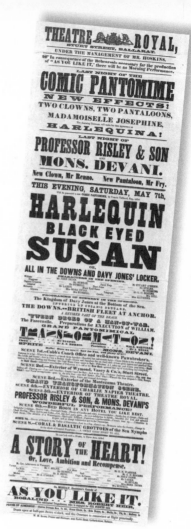

Risley and "son" with D'Evani, as they appeared on a May 7 playbill at Ballarat's Theatre Royal, on Sturt Street. X792/3 COURTESY, MITCHELL LIBRARY, STATE LIBRARY OF NEW SOUTH WALES.

come with Joseph Rowe's circus). Or they were talent who lived in Australia. When Risley began performing in the Theatre Royal in Melbourne, John Reddie Black (a popular singer who as a newspaper editor would later befriend Risley in Japan) was scheduled nearby. Also in Melbourne around the same time were the Yeamans (a famous husband and wife clown and equestrian team), who would later work for Risley. In Back Creek, New South Wales, Risley was competing with a "Professor Bushell," the "electro biologist," who would also pop up later in Japan; as a local reporter joked, there were, "I scarcely know how many professors."[29] While there appear to have been no Japanese in Australia, there was a Chinese acrobat who electrified Australian audiences, appearing on playbills with the astounding sobriquet of "Chin Foo Lam Boo," who may not actually have been Chinese. Meeting fellow performers generated opportunities, information on new Australian entertainment circuits, and possibilities for the future. Some of the circus managers Risley apparently met at this time would also later, with his help, import Japanese troupes into Australia.

Risley would remain in Australia for nearly two years, performing in Melbourne, Sydney, and smaller towns on the southeastern seaboard, as well as in the interior goldfields. With Master Charles and D'Evani, he also had a long run lasting over five months on the southernmost island and penal colony of Hobart, Tasmania, entertaining audiences that included the local British military garrison.

Ads for Risley's little band appeared in Australian newspapers with remarkable regularity. They make it possible to track his nearly nonstop movements in considerable detail, hint at his future plans, and show how he competed. For example, an 1859 playbill that appeared in Ballarat's *The Star* announced that Risley, Charles, and D'Evani would only be appearing at the Charlie Napier Theater for six nights, "their engagement in India precluding a longer stay." This engagement was apparently deferred, but it is evidence of the fact that, soon after arriving in Australia, Risley was already thinking of going even further west.[30]

Another playbill—for a show opening in Sydney's Temperance Hall on Pitt Street on May 12, 1860—illustrates how Risley was able to keep audience interest by incorporating other acts in his productions. Professor Risley and "son" are first announced as having appeared before Queen Victoria, Prince Albert, the Emperor of the French, the Emperor of Russia, the Emperor of Austria, the kings of Prussia, Sweden, Holland, Hanover, Naples, Pope Pius IX, and the governor of Tasmania, "His Excellency Sir H. E. F. Young and suite." Risley and Master Charles's act is headlined as "Drawing-Room Entertainment," featuring their "Classical Evolutions, illustrating the poetry of gymnastic science," and concentrating on "classical graces, beauty, and elegance." But they are also accompanied on the bill by the contortionist Monsieur D'Evani, as well as J. O. Pierce, a multi-talented vocal and instrumental star, and Signora Don, the opera singer and polka dancer. The audience was promised a change of program every night. In this and other performances Risley tailored his shows to local tastes, among other things incorporating humorous sketches of Yankee qualities, which made Australian audiences howl with laughter.[31]

There nevertheless remain a few puzzling unfilled gaps in Risley's movements while in Australia. For two months in the summer of 1859, he seems to have disappeared. At least one modern scholar has posited that he went back to America, but there would not have been time for this. His partner, D'Evani, even more oddly, appears in British and Tasmanian playbills at almost the same time, perhaps indicating that someone was impersonating him. Risley is sometimes also said to have engaged in gold mining in Australia, but this is far more likely to have been meant in a figurative sense. In the gold rush towns of Ballarat, Victoria, and Back Creek, New South Wales, he appears regularly in playbills and newspaper announcements. According to one good friend, Risley did hire some people to dig for him in Back Creek, but "from his claim he 'never saw the colour' (of gold)."[32]

When times were right, with the right acts, and with the right venue, entertainers could make a fortune off the miners. In the early days of the gold rush, one writer has noted, "the diggers, intoxicated at suddenly finding themselves in the possession of immense wealth, sought refuge from their own madness in every possible variety of amusement, recreation, dissipation." Parents of young women suddenly discovered that their daughters had fine voices, quiet store clerks suddenly revealed a talent for comic singing, and "fifth rate opera-singers, deserters perhaps from a Mauritius or Batavian troupe, were delighted, if not always astonished, to find themselves stars of the first magnitude."[33] For someone with real talent, the opportunities were nearly endless. One woman, Annie Griffiths, an Australian equestrian and actress, worked for Rowe's circuses on both of his Australian expeditions. In 1851–52, after the discovery of gold in Victoria, miners starved for entertainment and the sight of a young woman would come to Melbourne and "throw nuggets of gold into the ring," and also offer them to her father in hopes of being able to marry her.[34] Later, Annie and the man she ultimately chose (the famous clown and trick rider Ned Yeamans) would work for Risley in Yokohama.

The Theatre Royal in Hobart, Tasmania. © 2012 FIAMMETTA HSU.

As had happened to Risley in California four years earlier, when he had arrived too late to harvest the real riches, his timing in Australia was off. By 1858 the entertainment world had become much more competitive and the pickings poorer, brought about in part by a cooling of gold fever. Circus pioneer Joseph Andrew Rowe, chastened by his inability to make money on his second tour, gave up and went back to California in 1860. Unlike Rowe, Risley was aided by the fact that he did not have a full circus, he rarely used his tenting pavilion, and he had no animal acts; by keeping his troupe small and only adding extra performers as needed, he could keep his overhead low. Still, he was vulnerable. By mid-1860, D'Evani had disappeared from the playbills and apparently headed back to London. Risley, at forty-six, was reaching the physical limit for a gymnast. And Master Charles, his "son," could no longer be called an "infant prodigy." Charles was at an age where he was not only beginning a growth spurt, but starting to think more of his own self-interest.

In July 1860, Risley was staying at 208 Pitt Street in Sydney, New South Wales, when Charles disappeared. Risley ran an ad in the *Sydney Morning Herald* on July 20 claiming that Charles had vanished in suspicious circumstances and that "any person detaining him after this notice will be prosecuted according to the law." The following day, the paper ran a more detailed article, noting that detectives were searching everywhere for the boy; that it was presumed he had been kidnapped, "induced to go away with persons who intend to trade upon his skill and acquirements as a young athlete," and warning that the perpetrators were unlikely to succeed in their plot because the boy was so well known to thousands who had seen his performances. Professor Risley, greatly distressed and determined to clear up the matter, offered a reward of £50 for delivery of his "son," who was noted to be thirteen years old at the time.[35]

What really happened to Charles is not entirely clear, but in the first week of September the pair were back performing at the Olympic Theatre in Maitland, near Sydney. The papers praised their performances, but the weather was inclement, and they were performing to increasingly sparse audiences.[36]

Thereafter, Risley largely disappears from mentions in the Australian press. He presumably felt he had exhausted the local market, and he had begun to prepare for what would become a new, grand adventure. The 1860 United States census shows that Risley's wife Rebecca was living in Philadelphia with her sons John, now twenty-three, who was a "clerk," and Henry, twenty-one, who was working in a "variety store."[37] Risley, however, apparently had little desire to go home to join them. He may also have realized that the United States was about to become inhospitable to itinerant performers, for it was sliding rapidly toward armed conflict between "free states" and slave-holding states. Only six months later, in the spring of 1862, the United States would plunge into the bloody slaughter that we know of today as the Civil War. Rather than return home to America, the ever-on-the-move Risley decided to plunge deep into Asia and explore yet another, newly opened entertainment circuit.

Into Asia

*There is a strange class of roaming "artistes"—singers,
players, conjurors—of whose life and adventures nothing
is ever heard. . . . These performers . . . are to be met
with abroad wherever the English language is spoken, and
where it is not.*[1]
  —R.S. Smythe, "'Professionals' Abroad," *Cornhill
Magazine*, February 1871

Entertainers were often in the vanguard of globalization, and in the mid-nineteenth century they could be found in remarkably remote corners of the earth. Still, in 1861 it was highly unusual for Americans of Risley's stature to venture into the far corners of Asia. The Asian circuit was quite new. There was potential for great reward. Yet the risks were also great.

Solo artists rarely were a success. Dramatic companies required physical theatres or might be objected to on religious and other grounds, and it was hard to find replacements locally if an actor took ill or was absent. The circus was in fact one of the safer configurations for touring, especially if tents were used. Traveling and equipment costs were high, but circuses were fairly light and moveable and required little more than a vacant lot. In the colonies, they could be financially supported in part by native audiences, not just Europeans and Eurasians, and this was especially true if music was included and acts were tailored to local tastes, thus

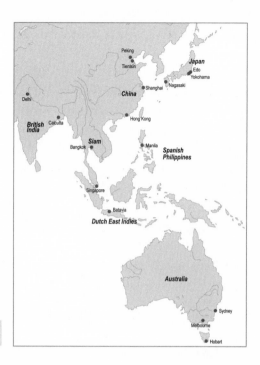

Map of Asia in Risley's era.

helping transcend language and cultural barriers. It also helped greatly to have some females as performers, because audiences were overwhelmingly male. A female performer could entice costly presents and celebratory picnics and suppers, and draw huge sums during benefits, especially from lonely European males. Of course, popular female performers were harder for a manager to retain and might draw the ire of conservative local authorities unless dressed properly. But as R. S. Smythe, author of an 1871 article on early troupes in Asia (who knew Risley), also noted, "a circus proprietor might as well appear without horses in his troupe as without women-riders."[2]

Even in the Victorian era, people often imagined entertainers' lives to be, as Smythe observed, "careless and quite charming." Yet in Asia, at least, this was hardly the case. Circus performers constantly faced the possibility of illness and injury, but here the fear of cholera and other contagious diseases was particularly strong. In the middle of the cholera season, Smythe wrote, "the man you met at breakfast was sometimes underground before dinner." In the Indian city of Agra (where the Taj

Mahal is located), when cholera was decimating the British garrison, a traveling circus company was once "engaged by the commandant to assist in cheering the spirits of the troops; and, accordingly, the riders, acrobats, and clowns continued their dance of death as long as a sufficient number of them survived to give a tolerable performance." A similarly macabre fate met a tiny theatrical troupe that arrived in Hong Kong from California in the winter of 1863. One of the actresses soon after died of cholera in Shanghai, another died in a cab on her way to the hospital at Rangoon, Burma, and a solitary actor who joined the Taiping rebels at Amoy "had his head cut off by his own party on suspicion of treachery." As for a little girl dancer with the stage name of "La Petite Cerito" (presumably no relation to Risley's dancer), she "was placed in a convent at Moulmein [in Burma], which some people will perhaps consider the worst fate of all."[3]

Calcutta

On December 20, 1860, Risley and Master Charles arrived in Calcutta (today's Kolkata), the capital of British India. They had sailed from Sydney, Australia on September 26, in a large 708-ton ship named the *Sonora*, on what must have been an exhausting nearly three-month voyage. Why it took so long is unclear, but fatigue may have been one reason their initial performance—originally scheduled for December 28th—was postponed. They would spend the next half year in Calcutta performing not only the usual acrobatic feats but also staging popular farces such as "Poor Pillicoddy" (where Risley played the main character) for members of the British community and military garrison. Risley would eventually put together a full circus, and in the spring of 1861 he would be joined by James Hernandez, his young friend and globally famous equestrian. But by then the weather would become miserably hot, and, as one observer predicted, it would "speedily make 'La Perche,' 'Herculean Feats of Strength,' &c., too much even for the Professor and his auxiliaries."[4]

Since Risley elected not to return to America after leaving Aus-

Spence's Hotel and St. John's Cathedral, Calcutta, with ships' masts visible in background, circa 1858-61. Albumen silver print, by John Constantine Stanley, 15.5 x 20.1 cm (6⅛ x 7¹⁵⁄₁₆ in.). Mount: 33 x 26.2 cm (13 x 10⅜⁄₁₆ in.). GILMAN COLLECTION, PURCHASE, CYNTHIA HAZEN POLSKY, GIFT, 2005 (2005.100.491.1). © THE METROPOLITAN MUSEUM OF ART. IMAGE SOURCE: ART RESOURCE, NY.

tralia, it is perhaps not surprising that he turned up in India. The 1860s symbolized the zenith of both Victorian culture and the British Empire, and Britain controlled Australia and New Zealand as well as large swaths of Africa and Asia. This provided entertainers a cultural, linguistic, and legal framework within which to travel, in an unfamiliar region, where any sort of performing arts infrastructure was highly limited. India was the "jewel in the crown" of the British Empire, and in Calcutta the British community was particularly large and well established, with imposing European-style buildings, a history already going back 170 years, and considerable wealth from industry and trade (including in opium). The more educated citizens were also remarkably global in their perspective, and local English-language newspapers kept them informed of events, not only in India, but in Europe, China, and even newly opened Japan. In Calcutta, itinerant entertainers of all stripes were welcomed by homesick and bored Europeans.

Risley and Charles faced considerable competition in Calcutta. Earlier that month the community had been entertained by a full circus called "Lewis's Great Australian Hippodrome." And there was another "professor" in town, this one of legerdemain, named Monsieur Theo, who had arrived for the holiday season. He had previously performed before the "Emperor of Java and the Rajah of Mysore," and he was capable of producing "bouquets of flowers, bisquits, cannon-balls, eggs, & etc.," from a hat. American entertainments also appear to have been in vogue. In early January 1861, there was a "Gigantic Panorama of the Mississippi" showing in Calcutta, claiming to show "over one thousand two hundred miles of its valleys, mountains, cities, &c. &c.," but to Risley's chagrin, no doubt, it was not his panorama. Instead, it was that of Henry Lewis, locally produced by another pseudo-academic named "Professor Johnson," who later would also give pyrotechnic displays to the delight of Calcutta residents and occasionally join Risley in his circus.[5]

On New Year's Day 1861, Risley and "son" staged their grand opening night at the Calcutta Town Hall, accompanied by the town band. It was an ambitious program for only two people. It consisted of eight parts, four performances interspersed with four musical interludes and showed the wide range of talents that Risley could marshal. Traditional Risley acts were demonstrated, including the famous "wonderful somersault from Soles to Soles which have delighted every beholder," and also the "incredible, Chain, Watch, Coin, Glass, and table feats, the last of which appears to set the laws of Gravitation at defiance." Then there were perch acts, with the still physically powerful Risley supporting Charles in various postures atop of a high pole, while dancing around the stage doing La Cracovienne. This was followed by singing and farces by Risley and Charles. The farces included "American travels, and California Pike county Candidate for Governor Stump's speech and original comic Yankee Polka by the Professor." The speech presumably was a version of Master Charles's parody of political grandstanding that had so impressed politicians in New Zealand. Two weeks later the same basic program was repeated, with the addition of the "Medley Song" by Risley to liven up his always-humorous "American Travels" skit. The medley included classic American minstrel tunes such as "Alabama," "Buffalo Gals," "Jimmy Crackcorn," and the now politically incorrect "I Once Knew a Darkee," as well as "The Star-Spangled Banner." But the selection also revealed Risley's ability to cater to local audiences, for he made sure to end with the decidedly British "Rule Britannica." Admission to these shows was six rupees to the dress circle and three rupees for unreserved seats.[6]

The performances were well attended. The *Bengal Hurkaru*, a local English-language paper, gently criticized the lack of variety, the overly long intervals, and the lighting of the stage, yet it heaped praise on Risley and Charles, especially on their "grand sommersault" act, and assured readers that Risley

> . . . retains all the easy grace and elegance that marked his performance when he first made his bow to a London public. . . . But for Risley—this class of entertainment would have remained for the edification solely of the "yokels." . . . Risley at once made the entertainment "classic," and it has ever since been highly patronized by every class from the highest lady to her humblest subject.[7]

Risley, the consummate entertainer, also performed at private parties, such as one staged by a jewel-bedecked Baboo Khelut Chunder Ghosa, a local *zemindar*, or wealthy Hindu landowner, on the occasion of the man's thirty-second birthday. And Risley was already planning something much more spectacular. He was building a temporary but huge amphitheatre on Calcutta's esplanade, the *maidan*, complete with a circus ring in the center, surrounded by seats, and a stage with a drop scene at the opposite end. It was far more than a tent, and a real building, with whitewashed matted walls, a temporary roof disguised with a heavily ornamented ceiling, and illumination provided by gas lights. Later, when there were complaints about it being hard to hear the performers, he added special sound boards. To fill his facility, he also put together a full complement of performers—a true circus—drawing upon his vast network of professional acquaintances, some of whom were presumably already on the Asian circuit and in India. In early February, he ran notices in the local newspapers, inviting "any persons conversant with Theatrical business, of both sexes," to call upon him for an audition at Room no. 3 of Calcutta's grand European-style Spence's Hotel.[8]

On February 11, Risley opened an impressive new production in his brand new "Royal Ampitheatre." He had secured the services of the bands of both Her Majesty's Fifth Fusilliers and the Sixth European Regiment, and offered a program that included not only his usual acts with Charles and his own "Yankee Excentricities" skit and polka dancing, but the following additions: clown and trampoline acts; Monsieur Florentine on the horizontal bar; equestrian performances in the ring by Signor Carlos, staging "the Wild Prairie Indian," with a special appearance by Risley's own St. Bernard dog, Governor; a "wonderful globe ascension" by Signor Fernando; the double trapeze by the Italian brothers; and graceful equestrian scenes in the ring by Master Henrico Eroni. Prices were also lowered, with dress circle tickets going for five rupees, and ordinary rotunda tickets for one rupee. At the time, some British civilians were salaried at three thousand rupees a month, while even the lowliest clerks received twenty, so it was quite a bargain.[9] The strategy worked, for the ampitheatre was packed.

That Risley was able to stay in Calcutta so long, giving near-daily performances, is a testimony to his skills as a producer. He was able to vary performances and always keep the shows interesting. He gave a private show for the fabulously wealthy Maharaja of Burdwan, but he generally stayed in his pavilion and amphitheatre. He added new entertainers as they arrived on the scene and new performances. Not only did his dog get to perform, but so, too, did his beloved and highly trained piebald mare, Cleopatra. The local papers heaped praise on him well into May.

Risley's fortunes seemed about to receive a further boost in late April, when James Hernandez, the sensational equestrian, arrived in

Calcutta to join his circus. But this was instead the beginning of a spell of bad luck. A grand performance was staged, introducing Hernandez on May 2, and it received highly favorable reviews, the *Bengal Hurkaru* being especially amazed by Hernandez's legendary somersaults on top of his dashing steed. Yet the same paper remarked that the attendance was disappointing. Risley, it noted, was preparing to leave soon for England, where he would procure a "first class Corps de Ballet," which he would bring back for the "cold season."[10]

In May, the monsoon from the southwest helped break the oppressive Calcutta heat, which often exceeded a muggy one hundred degrees Fahrenheit. In such weather it is hard to imagine how a circus show could be enjoyed, let alone endured, in an enclosed pavilion by either the audiences or the performers. Mercifully, perhaps, on May 8 and 9, a violent squall badly damaged both the pavilion and amphitheatre. On the eleventh, Risley ran an announcement, stating that due to the "inclement weather that prevails at this season of the year, and the damage done to the Amphitheatre, he is necessitated to postpone his benefit till further notice."[11] The announcement would be repeated for several weeks, but then news of Risley vanished from the local press.

Singapore, Batavia, Hong Kong, Bangkok, and Manila

Risley next appeared in Singapore, a bustling city on an island just north of the equator, at the southern tip of the Malay Peninsula. Like Calcutta, Singapore was part of the British Empire and an important center for trade, with a substantial population of English speakers. On June 8, the English-language *Straits Times* announced that Risley would be arriving imminently from Calcutta with Hernandez and would give a few performances en route to China. The paper duly noted Risley and Hernandez's international fame and reminded readers that the latter was already an old favorite (Hernandez having visited Singapore previously with George W. B. Lewis's Australian Hippodrome). On the same day as the announcement of Risley's pending arrival, the paper also reported the arrival of the Olympic Circus, another Westerner-staffed equestrian troupe then touring Asia. Records of Risley's movements in Asia are spotty, but from reports of the Olympic Circus in the *Straits Times* we can see that Singapore had been on the Asian circus circuit since 1850, and that the same circuit included Hong Kong, Calcutta, Bombay, and Madras, as well as Batavia (modern Jakarta), Surabaya, and Semarang, on the island of Java in what was then the Dutch East Indies, or today's Indonesia.[12]

Shortly after arriving in Singapore in June, but prior to opening his show, Risley scored an increasingly rare global publicity coup. Ever since leaving California, his name had entirely disappeared from United States media, which was busy covering the tense lead-up to the Civil War between North and South. That changed when, on July 4, 1861, American residents of Singapore and visiting ship captains gathered to celebrate independence and toast the Union. Risley made sure that he attended and, after a fireworks display, he "enlivened the company with several excellent and amusing songs."[13] It was an astute move, for the local newspapers and even the far away *New York Times* later delighted in reporting his patriotic contribution. Because of the time it took for information to travel in those days, the attendees at the party had only days earlier learned, with disbelief, of opening shots in the Civil War having been fired in April. They were all Union supporters and hoped for a quick resolution of the conflict.

When Risley's troupe finally did open in Singapore, it was a great success followed by a great tragedy. On July 13, the *Straits Times* observed that Singaporeans often did not seem to favor public amusements, preferring instead to relax at home after working all day. Moreover, other troupes in the past, including the circus of the Australian, George Lewis, had "gone away disappointed and with empty pockets." Yet when Risley appeared in his Royal Pavilion in a circus tent on High Street on July 12,

> not only was every seat occupied but all the available standing space was crowded, and we saw numbers of people who were unable to obtain admission, and who

V. R.

RISLEY'S
ROYAL PAVILION.
OLD SAILORS' HOME.
High Street.
SINGAPORE.

COMPLIMENTARY BENEFIT TO PROFES-
SOR RISLEY.
Under the kind Patronage of many of the leading
inhabitants of Singapore and the Captains
of Vessels in Port.

AN ENTIRE CHANGE OF PRO-
GRAMME.
Tuesday Evening, 6th August, 1861.
PROGRAMME.

PART 1st
THE AERIAL FLIGHTS, BY
THE COMPANY.
The Egyptian Pyramids by Members of the Com-
pany in which will be represented for the first
time here
The celebrated statues of the Sculptor Rafael.
THE CELEBRATED TRICK MARE.
"CLEOPATRA."
Expressly Trained by Mr. FORESTINE will ex-
habit the extraordinary feats of docility.

THE DRAWING ROOM ENTERTAINMENT
By Professor Risley, Son and Pupil,
As performed by him with such immense
success, before the Queen of England
and other crowned heads of Europe.

A INTERMISSION OF TEN MINUTES.

Part 2nd.
THE STAGE STRUCK OPERA
SINGER.
BY PROFESSOR RISLEY.
For the First Time Here.

The Dying Moor, in defence of his
Flag. By Signor Carlo.

THE DOUBLE SPANISH RINGS.
A Wonderful performance, by the Italian
Brothers.

Overture by the Band.
CLASSICAL TABLEAUX.
BY MADAME HARLOWE,
MISS SINCLAIR,
Their first appearance. Professor Risley
Master Risley and Signors Ferdinand,
Carlo and Eugene.

THE CATHERINE WHEEL,
With a brilliant display of Fireworks
BY MR. FORESTINE.

The whole to conclude with the laughable
Extravaganza entitled,
PLANTATION LIFE IN OLD KENTUCKEY
By Professor Risley and the Members of the Company.
In which two celebrated Artists just arrived from America will make their first
appearance.

QUEEN'S JESTER ...... MASTER RISLEY.
CLOWN OF THE RING ... MR. NORTH.
PRICES OF ADMISSION.

Reserved Seats .... 2 Dollars
Dress Circle .... 1 Dollar.
Rotunda .... 50 Cents.
Tickets to be had at the Principal Hotels and at
Messrs. John Little and Co. and Taylor & Co.
NO SMOKING ALLOWED.
The performance will commence punctually at
8 o'Clock, Doors open at ½ past 7.
☞ All business communications to be ad-
dressed to the Agent, Hotel De L'Esperance,
where Professor Risley's Book of Testimonials
may be seen, and where Reserved Seats may
be secured.

Risley playbill for December 6,
1861. *THE STRAITS TIMES,* DECEMBER
6, 1861.

were reluctantly turned away from the doors. . . . The riding and pantomimic performance [of Hernandez] was received with storms of applause, but the culminating point of interest was reached when Master Risley and his father made their appearance. The performances of young Risley were really splendid, and showed the careful training which he had evidently received.[14]

Six days later Hernandez, the twenty-seven-year-old, fearless equestrian star at the prime of his life, was dead. And instead of dying dramatically in the ring, falling from his steed upon performing a spectacular somersault while riding at full gallop, his death proved to be far more prosaic. While staying at the Union Hotel, he suddenly and mysteriously died. According to the reminiscences of a singer and fellow barnstormer of the era, Joe Taylor, Hernandez fell out of bed and broke his neck, but this seems too implausible for someone of his young age and athletic abilities. One can only speculate, but Hernandez was known to be a heavy drinker, and after years of falls and perhaps concussions he may suddenly have collapsed from other causes.[15]

The show had to go on. Playbills for August 6 show that a special benefit was held for Risley, sponsored by notable European residents of Singapore, prior to his leaving for "China" and eventually "San Francisco." It was quite an extravaganza. There were aerial acts; "extraordinary feats of docility" by Risley's celebrated trick mare, Cleopatra; drawing room entertainments by Risley and his son and pupil; a performance of "The Stage Struck Opera Singer" by Risley; "The Dying Moor, in defence of his flag," by Signor Carlo; the double Spanish rings by the "Italian Brothers"; a performance by a band; a display of fireworks; a comic presentation of "Plantation Life in Old Kentucky" by Risley and other company members; and a Classical Tableaux by Madame Harlowe and Miss Sinclair. The last act, according to the local press, introduced some "lady artistes" for the first time into Singapore.[16]

To top it all off, interested parties in Singapore could also go to the Hotel De L'Esperance and view "Professor Risley's Book of Testimonials." And only one week later, Risley showed the "Panorama of

Met toestemming van den Resident van Batavia.

Maandag, 28 October,
EENE EERSTE VOORSTELLING
van
RISLEY'S CIRQUE,
in het nieuwe gebouw op Tanah-Lapang
Glodok

Het **PROGRAMMA**, dat nieuwe en gevarieerde
toeren aankondigt, zal algemeen verspreid worden.
Prijzen der plaatsen:
1ste Rang ƒ **3.**—, 2de Rang ƒ **2.**—, 3de Rang ƒ **1.**—,
terwijl er eene **getraliede loge** voor de
Chinesche Dames ingerigt is à ƒ **2.**—.

(3701) KINDEREN beneden de 10 jaren betalen
de helft.

GRAND GALA NIGHT
Theatre.

Under the distinguished Patronage of
His Excellency the
GOVERNOR GENERAL.
Professor RISLEY,
begs to intimate to the public of Batavia, that
he is making
GREAT PREPARATIONS
for his Benefit.

Due Notice of which will be given.

N. B. On this occasion the Professor will be assisted
by **20 Artistes** (5719)

Advertisement for October 28, 1861, performance of Risley circus in Batavia (modern Jakarta), in both Dutch and English. In the Dutch East Indies, Risley sometimes also ran the ads in French. *JAVA-BODE*, OCTOBER 26, 1861.

the Mississippi" in Singapore to great acclaim. It was presumably the result of some deal that he had made with the proprietors who had been showing it in Calcutta. How they had managed to get this giant and unwieldy mass of canvas and wood frame all the way from either Europe or America, or even from Calcutta, through ocean squalls and extreme heat and humidity, is unclear, but it was a big hit. With Madame Harlowe providing musical accompaniment on the piano, Professor Risley served as narrator, "rich as usual in his inexhaustible fund of wit, humour and anecdote."[17]

On August 24, Risley's circus gave what was billed as its last performance in Singapore, with a special benefit for the young Australian equestrian named "Master Eroni," who helped to fill in for Hernandez's absence. After that, the whereabouts of Risley and his circus become quite blurred. He did not go to China directly, as the newspapers in Singapore had suggested he would. Instead, he embarked further off the beaten path in Asia.

★

In mid-September Risley showed up in Batavia, or today's Jakarta, then the capital of the Dutch East Indies, or what is now Indonesia, where he would spend another six months. Batavia, like Calcutta and Singapore, was part of a European empire, in this case that of the Dutch, who had controlled much of the Indonesian archipelago for over two centuries. As a result, there was a framework in place for traveling entertainers, and, as advertisements in the local Dutch-language *Java-Bode* newspaper illustrate, while Risley was there he again faced considerable competition, particularly from Australian entertainers. George W. B. Lewis's Australian Hippodrome was also present, with beautiful horses and a troupe of twenty "ladies, gentlemen and children."[18]

On September 18 Risley began doing gymnastics to accompany Henry Lewis's Panorama of the Mississippi, which he had also brought to town. On the twenty-third, however, he opened with his full circus amphitheatre, sponsored by the commander of a U.S. Navy ship, the twenty-gun *John Adams*, which happened to be in port. Batavia was an international community, so Risley sometimes ran ads in the *Java-Bode* in Dutch, French, and English. They show that in addition to his "son" and "pupil," he had female performers such as "Madam Ferdinando" and "Mademoiselle Marion," as well as males such as Messrs. Eugene, Forristine, J. North, and Eurona and "Senors" Carlo, Ferdinando, and Angelo, and he was still accompanied by his old friend Dickerson. The performances, in addition to gymnastics, continued to include equestrian acts.[19] Risley would perform on the island of Java through the beginning of 1862, staging benefits and occasionally appearing under the patronage of the Dutch governor-general. He would also move outside of Batavia to other population centers on Java, such as Semarang and Surabaya.

★

On September 26, 1862, in faraway Shanghai, an announcement appeared in the *Daily Shipping and Commercial News*, a local English language paper. It said:

IMMENSE ATTRACTION PROFESSOR RISLEY
and the most Numerous and Talented Company of
Artistes, with Ten unrivalled Horses, will shortly arrive
in Shanghai. Full particulars will appear hereafter.[20]

Yet Risley did not actually arrive in Shanghai until the fall of 1863, a year later. In the interim, he was caroming among countries in Southeast Asia with his full circus, and his movements are again shrouded in the fog of poorly documented history. Joe Taylor, the well-known minstrel singer who also traveled throughout Asia around this time, in a later book of reminiscences tells the story of Risley auditioning with the King of Siam (Thailand) for permission to perform with his circus in Bangkok. According to Taylor, Risley took some of his performers along with him to the audition. When introduced to the circus clown and being told the role of a clown, the King demanded to be made to laugh. By carrying out a silly, impromptu slapstick routine of pretending to knock each other down, Risley and his performers succeeded in making the king laugh and thus gained the permits they needed.[21]

In November 1862, Risley was back in Singapore. He gave special performances with his full circus, and an entirely new program that included "an eight horse entrée with entire new trappings." He had his old, longtime friend and band leader, Philip Dickerson, acting as secretary and a performer named "Old Joe" appearing in a starring role. The *Straits Times* was then filled with articles, not only on local news but on the American Civil War and Lincoln's Emancipation Proclamation, politics in Italy, the price of opium in China, and political turmoil in Japan. Still, on December 6 it included a good review of Risley's circus, especially of Master Charles, who stood on a table and bent backward to drink from a glass on the ground, and of the young equestrian Master Eroni, who performed bareback somersaults. Yet it indicated that a byplay included in the program was "tiresome."[22]

For the lucrative Christmas season, Risley was in Hong Kong, not Singapore. He arrived in the second week of December on the P&O Line's steamship, the *China*, with an equestrian troupe of twelve artists, ten horses, and performing ponies. He quickly set up in a pavilion (behind the British government offices) capable of holding "1,000 persons, paraphernalia, &c.," and put out notice that he could not stay long, while at the same time vowing to give "a touch of his quality" to the local people. True to character, he deposited "a mass of testimonials" in the hands of a Hong Kong paper's editor who, impressed, took them to "prove that he is eminent in his profession. He has performed before many Royal personages, amongst others our most gracious Queen."[23]

Risley stayed in Hong Kong for nearly a month, and despite the inclement weather the English-language *China Mail* gave his New Year's Day performance a hearty review. "His own skill as an athlete is of a very high order," the paper told its readers, "and he is well supported by his son and a numerous troupe of performers. Those who wish to see graceful horsemanship, fine physical training, or light, amusing circus performances, should favour the Professor with a visit." As in Calcutta, Risley varied his performances, inviting the local military band on some days and, on January 8, incorporating the famous American minstrel group, the Ethiopian Serenaders, who happened to be in town.[24]

While in Hong Kong Risley probably did not have going to Japan on his mind, but he would have been increasingly aware of it. As in Calcutta, Singapore, and other parts of the British Empire, the local English-language newspapers had a uniquely global perspective. They were filled with articles not only on events back in Europe and the Americas, but also New Zealand, where conflicts with the indigenous Maori continued; on closer troubles to the north, in Shanghai, where the Taiping rebellion was raging; and on Japan, where disgruntled samurai were occasionally attacking foreign diplomats and traders and threatening British interests. Many British readers were particularly irritated with the Japanese Shogunate's slowness in opening Japan to international trade. The mindset among imperialist Europeans and even democratically minded Americans was that no nation had the right to refuse to trade with them. The more bombastic of them predicted war.

★

Risley visited at least one other major population center in Southeast Asia, Manila—in the Philippines—where he arrived at the beginning of February 1863. Just as Java was part of the Dutch empire, and India, Singapore, and Hong Kong part of the British, in Risley's era the Philippines was controlled by Spain. In Asia, the Philippines was also one of the oldest European colonies, having been claimed for Spain by the first circumnavigator of the earth, Ferdinand Magellan, in 1521. When Risley arrived in Manila in 1863, he did not merit mention in the American media, which was preoccupied with the Civil War. But reflecting his global fame and competing interests of the European colonial powers in Asia, his presence in Manila was duly noted in newspapers in far-away Spain and Holland, as well as the much closer British-controlled Hong Kong.

The year 1863 was a particularly tragic one for the Philippines, with a series of seemingly unending natural disasters. Around the time Risley arrived, Manila was struck by a terrible fire, and thousands of structures in the poorer area of the city were destroyed. There were also huge gales, and when it was not raining it was blisteringly hot in the daytime, all contributing to a general sense of foreboding. On February 8, the Manila correspondent for the Hong Kong–based *China Mail* noted with apprehension that strong earthquakes had been reported on the nearby island of Panay; he earnestly hoped they would not occur in Manila. Risley's performances, he observed, were not doing particularly well.[25]

In a more informative report written exactly two months later, on April 8, the same Manila correspondent wrote that Risley—the "celebrity of the day here"—had been dramatically affected by the gales. He had been caught on a nearby lake, and at one point reported as "drowned," but "the gods threw their shield around their favorite, and on the night of the 5th he reopened his magnificent Colisseum, and with his son, Master Charles, pupil master Rony, the brilliant Madame Hendrick Stebbings, and Messrs Carlo, Stebbings, &c., &cs., fairly electrified us with gymnastic and equestrian feats." In fact, Risley's reopening was so successful that a petition was sent to the local Archbishop of the Catholic

Church (always extremely powerful in Spanish territories), asking him to allow friars and nuns to attend Risley's circus. As the correspondent lamented, "surely there can be no earthly (or heavenly) reason why these pious souls should be debarred such an innocent pleasure."[26]

The sole complaint of some attendees at Risley's circus seems to have been that they did not get a chance to see a "Miss Sybil Gorilla." Exactly who, or what, Miss Sybil was, is unclear, for Risley was known for the quality and propriety of his circus shows; he rarely exhibited animals unless they were part of an equestrian act or a performing dog show, and he never seems to have included the human "freaks" that P. T. Barnum and other American circus impresarios loved. According to the local correspondent, Miss Sybil did not appear because "Professor Risley is unwilling to take her from her studies. She has already learnt her alphabet, and has commenced monosyllables, and the Professor has assured a friend of mine (seriously) that he is confident of being able to teach the young lady to articulate! When this is effected how many secrets may we not learn of animal economy!" He went on to note that some local wag had put together a limerick to honor Ms. Sybil:

> There was a young gal in Manila,
> So excessively like a Gorilla,
> That when she went out,
> All the natives would shout,
> "There goes Charley Risley's Sybilla."[27]

By early May, Risley had moved his circus to Antipolo, a town a few miles to the east of Manila. Shortly thereafter, on June 3, 1863, the *China Mail* reporter's aforementioned fear about an earthquake hitting Manila came true. Writing a day later, he said:

> On the 3d instant, at half-past seven in the evening, a
> circumambient flame was seen to rise from the earth and
> gird the city of Manila . . . , and at the same time a most
> terrific quaking of the earth took place. It lasted scarcely
> a minute, but in that short space nearly the whole of

View of the American concession in Shanghai, circa 1860, by Lancelot, from a watercolor by English artist Major Fisher. *LE TOUR DU MONDE: NOUVEAU JOURNAL DES VOYAGES*, ED. EDOUARD CHARTON (PARIS: LIBRAIRIE HACHETTE, 1ST SEMESTRE, 1864).

Fair Manila has been reduced to a heap of ruins. The abomination of desolation has taken possession of her palaces, her temples, and her dwelling-places, and death and destruction have ridden triumphantly over the land.[28]

Of Risley's fate, the correspondent mentions nothing. However, Risley's old friend, the aforementioned minstrel Joe Taylor, also on the Asian circuit, mentions in his autobiography that he had been scheduled to meet Risley in Singapore at one point and perform with his troupe as "Black Clown." Taylor does not give a specific date, but he mentions that Risley was caught in an earthquake in Manila, "which almost entirely destroyed his outfit." His comment is reinforced by a playbill of Risley's printed several years later, in 1867, in a Baltimore, Maryland newspaper. The playbill lists as an "Interesting Fact" the information that Risley's "theatre" had once been destroyed in Manila and that he had lost ten-thousand dollars in gold as a result. Incredibly, it was Risley's second time to lose a fortune and narrowly escape with his life during a major earthquake.[29]

Shanghai

On October 13, 1863, Risley finally arrived in Shanghai with a twelve-man equestrian circus on the steamer *Carthage* from Hong Kong. He would remain in Shanghai for the next few months. He had endured great hardships in Asia since leaving Australia, and Shanghai would only offer more. But it would become the final launching pad for his adventure to Japan.

In 1863, Shanghai was a bustling international settlement at the mouth of the Yangtze River. Like Singapore, it was a center of trade with many European residents, but it was engulfed in a far more turbulent political storm. Indeed, it is difficult to imagine a more problematic place to take a full circus in the mid-nineteenth century, unless it was Japan.

In the 1860s, China was an independent empire ruled by the increasingly weak Qing Dynasty. The colonial powers of Europe, in an expansionist mode, had begun to nibble on the edges of its territory. Much like Japan, China had long tried to restrict contact with the outside world, but during the two so-called Opium Wars of 1839-42 and 1856-60, the British had forced China to cede it Hong Kong and to open several Chinese ports, including Shanghai, to trade, and especially to trade in opium. Bustling settlements of British, Americans, and French had subsequently sprung up alongside the native Chinese community.

Around the time Risley arrived, even normally prosperous Shanghai was suffering greatly from a terrible civil war in China. Known as the Taiping Rebellion, it lasted until 1864 and was only suppressed with the aid of British and French forces. One of the bloodier civil wars in history, the Taiping Rebellion was arguably also one of the oddest. Indirectly a response to the weakening of the Manchu-controlled Qing Dynasty, and the humiliations imposed on China by the European powers, the rebellion was led by a charismatic man named Hong Xiuquan. He believed himself to be the younger brother of Jesus Christ, with a duty to spread Christianity and establish a new order, but his vision was ultimately apocalyptic, resulting in the deaths of an estimated twenty million people and devastating much of southeastern China. Shortly before Risley arrived, fighting near Shanghai had caused an influx of hordes of starving refugees into the area, and unsanitary conditions had triggered massive outbreaks of infectious diseases, especially cholera. Westerners residing in Shanghai were protected by their own militaries, mercenaries, and a Chinese force led by a filibustering American soldier of fortune and two Britishers. Still, as China expert and historian Jonathan D. Spence writes, ordinary residents carried arms "as a matter of course; the inventories of their possessions often show shotguns, rifles, and revolvers, along with the brandy and cigars, the furniture, crockery, dogs, and bedding."[30]

In the foreign settlements of Shanghai itself, many at first prospered amid the chaos. Around 1863, the city was a booming center of the trade in silk and opium, munitions, and food and tea. The river port was filled with foreign ships, and in the European settlements there was already the Bund, a waterfront of imposing, European-style buildings, including banks, and hotels for all ranges of income, with rooms from the Spartan to the luxurious. There were even photo portrait studios, churches, billiard saloons, and a ten-pin bowling alley. The bowling alley was courtesy of the American residents, whose influence had been greatly weakened by the Civil War, when all U.S. naval vessels in the area were ordered back home. This boom may have been what drew Risley to Shanghai, for speculation was rampant, and at one point it seemed possible to multiply any investment hundreds of times over. But by the end of 1863, just around the time Risley arrived, what a long-time resident described as "a feverish bustle in business, and extravagance in private life" crossed a threshold, and the boom went bust.[31]

The economy and a raging civil war aside, residents of the settlements, like those in European colonies throughout Asia, craved entertainment and looked forward to nearly any diversion. Risley's circus was not the first to visit Shanghai; a year earlier, George W. B. Lewis's Australian Hippodrome had been there, but it had not done well. And during Risley's stay in the city he had some competition, for there was a newly arrived musical act in town, consisting of a singer named Miss Amelia Bailey, backed by a pianist named James Marquis Chisholm and the Rhenish band. Still, when Risley arrived with his circus, the local English-language paper hoped that it would be a "valuable means of dispelling the ennui inseparable from winter in China."[32] Much to the delight of the men in the settlement, he had three females in his troupe.

Many Shanghai records from this period have been lost, but the content of a Risley playbill was copied in a New York newspaper fifty years later, and it shows "Risley's Mammoth Circus of All Nations" as being "under the distinguished patrons of Foreign Diplomats." After mentioning Risley's "world-wide fame in London, Paris, Hamburg, Berlin, St. Petersburg, and all the Principal Cities of Europe and America," it outlines an impressive program. There is, oddly, no specific mention of Risley's protégé/son, Charles.

TALENTED GYMNASTS

Stud of highly trained horses and ponies
Madam Fernand . . . . Pantomimist.
Madam Augustine . . . . Expert Menage Act.
La Petite Marie . . . . Infant prodigy.
Italian Brothers . . . . Unrivaled Gymnasts.
Mons. Eugene . . . . The Modern Sampson.
Senor Carlo . . . . Melmore cu Cheval.
Mr. Tate . . . . Australian Horseman.

GRAND ENTRÉE AND EASTERN CAVALCADE

The ladies and gentlemen, on trained steeds, in splendid costumes.
Mr. TATE, on his bareback steed, "Flying Voltigeur."
LA PETITE MARIE, Rosebud of Cashmere's Double Horse Act.
ITALIAN BROTHERS . . . . Flying trapeze.
Company Vaulters, in astounding somersaults and flying leaps.
PROFESSOR RISLEY and Pupil, in their wonderful La Perch Equipoise.
SENOR FERNANDO . . . . Modern Atlas.
FAIRY TRICK PONY. "BEAUTY SPOT."
CLEOPATRA, the highly trained horse.
JACK DOWNY, the educated bounding Gorilla.
MASTER ERONI, the wonderful daring Australian rider.

Mr. FRED WILSON, Versatile Conversationalist
Clown and Clog Dancer.
Mr. EUGENIE, the Marvelous Ladder Performer.[33]

Not all the performers had been brought by Risley. Fred Wilson
was a noted minstrel who happened to also be serving as the U.S. Marshal for the American settlement in Shanghai at the time (at the beginning of December, Risley would also sing with Wilson). And there were
other substitute performers, also on the Asia circuit. Some had worked
with Risley in California and had come to join him and his circus (an
example being Lizzie Gordon, apparently the same woman who, along
with her daughter, La Petite Cerito, would later sue Risley for back
wages).[34] Some, if they survived Shanghai, would eventually join Risley
on his adventure to Japan.

After a successful opening in Shanghai, things seemed to go downhill for Risley. It was an intensely cold winter, with sleet and snow. The
settlement, still worried about the surrounding Taiping rebellion, was
now also concerned over a possible attack by an American Confederate pirate cruiser—the *Alabama*—that was prowling in the area. Despite
the fact that Risley was in the settlement for nearly five months, the
main local English-language paper, the *North-China Herald*, contains
surprisingly few mentions of his circus. When his name does come
up, it is usually him alone, and in conjunction with an appearance
with other performers, such as a singing appearance with Fred Wilson,
the U.S. Marshal and minstrel, or with Amelia Bailey and her pianist,
Marquis Chisholm.

Far away from China, a British paper that covered the region
later gave Risley the type of international publicity he did not want.
It described his sojourn in Shanghai at this time as having "not been
attended by much benefit to his pocket. . . . He has had so many difficulties to contend with, no Circus, no Theatre, bad weather at commence-
ment, sickness, &c, &c, that we have been astonished at his perseverance."
The same paper also noted that on January 4, Patrick Tate, an Australian
equestrian rider and member of Risley's troupe, died in the Shanghai
hospital of smallpox.[35]

Chisholm, the pianist who accompanied Risley when he sang with Amelia Bailey, gives even more detail on Risley's bad luck in this period. In a book he later wrote on his experiences in Asia, he says, "Two of Risley's best horsemen died, one of them being Mr. Tait, a very graceful and daring rider. Risley himself was almost always sick, and the greater number of his horses, and even Jacko, the performing monkey, were unable to appear, so prostrated were they by this sickly climate." In addition, Risley's leading female star deserted him and got married.[36]

Thoughts of Japan

From Shanghai, Yokohama is about a thousand miles removed, but Nagasaki is only about five hundred miles due east. Indeed, throughout its long period of isolation from the outside world, Japan had allowed tiny Dutch and Chinese trading posts in the southern port of Nagasaki and thus maintained at least limited connections with China. And by 1863, Japan's official policy of seclusion had at least partially ended and Yokohama had opened as a port. Steamers were thus arriving in Shanghai regularly from both Nagasaki and Yokohama, bringing not only lumber and other goods, but also reports of the latest developments in Japanese industry and politics to Europeans, hungry for information on the still-little-known country.

Like China, Japan had been forced by Western powers to open select ports to trade, but it had done so only with great trepidation. As one writer to the English-language *North China Herald* noted in 1863, the first treaties signed between Japan and the Western powers had been "extorted from the unwilling Japanese by a display of power in the shape of ten-inch guns and cutlasses."[37] The result was political upheaval. In Shanghai, the *North-China Herald* was filled with regular accounts from travelers returning from Japan, many of whom were excited about the changes taking place there and the potential for new trade and business and possibly riches. But the newspaper was also filled with rumors that the Japanese government was about to take the country back into seclusion again and expel all foreigners. There were even reports of disgruntled two-sworded samurai staging vicious attacks on foreigners in the few tiny settlements where they were permitted to live.

Given these reports, why did Risley decide to leave Shanghai and take a circus to Yokohama, where conditions were regularly reported to be tense, if not dangerous? We will probably never know exactly what motivated him, but during the short period he was in Shanghai, curiosity about Japan reached feverish new heights.

In February 1864, Shanghai was visited by Rutherford Alcock, the head of the first British legation in Japan and the author of a hot-off-the-presses book, *The Capital of the Tycoon*, about his three years of residence there. Alcock's book had fueled the boom in curiosity about Japan around the world, and especially in Britain. In it he had commented on the Japanese love of entertainment and waxed effusively on the superiority of Japanese jugglers and top-spinners. The latter he had witnessed at the house of his American counterpart in Yokohama, writing that the top-spinners have achieved "greater excellence than any other people" in the world.[38] If Risley, the ever-curious professional entertainer, read or heard Alcock's stories, how could he not have been seized by a desire to go to Japan?

Risley may also have been influenced by some other European entertainers then in Shanghai, who had already been in Japan. As it turned out, Amelia Bailey, the pianist James Marquis Chisholm, and the Rhenish band with whom Risley occasionally performed in Shanghai had just returned from Nagasaki. They had been some of the very first professional European musicians to sail to newly opened Japan. And perhaps because the citizens of Nagasaki had long hosted the tiny Dutch and Chinese trading posts and were more used to foreigners, they had given Bailey and her team a rousing welcome. Bailey, Chisholm, and others in her troupe may have conveyed some of this excitement to Risley.

When Risley was in Shanghai, there were also some genuine Japanese in the city. It was still illegal for Japanese citizens to travel abroad, but four young samurai from the Satsuma domain (including twenty-one-year-old Ueno Kagenori, who later would become a famous diplomat), wanted to learn English so badly that they had stowed away on a ship, hoping to go to Europe, and then gotten stuck in Shanghai. Moreover,

Left to right: Kawazu Izunokami, Ikeda Nagaoki (also known as Ikeda Chikugono-kami), and Kawada Sagaminokami, photographed in Paris in 1864. OSATAKE TAKESHI, *ITEKI NO KUNI E : BAKUMATSU KENGAI SHISETSU MONOGATARI* (TOKYO: BANRIKAKU SHOBŌ, 1929).

at the beginning of 1864, the settlement was visited by an official delegation of Japanese on their way to Europe as emissaries from Japan's feudal government. This delegation, only the second sent by the Shogunate to Europe, left Japan in 1863 and arrived in Shanghai in early 1864 on its way to France, via India and the pre-canal Suez. It was only in Shanghai from February 15 to 20, but as the local paper excitedly reported, it consisted of three official samurai "ambassadors," supported by "thirteen officials and a retinue of twenty-four attendants."[39]

Led by an improbably young and dashing twenty-seven-year-old samurai named Ikeda Nagaoki, the delegation was an anachronism of history. Sent by the Shogunate to placate the anti-foreign *sonnō jōi* faction of Japan, it was supposed to explore with France the possibility of closing the newly opened foreign settlement at Yokohama, and to explain the recent murder of a French official. The mission resulted in a now-iconic photograph of the band of two-sworded samurai posing in front of the Sphinx in Egypt, but it was doomed from the start, as the European powers were in no mood to negotiate. Since the official goal of the mission's members was to expel foreigners from Japan, it is hard to imagine these samurai in Shanghai meeting and encouraging Risley to go to Yokohama. But, as contradictory as it seems, it is entirely possible that during moments of inebriated congeniality they may have suggested to him that the Japanese people, in principle, would love his sort of entertainment. Many held no personal animosity toward individual foreigners. While in Europe, Nagaoki switched from being a member of the anti-foreigner faction to an advocate of more openness to the West. On return to Japan, he was put under house arrest for his beliefs.

In Shanghai, the samurai were the talk of the town. For the retinue's members, it was their first exposure to European, not to mention Chinese, society, and they made some uproarious mistakes. In a bathroom, they once mistakenly washed their hands in urine-filled chamber pots. One member was arrested by an overzealous policeman for walking around town with his two swords openly displayed. Chisholm, the pianist with whom Risley had performed, writes that he played for the samurai on three evenings, and that " . . . it is no breach of confidence to say that, what with the champagne and the exhilarating influences of their national melodies, my Japanese audience got rather elevated during a two hours' entertainment. They were a very nice lot of fellows." At the Astor Hotel where they stayed, Chisholm notes that they attracted further attention by breaking panes of glass in order to ventilate a room in which they were sitting, peppering their champagne with cayenne, and voraciously drinking the water in their finger bowls.[40]

There was one final other fact that may have encouraged Risley to think of traveling to Yokohama. After Commodore Perry and the Americans forced Japan to begin interacting with the outside world and engage in limited trade, one problem the Japanese faced was that they had no experience with currency exchange. By treaty, European and American consular officials and visiting naval ship crews were given special privileges when exchanging Japanese coins (known to foreigners as "itziboos") for Mexican dollars (the primary currency for exchange) and vice versa. They were, in effect, guaranteed of turning a tidy profit by simply visiting Japan. Even though the tiny foreign settlement at Yokohama could be regarded as an extreme hardship post, it was highly popular among foreigners, many of whom were flush with profits from the exchange rate, which they could also spend on entertainment.

In 1864, Japan, and the settlement of Yokohama, was a dangerous new frontier for Europeans. But Risley was always a gambler, and for him, the idea of going to a brand new place—where his form of entertainment might be novel and highly welcomed, and where there might be a chance of turning a tidy profit—was probably too much to pass up. It would also take him away from Shanghai. According to the pianist, Chisholm, when Risley left on February 20, on the *Kirkconnel*, "he was so enraged by the misfortunes which had followed him while in Shanghai, that he kicked off his boots and cast them into the river, exclaiming, 'There, I'll take none of the dirt of that big graveyard along with me!'"[41]

Yokohama, Japan

*Tumblers, mummers, mountebanks, conjurors and jugglers
exercise their callings to the delight of the common people,
and are frequent in the public streets.*[1]
—S. B. Kemish's *The Japanese Empire* (1860)

On March 6, 1864, Professor Risley arrived in Yokohama after a two-week sail from Shanghai on the 253-ton British *Kirkconnel*. He had an equestrian troupe of ten performers and eight horses with him, and he was about to become the first person to introduce Western-style circus to Japan. It was an audacious, if not foolhardy, business decision, for Risley had no guarantee that Japanese audiences would welcome him, or even that he could expect success in the tiny foreign settlement at Yokohama. And he could never have imagined where his adventure would lead him.

The Settlement

In 1864, Yokohama bore scant resemblance to the modern metropolis it is today. It resembled the Shanghai settlement in China in that foreigners had been allowed to reside there and trade, but it was much smaller, having only been opened to the outside world five years earlier. Yet by 1864, what had once been a tiny fishing village already had a customs house,

Panorama of Yokohama, from a photograph by W. Saunders of Shanghai. *ILLUSTRATED LONDON NEWS*, SEPTEMBER 13, 1863.

warehouses, churches, hotels and clubs, banks, an English-language newspaper, a bowling alley, and even a few two-story buildings. Unlike Shanghai, where opium was one of the main commodities of trade, in Yokohama the exports were tea and silk and some cotton. Having been self-sufficient for over two hundred years, the Japanese did not import much yet, and trade was not as lucrative as had been hoped.

The foreign residents of Yokohama were a motley bunch of diverse nationalities and colorful personalities. British and Americans, Germans, and French were the most numerous. Most did not plan to stay long, and if they were not working as consular agents or stationed as part of the military garrisons of the European nations, they were usually merchants of uneven quality, extravagantly described by one diplomat as "the scum of Europe."[2] As was true of Shanghai, the vast majority were young, single males. Yokohama also included a large neighboring Japanese community and, across a swampy area, an entertainment zone with numerous houses of prostitution. Fires, cholera, and smallpox were always feared in the community, but venereal disease was particularly rife. Foreigners who stayed longer tended to take Japanese mistresses, and occasionally wives, and many fell in love with the country. Charles Wirgman was the publisher of a pioneering British-style cartoon and humor magazine in Yokohama called the *Japan Punch* (and the local illustrator/correspondent for the *Illustrated London News*). At the end of 1865, with massive exaggeration, he described his adopted town as having a total population of about three-thousand, broken down this way:

> . . . 3 merchants, 480 bill-brokers, 18 ministers, 27 con-
> suls, 60 legation and consular attaches, 100 storekeep-
> ers, 200 auctioneers, 50 butchers, 400 bakers, 70 silk
> inspectors, 1 tea taster, 3,377 grogshop keepers, numer-
> ous I-have-this-day-established-myselfers, 4 photogra-
> phers and half an artist, several editors and one Porcine
> Judge. . . .[3]

In Yokohama, the foreigners were even more strictly controlled than in Shanghai. J.R. Black, a Scottish singer who came to Yokohama in 1864 on the Asian performance circuit and stayed, later described the early settlement as having resembled a small guarded island. It was bordered by the bay, rivers, and a swamp. Bridges connecting the town to the outside world had gates that closed at sunset and guardhouses housing officials who carefully inspected all comers and goers for contraband.[4] Special permission was required to travel in and out of a twenty-five mile range specified by treaty and especially to visit nearby Edo (Tokyo), where the Shogunate was based.

The Shogunate was a feudal, military dictatorship that still ruled over *daimyō*, or territorial lords, from Edo in place of the emperor, who was kept secluded in Kyoto several hundred miles to the southwest. For nearly 250 years it had pursued a policy of near-total isolation from the outside world, keeping Japan at peace, but also keeping it in a state of near stasis politically and technologically. The first Westerners who arrived in the mid-nineteenth century probably felt like the protagonist of Mark Twain's famous novel *A Connecticut Yankee in King Arthur's Court* about an American transported back in time—in this case into an era of swords and bows and arrows and matchlock guns and no modern machinery at all. Only ten years before Risley's arrival, Commodore Perry and the U.S. Navy had by threat of force induced the Japanese Shogunate to sign a "Treaty of Amity and Friendship," which had been followed by a more comprehensive treaty in 1858. With this treaty, Japan had reluctantly agreed to diplomatic relations, the opening of a few new ports, the right to trade, extraterritoriality for foreign residents (meaning they would not be tried in the Japanese legal system), and the presence of Christian mis-

The entrance to the foreign section of Yokohama. *ILLUSTRATED LONDON NEWS*, AUGUST 1, 1868.

sionaries. It was a huge shift, accompanied by much domestic humiliation, introspection, and upheaval, and, after Risley departed, it would eventually lead to civil war, revolution, and restoration of the emperor.

The Shogunate's problem was not just foreigners. It had to contend with progressive forces in Japan that wanted to modernize the country more rapidly and open it to the West, and conservative forces that wanted to throw all foreigners out and restore the emperor to power.

Ideally, the Shogunate would have liked to have kept the Yokohama foreigners in a state of isolation and semi-imprisonment, much as they had kept a small cadre of Dutch traders for two centuries on a tiny island in Nagasaki Bay, far to the south. With good reason, they feared that what had happened to China might happen to them, that their nation might be carved up or even colonized like India or Indonesia or the Philippines or Vietnam. But with the success of the Americans in establishing relations and signing a treaty of commerce, the major European imperial powers had one-by-one demanded equivalent rights from Japan and used their naval and military might to assert their superiority. Often, at what seemed the slightest provocation, they would demand outrageous financial indemnities. As the American, William Elliot Griffis (who arrived in Yokohama six years after Risley), later wrote of this period, exaggerating only slightly:

> A favorite threat of atrabilious Frenchmen, blustering Russians, and petty epaulet-wearers of all sorts, when their demands were refused, was to strike their flag, go on board a man-of-war, and blow up the native town. Yokohama still stands, having survived bombardments in five languages.[5]

Many foreigners found the Japanese extremely friendly and polite, and many fell in love with the country and its people. But in certain conservative circles in Japan, fear and hatred of foreigners was intense. And so was loathing of the feudal Shogunate for its inability to stand up to the foreigners and its having signed a series of unequal treaties. Under the slogan of *sonnō jōi* (revere the emperor, expel the barbarians), there was a growing movement to overthrow the Shogunate, repeal the treaties, expel the foreigners, restore the emperor to power, and restore Japan's national pride. Japan had not yet fallen into a civil war like China, but its political situation was precarious and volatile, and anti-foreigner sentiment even more intense.

Introducing Western Circus

When Risley arrived on March 6, 1864, the European residents of Yokohama were feeling a bit more secure. In 1862, two-sworded samurai from the southern Satsuma domain had hacked a Britisher to death near Yokohama (and severely wounded two others) for what they regarded as insolence. This had caused a mini-war to erupt the next year in the south between Satsuma and the British navy. Yokohama's foreign residents, who had to live in dread of being expelled from Japan, now also feared being assassinated by bands of disgruntled roving, masterless samurai, or *rōnin*, who felt that the traditional feudal order in Japan was threatened by contact with the West. As the editor of Yokohama's English-language *Daily Japan Herald* wrote only ten days after Risley's arrival, things were quite peaceful, but only the previous year residents had "slept with the revolver by the one side—and the ready-charged carpet bag on the other."[6] It was all relative, of course. During Risley's nearly three years in Yokohama, the fears continued. Even as late as 1870, when Griffis arrived in Japan, he would write that few left their homes without one of "Smith & Wesson's best" and that "a nightmare of samurai, swords, blood, bleeding heads and arms, grave-stones, and grim death brooded over the foreigners."[7]

Risley took his time to carefully set up his circus in Yokohama. On March 26, *The Daily Japan Herald* ran a sympathetic article, announcing his arrival and encouraging the foreign residents of the settlement to go see his show. Risley, the editor noted, "has in the course of his circuit, met with a series of sad misfortunes; the death of some of his company,—the loss of several of his favorite horses—and other things of a like character which has required a stout heart and the sympathy of the public to overcome."[8]

The same edition of the paper ran a large advertisement for the opening of the circus on March 28. There was no mention, again, of Risley's protégé, Master Charles, and his fate is a mystery. It did, however, advertise the fact that Risley's equestrian troupe was the first ever of its sort in Japan, and it noted that the show would be augmented by the newly arrived, "highly accomplished actress Miss Lizzie Gordon and the celebrated danseuse, La Petite Cerito." The program was to consist of the following:

> Grand Entrée of the Company,
> Gymnastic Exercises,
> Equestrianism,
> Eccentricities,
> The Wonderful Polka—"La Perche,"
> The Hungarian Brothers,
> The Macassar Trick Pony—"Spot Beauty."

Admission was not cheap. Prices were three dollars for the dress circle and two dollars for second-class seats. For Japanese, who were also encouraged to come, the prices were in the local currency of two and one *itziboos*, respectively.[9]

The opening show was quite a success, even if the audience was small. As the *Japan Herald* reported, there were about 250 foreign residents and 200 Japanese. The gymnastics of the Italian Brothers, the singing of Lizzie Gordon, the dancing of La Petite Cerito, the daring back-somersault of the Australian equestrian Rooney (presumably "Eroni"), and the trained dogs of Mr. Eugene were particular hits. The paper further noted the absence of "vulgarities or improprieties" or "clap-trap pretense" in the troupe's performances, and encouraged others in the community to go see them. Shows continued on a regular basis, and their reception attracted attention far from Japan. The San Francisco *Alta* later ran a report from its Japan correspondent, who described the "wondering, gaping eyes" of the Japanese audience. The *London and China Telegraph* reported, "The Japanese seemed delighted beyond measure with the feats of horsemanship, and with the high training of the dogs, all of which is something quite novel to them."[10]

Japanese had never seen a Western-style circus, and most of them had probably never seen foreigners, either. In 1864, the cultural gap between Europeans and Japanese was truly vast. Almost no one in all Japan spoke English, and Japanese-speaking foreigners could probably be counted on one hand, so communication in Yokohama was often done in an invented pidgin-language. The Japanese were also still part of an elaborate feudal system that divided citizens into a semi-rigid hierarchy of four classes: samurai, farmers, craftsman, and merchants (in that order). Samurai still wore two swords and enforced the social order. Nearly everyone was a semi-vegetarian and, other than fish or occasional fowl, ate no meat. Christianity was still banned. Because for nearly two and a half centuries Japanese had been forbidden to travel abroad, most people had never seen any sort of the complicated mechanisms, machinery, or gadgets produced during the West's scientific advances. Thus, ever since Yokohama's opening in 1859, its little settlement of exotic foreigners had become the object of extreme fascination among the Japanese. An entire

"Equestrian Acts of Foreigners." (Risley's Troupe) performing in Yokohama in early March, 1864. NATIONAL DIET LIBRARY WEBSITE.

school of hugely popular, mass-produced woodblock illustrations, called *Yokohama-e*, or "Yokohama pictures," developed to satisfy this curiosity. They showed big, hairy, long-nosed foreigners in strange clothes and leather shoes, engaged in all sorts of odd rituals, strolling on the Western-style Yokohama waterfront, dancing, eating, drinking, whooping it up with geishas, sledding down hills, taking photographs, or riding in exotic wheeled carriages.

Among the *Yokohama-e* produced in 1864 are some showing a Western-style circus by now-famous woodblock artists such as Utagawa Yoshitora, Tsukioka Yoshitoshi, and Utagawa Yoshikazu. They show daring equestrians performing acrobatic feats on the backs of dashing horses, acrobats hanging from trapezes or tossing knives while balancing on rolling balls, and four musicians providing musical accompaniment. These are generally regarded as the first illustrations in Japan of a foreign circus, and the fact that multiple artists depicted the same scene testifies to the huge impact Western-style circus had on Japanese at the time. Yoshitora's prints, while not the best executed, are the best known, and he titled his illustrations as "*chūtenjiku* acrobats from abroad." *Chūtenjiku*, a now-archaic word written with rarely seen ideograms, literally meant "Middle India," but in this case it is simply a metaphor for a strange and exotic place. For years it was not clear which circus Yoshitora had depicted. Only as research on early Western circus in Japan has developed in the postwar period has it become evident that these beautifully colored woodblocks show the performances of Risley's troupe in Yokohama.

Stuck in Japan

Albert W. Hansard, the first editor of the local *Japan Herald*, was particularly supportive of Risley, and he tried to drum up interest for him. He had seen Risley in New Zealand years earlier, successfully entertaining not only the elite of the colony but also several hundred "savage Maori" natives. The Maori, he reflected, had been better behaved than many of the Yokohama foreigners in the audience. Yokohama was a port town and often suffered from rowdy drunken sailors. During the Risley circus performances, there were some ladies in the audience, and Hansard was bothered by the fact that a few vulgar men had insisted on smoking in their presence; he proposed banning smoking in the ladies section. At the same time, he also wrote with approval of a stunt personally performed for him by Risley himself. It involved Risley using his rifle (made by the legendary English gunsmith Joe Manton) and with a single well-placed shot drilling a clean hole in a dollar tossed into the air. True to form, Risley of course challenged anyone in the community to match his feat.[11]

Audiences in the small Yokohama settlement were limited, but with the special permission of naval captains Risley was able to expand his reach by staging performances for the sailors of the British fleet in port. On April 21, he staged a special benefit for Lizzie Gordon before she returned to California, and in it Master Rooney for the first time ever performed a "trampoline sumersault over twenty soldiers with fixed bayonets."[12]

After a month or so, Risley's circus ran out of steam. The Yokohama audiences were simply too small, and while Risley may have hoped to be able to tour throughout Japan, it was still prohibited and too dangerous. Risley had apparently planned to stay only a brief time in Japan, and then return to America, but perhaps because the Civil War was still raging, he decided against it. Subsequently, most of his performers left him in Yokohama. Effectively stranded with his horses and equipment, it was again time to try something new.

Risley was able to contact two old friends from Australia, who happened to be on the Asian circuit. They were the Australian equestrian performer and tightrope walker Annie Yeamans and her husband Ned, a famous clown and horse-trainer, who had also become stuck in Shanghai, where cholera was virulent and the performing group to which they had been attached had come undone. Risley asked them to come to Yokohama and help him out, and they were more than willing, simply to get away. As Mrs. Yeamans, who went on to become a famous stage actress in the United States, remembered almost half a century later:

> Then we had a chance to go to Yokohama. There was
> a man there who had a circus without any performers.
> They had all deserted him and gone home, and there

were the horses eating their horses' heads off, and he
had nothing for them to do, so he sent for Mr. Yeamans.
That was a twenty day's sail, and when we got there,
there were no performers. I was the whole circus, and
gave songs and dances, and, in addition, we used to give
farces. Risley was the man. He had some Japanese performers to help out. . . . Then, in addition to the circus,
Risley had a hotel and bar attached, and on gala nights I
used to be barmaid as one of the attractions.[13]

According to Mrs. Yeamans, Risley received her and her husband in
Yokohama with tears in his eyes. She recalled how she would ride horses,
do acrobatic feats on the swinging trapeze, appear in a concert doing
songs and dances, and, after the concert was done, serve as the barmaid
in Risley's hotel—all in one day.[14]

In a 1911 article authored near the end of her long life, Mrs. Yeamans remembered a timeline that contradicted both her earlier statements and the historical record in some details, but is still revealing. She
claimed that she and her husband had met Risley not in Yokohama, but
when stranded in Shanghai. With him, they had put together "a company of players, recruiting our members from other temporarily disabled
brethren and sisters in woe," and gone to Japan to offer "various sorts of
entertainment for the delectation of our almond-eyed friends and such
Europeans and Americans as happened to be there." Of Risley, she accu-
rately recalled, like them he had been a "professional soldier of fortune,"
who "had nothing much but hope and optimism, and his ability as a
performer, as stock in trade."[15]

Indeed, after losing his circus in Yokohama, Risley demonstrated an
extraordinary, almost desperate entrepreneurial spirit. Settlement records
show that he quickly became the proprietor of the local Flying Horse
Tavern. In the *Japan Herald* and other publications, advertisements and
articles mentioning him also appear with considerable regularity, illustrating his high level of local fame.

At the end of July 1864, Risley may have had no performers other
than the Yeamans, but he had his horses and had opened up a "Riding

Establishment" opposite the Grand Café du Japon. There, he hired out horses, gave private lessons in horsemanship, broke and trained horses, and also staged free equestrian and gymnastic trials for amateurs, with prizes awarded weekly.

In September, the settlement was abuzz with talk of the Battle of Shimonoseki to the south. The Chōshū domain, controlled by the anti-foreigner *sonnō jōi* faction, had fired upon foreign warships and then been thoroughly pummeled in vengeance by a combined fleet of British, French, Dutch, and American warships. More than ever, entertainment was needed.

In November, when Risley, along with Mr. and Mrs. Yeamans, opened up an amphitheatre for entertainment, the *Japan Herald* encouraged them all with the line, "we appreciate your courage—never give up." By December, it was well attended, and as Mrs. Yeamans's recollections hinted, Risley had apparently incorporated some local, native acts, for the paper noted, "The Japanese performances were really wonderful, and we recommend all to witness them." Risley himself was also performing, but Mrs. Yeamans was proving to be a "universal favorite." In a true sign of success, the paper noted the popularity of the performances but recommended that more space be made available for the "Ladies." Early in 1865, the name of the amphitheatre was changed to the Royal Olympic Amphitheatre, becoming what is now regarded as Japan's first true Western-style theatre. In February and March, grand programs were held that included a burlesque of "Fra Diavolo," and dances and singing of "Pretty Polly Perkins of Paddington Green" by Mrs. Yeamans, accompanied by the band from the Twentieth Regiment of the British garrison. By the end of May, the Yeamans had finally earned enough money to return to the United States.[16]

As the very hot summer of Yokohama approached, Risley hit upon an idea that he had learned of in Shanghai, and that was to import ice from Tientsin (today's Tianjin) in China. It was brought in by boat, covered in straw, and had to endure such onerous inspections by Japanese customs agents that it is amazing it did not all melt. On May 13, 1865, Risley used the exact format he had seen ads use in Shanghai's *North China Herald* to announce in the *Japan Herald* that he would begin selling ice—"pure spring-water, crystal ice." It was a radical enough idea that it later generated a parody piece in the local humor magazine, *Japan Punch*, with the editor announcing, "Notice: We have this day established ourselves at this Port as ice merchants and Professors—Grizzly and Co." But on May 13, Risley also announced that he was building an "ice cream saloon," adjoining the Royal Olympic Theatre. This would become the first ice cream ever made available in Japan.[17]

By the summer of 1865, the Civil War in the United States had finally ended, and on July 8, news of the April 15 assassination of President Abraham Lincoln reached the Yokohama settlement. By September, following the success of his ice scheme, Risley had decided to create a dairy business, which also did not exist then in Japan. To that end, he auctioned off six of his prized horses, along with side saddles, regular saddles, and a buggy and harness. After securing financial backing from members of the Yokohama community, including that of the local U.S. consul, George S. Fisher, he sailed to San Francisco in December on the *Ida Rogers*, one of the fastest clipper ships of the time. It took thirty-eight days through heavy seas, but the local *Alta* paper reported his arrival in considerable detail, reminding readers of Risley's global fame as an entertainer and noting that the peripatetic entertainer had finally decided to settle down as a merchant in Japan.

> No matter how elaborate the workmanship and handicraft of the Japanese may be, they cannot provide the outside barbarians with cow's milk or butter. To supply this want, Mr. Risley revisits California, to purchase the full stock in cattle, horses, sheep and swine, to make a farm perfect. . . . With the view of civilizing the natives, Mr. Risley proposed to cultivate a farm on the regular Yankee principle, in aid of which the Japanese government made a concession of land, and Mr. R. is here to procure his stock, etc.. . . . Mr. Risley is a man of great perseverance and energy, and the result of his enterprise will be, no doubt, the means of creating a better feeling between the Japanese and the Americans.[18]

After purchasing six fine cows and calves in California to start a herd, Risley sailed back to Yokohama on the *Ida Rogers*. He arrived on February 24, 1866, after again experiencing rough seas and being blown far off course, in what ultimately became an astoundingly lengthy seventy-day voyage. His cattle nearly died from lack of water, but soon he was advertising fresh dairy milk in the local paper, another first for Japan.

One of the best accounts of Risley during this time comes from J. R. Black, the formerly itinerant Scottish singer, who had settled in Yokohama and assumed the editorship of the *Japan Herald* in 1865. Black had met Risley in the Australian goldfields, at Bendigo and Back Creek, and in Yokohama he was always supportive of him. As he wrote later in his book, *Young Japan*:

> [Risley] was particularly cut out for the kind of Bohemian life he had chosen. He was a wonderful rifle shot; a good billiard player; up to everything that lithe and active men rejoice in. He knew thoroughly well the usages of good society, and could hold his own with high or low. His fund of anecdote was marvelous; and he could keep a roomful of people holding their sides with laughter, without the least appearance of effort, or the faintest shades of coarseness. Yet after his very successful European career, he did not manage to progress. . . . [H]ad he been content to make [the dairy] his business, and stick steadily to it, he might long ere this have been a thoroughly independent man.[19]

Black interviewed Risley upon his return to Yokohama, and in his book he includes one of the rare written renderings of Risley's unique manner of speech, and his mixing of the vernacular with the proper.

> Waal! Got back you see; though I know the bettin' was against me—but we had a narrow squeak for it as ever you saw. But here I am! And I've got six as fine cows as ever were milked—and six fine calves too. But it's God's

Professor Risley and his cows. *THE JAPAN PUNCH*, 1866.

mercy I've got them here; for I never was nearer losing anything in my life. Not a drop of water left. . . . We were close to Yokohama a month ago—and blown right off to the north, and had to beat up against a dead head wind, and thought we should never get here.

Black also saw in Risley's attitude to his animals a "real kindness of heart, which was his best trait."

I can't bear to see a poor dumb animal suffering—but—if you'd only seen the poor creatures! As I passed along in front of them they'd try to lay hold of me, as if to ask 'why don't you bring us some water?' I really hardly knew how to endure it. At last, I'd made up my mind that they must die, and was only thinking whether I should throw them overboard or let them die—and not yet able to make up my mind—when

God was merciful and sent a night's rain. I worked like a horse; and all that night I was employed in catching water—I did—all with my own hand! There! You may judge how I worked. Every bucket-full passed through my hands. Waal! You may smile—but it did, you know! And the cows were saved. I never was so relieved in my life.[20]

Almost as soon as Risley had arrived and started his diary, he was off again to Tianjin to get more ice for the summer. Ads for Risley's dairy operation show that he struggled on until he left Yokohama at the end of 1866, but several of his cows died, resulting in his being lampooned—yet again—in the *Japan Punch*. Wirgman's cartoon of Risley, in a parody of a popular song called the "Broken Hearted Milkman," depicted him standing forlornly in a field surrounded by dead cattle.[21]

A Different Approach

Before assuming editorship of the *Japan Herald* in Yokohama, J. R. Black had occasionally held paid performances once a week at his own bungalow, for members of the Yokohama community. Calling them "Evenings at Home," he would sing his favorite songs, accompanied on the piano by Marquis Chisholm (who had also accompanied Risley in Shanghai). At the end of August 1864, however, Black began to add other entertainments. A September 3 advertisement in the *Japan Herald* indicates that he was not only performing patriotic songs for the local British garrison, but including Japanese performances as well. In particular, he showcased the act of a renowned juggler named Asakichi, who could perform the "butterfly trick." This involved using a fan to make little origami butterflies appear to flit and float like the real thing, and it was already famous among foreigners. The next week, he followed up with another evening starring—in addition to himself and Marquis Chisholm on piano—a famous Japanese juggler from Edo, named Namigorō, with his son and daughter doing slackrope walking and top-spinning acts, respectively.

Professor Risley and sons, circa 1843–45. Ink with applied color on paper, 14x9 inches, SN1546.134.8. FROM THE CIRCUS COLLECTION, THE JOHN AND MABLE RINGLING MUSEUM OF ART, THE STATE ART MUSEUM OF FLORIDA, A DIVISION OF FLORIDA STATE UNIVERSITY.

 Imp. J. Rigo et Cie LE PROFESSEUR RISLEY ET SES DEUX FILS.

OLD THEATRE ROYAL,
KING STREET, BRISTOL.

LESSEE, — — JAMES HENRY CHUTE.

GLORIOUS TREAT FOR THE HOLIDAYS!

FOR SIX NIGHTS ONLY,
COMMENCING MONDAY, DEC. 27th,
AND TERMINATING SATURDAY, JAN. 1st.

UNDER THE PATRONAGE OF
THE PRINCE AND PRINCESS OF WALES.

RETURN AND FAREWELL VISIT
of
PROFESSOR RISLEY'S
ORIGINAL IMPERIAL
JAPANESE
TROUPE

CONSISTING OF TWELVE MALE AND FEMALE ARTISTES, COMPRISING

Tumblers, Tight-rope Performers, Acrobats, Jongleurs, Top Spinners, Sleight-of-Hand Performers, Balancers, Polanders, &c.,

From the Court of Yeddo, in Japan, travelling by special permission of the Tycoon.

The above Troupe performed a few weeks since in Clifton and Bristol to crowded and admiring audiences, filling the Colston Hall to repletion, hundreds being unable to gain admission. Now that the merits of this most talented Troupe are so well known in Bristol and its environs, pronounced by the Press and the Public to be the BEST AND MOST LEGITIMATE ENTERTAINMENT that has ever visited the city, Professor RISLEY, having arranged with the Proprietor of the above Theatre, will, by Special Desire, give his

FAREWELL PERFORMANCES
FOR SIX NIGHTS ONLY,
COMMENCING MONDAY, DECEMBER 23th,

In order to amuse the Juveniles at this Festive Season, Professor RISLEY has specially engaged

Mons. HENRIQUEZ'S CELEBRATED
TROUPE OF DOGS AND MONKEYS

That have lately created such a furore in the Metropolis, having performed to audiences of over Half-a-Million of persons, and will appear here at each performance.

GRAND FASHIONABLE MATINÉE,
On MONDAY & WEDNESDAY, DEC. 27th & 29th.
COMMENCING AT HALF-PAST TWO. Doors open half-an-hour previously.

LEFT: Professor Risley and sons, circa 1843–45. F TS 931.10, HARVARD THEATRE COLLECTION, HOUGHTON LIBRARY, HARVARD UNIVERSITY.

ABOVE: Color poster for Professor Risley's Imperial and Original Japanese Troupe advertising year-end performances at the Old Theatre Royal, in Bristol, England, 1869. © THE BRITISH LIBRARY BOARD, EVAN.2806.

National Museum of Japanese Histo

One of the most spectacular quasi-circus bromides produced in mid-nineteenth-century Japan. A large triptych woodblock print, showing Hayatake Torakichi and his Osaka troupe, performing in Hirokōji in Nishiryōgoku in the mid-nineteenth century. In a narrative format, it demonstrates their "kyokuzashi" (tricks on top of poles), jumping across paper-covered lanterns, and spinning tops, in the midst of a huge set. COURTESY OF THE NATIONAL MUSEUM OF JAPANESE HISTORY.

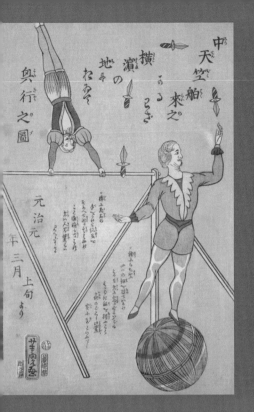

Triptych, viewed from right to left. "Performance in Yokohama of Foreign Acrobats from India." Woodblock *Yokohama-e* by Yoshitora, showing Risley's circus in March 1864. NATIONAL DIET LIBRARY OF JAPAN WEBSITE.

Triptych, viewed from right to left. "Equestrian Acts of Foreigners." Woodblock *Yokohama-e* by the now famous Tsukioka Yoshitoshi (shown here as Gyokuô Yoshitoshi), illustrating the dramatic acts of Risley's circus in March 1864. NATIONAL DIET LIBRARY OF JAPAN WEBSITE.

浅草観音
於境内ニ奥行仕候

大坂下り
櫻絹駒司
櫻絹幸吉

LEFT: Acrobats from Osaka performing on grounds of Asakusa temple in Edo (Tokyo). Edo period, 1857 (Ansei 4), 2nd month. Woodblock print (*nishiki-e*), ink and color on paper by Utagawa Kunisada II (Kunimasa III, Toyokuni IV), 1823–80. Publisher: Maruya Jinpachi (Marujin, Enjudō). Vertical *ōban*. MUSEUM OF FINE ARTS, BOSTON, WILLIAM STURGIS BIGELOW COLLECTION, 11.41491. © 2012 MUSEUM OF FINE ARTS, BOSTON.

ABOVE: Originally monochrome but later hand-colored woodblock print, or poster, advertising the Hamaikari Troupe. Text emphasizes the elaborate and wonderful props and gadgets the Hamaikaris used for their acts and highlights the role and strength of Hamaikari Sadakitchi, Denkichi, and Umekichi. The Hamaikari family would form the core of Professor Risley's Imperial Japanese Troupe. Undated, but probably produced

"Foreigners, Performing Equestrian Acts in Yokohama." Masterfully executed wood-block *Yokohama-e* by Utagawa (or Issen) Yoshikazu, showing acts of Professor Risley's circus, circa 1864, in great detail. A tryptich, with text emphasizing how much fun the equestrian and acrobatic acts were and marveling over how people over the world can enjoy the same things. CHADBOURNE COLLECTION OF JAPANESE PRINTS, LIBRARY OF CONGRESS PRINTS AND PHOTOGRAPHS DIVISION, WASHINGTON, D.C. 20540 USA.

Undated color woodblock print by Utagawa Yoshiharu (1828–88), originally designed to advertise the Hamaikari troupe within Japan. The Imperial Japanese Troupe apparently later added the list of all their individual member names to this older print, in

National Museum of Japanese History

both English and Japanese, and used it to advertise their performances in Britain and the United States. The absence of top-spinner Matsui Kikujirō's name indicates the list was added after his death on April 8, 1868. COURTESY, NATIONAL MUSEUM OF JAPANESE HISTORY.

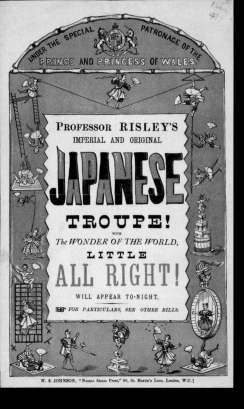

Color poster for Professor Risley's Imperial and Original Japanese Troupe in Britain, circa 1869–70. © THE BRITISH LIBRARY BOARD, EVAN.489.

In the late nineteenth century and even into the early twentieth century, Japanese acrobats and Japanese-themed acts continued to be popular on stage, in circuses, and in advertising.

LEFT: Another "Original Little All Right" in a trade card advertisement for Col. T. E. Snelbaker's Majestic Consolidation, a variety troupe active in the 1880s. COURTESY OF DR. ROBERT H. SAYERS.

RIGHT: Japanese acrobats advertising George A. Clark's cotton thread, in 1879. AUTHOR'S COLLECTION.

FOLLOWING PAGE: "The clever acrobats of the Oriental Company perform amazing tricks." Scene from Lothar Meggendorfer's famous children's pop-up book, *International Circus,* first published in 1877. MEGGENDORFER, LOTHAR. *INTERNATIONAL CIRCUS: A REPRODUCTION OF THE ANTIQUE POP-UP BOOK.* LONDON AND NEW YORK: KESTREL BOOKS; VIKING PRESS, 1979.

The latter resembled the top-spinning games enjoyed by Western children, taken to new and impossibly dramatic heights.

Nearly a year later, in September 1865, Risley also began to feature Japanese performers in his new Royal Olympic Theater. Whether he was inspired by Black or not is unclear, for it is worth noting that he had also been holding some sort of Japanese performances much earlier in his "Ampitheatre." Either way, on September 26, 1865, Risley went full force, with a dramatic advertisement in a new English-language newspaper, the *Japan Times Daily Advertiser*. With great flourish, it proclaimed that the show would start on the 28th, under the patronage of a long list of Yokohama diplomatic dignitaries of various nationalities, including all the local, high-ranking British admirals and generals. The ad trumpeted:

> PROFESSOR RISLEY has the honour to intimate that, at the request of some of the most influential gentlemen in the community, he has sent to Yedo and succeeded in engaging several of the best JAPANESE PERFORMERS of LEGERDEMAIN, TOP-SPIN-NING, GYMNASTICS, and of the celebrated "BUT-TERFLY TRICK."[22]

The entertainment, alas, did not go as well as Risley had hoped. The next week, the *Daily Advertiser* wrote a review of the program that, unusual for Risley's productions, was quite critical. Although the event was extremely well attended, with the audience anticipating some of the marvelous and rumored Japanese entertainment, the reviewer said that he had never sat through such commonplace performances, and that were it not for the presence of the band from the British Twentieth Regiment "somnolence would have fallen over the majority of the audience." The gymnastics were poor, as was the rope walking. When Risley appeared onstage, the reviewer wrote that he was at first met warmly but snidely added that "we should think that the warmth of his reception was due to the ice which he imported to cool their liquors in the hot weather, rather than the entertainment with which he sought to inaugurate the cold [of winter]." Unfortunately, Risley also had to tell the audience that the much anticipated butterfly trick would not be performed, with the result that the reviewer scolded Risley for so disappointing his audience, warning him that in the future "he must speak by the card, or equivocation will undo him." Risley's later excuse, the reviewer noted with undisguised disbelief and disapproval, was that despite having paid the butterfly trick performer a larger sum than usual, "the conjurer on the night of the performance [had] refused to exhibit the trick."[23]

That night, Risley not only failed to meet the high expectations of the reviewer (who had clearly seen many Japanese performances before), but also of his audience. If anything, the fiasco reinforced in his mind the high demand among Western audiences for quality Japanese entertainment, the need to provide them with the absolute best in performers, and the pent-up curiosity about exotic acts like the butterfly trick.

Circus Approximate in Japan

Although Risley is known today as the person who introduced the circus to Japan, it would be a mistake to assume that Japan had nothing resembling a circus. Many of the tricks and acts had been imported from China centuries earlier, but changed, refined, and eventually made uniquely Japanese. By the time Risley arrived, Japan already had all the ingredients of a Western circus, except for the nomenclature, the style, the form, and the oval or round circus tent.

The word "circus" can be traced back to the Roman Empire, where performances and contests were held in circular or elliptical arenas, such as the "Circus Maximus." Our modern sense of the word is said to have developed in the late eighteenth century, when innovators such as the renowned equestrian Philip Astley (1742-1814) developed an approximately forty-four-foot circular ring to demonstrate equestrian tricks. This eventually became a global standard for ring size, since it allowed performers and horses to use centrifugal force to keep their balance and to internalize the dimensions of the ring no matter where they went.

Astley and others gradually added more entertainment such as acrobats, clowns, musicians, and even animal acts. Eventually performers also began touring with circus tents.[24]

Among Europeans and Americans, reports of exotic Japanese acrobats, jugglers, top-spinners, and other entertainers had circulated for many years, long before Commodore Perry's expedition to the reclusive land in 1853-54. Engelbert Kaempfer, as physician to the Dutch in Nagasaki in 1690-92, had the rare opportunity to travel to Edo. He later wrote a book on Japan, translated into multiple European languages, which would remain one of the few reliable references on the mysterious country until the middle of the nineteenth century. Going through the city of Osaka, he commented, "Mountebanks, Juglers, who can show some artful tricks, and all rary-shew people, who have either some uncommon, or monstrous animal to shew, or animals taught to play tricks, resort thither from all parts of the Empire, being sure to get a better penny here than anywhere else."[25] Much later, reports also came from the Russian count, Vasili Golovnin, who was imprisoned in the north for two years between 1811 and 1813 for violating Japan's seclusion laws. Even rescued Japanese castaways commented on the phenomenon. Joseph Heco, saved by an American ship, in his English-language tale of survival published in 1850 wrote of his excitement at having seen jugglers and acrobats in Edo as a boy. By 1862, the British magazine *Blackwood's* would summarize the prevailing stereotypes of still-mysterious Japan as follows:

> There is no doubt that there exists a spiritual and a temporal emperor—that the population are addicted rather to cleanliness than to clothes—that the country is pretty, the tea-houses seductive, the arts and sciences advanced, and that the jugglers can do the butterfly trick—that the women blacken their teeth and pull out their eyebrows, and that the men rip themselves up;—these and other glaring characteristics, which it would be impossible to overlook, are descanted upon by every successive traveler.[26]

Still, the most detailed accounts came after 1856, when the first foreign diplomats visited Japan in the wake of Perry and, unlike him, were even allowed to visit Edo, the nation's capital. Townsend Harris, the first American consul-general, arrived in 1856 and spent nearly two years negotiating a critical trade treaty. Despite great isolation in the tiny town of Shimoda (south of Yokohama), frustration with Japanese officialdom, illness, and the fact that his prized interpreter, Henry Heusken, was hacked to death by rogue samurai from a *sonnō jōi* faction, Harris sent back many sympathetic reports of Japan. In a July 3, 1858 letter, he noted that jugglers and top-spinners were some of the most popular amusements among the Japanese, and that he had seen delightful performances of both. He had been highly impressed by a juggler's butterfly trick, but even more so by a top-spinning performance, which seemed particularly magical and delightful to him. And he was nearly as impressed by the presentation of the tricks as by the tricks themselves, for he notes the panache of the performer who "talked to the tops" as they spun and made dramatic flourishes with each movement.

> A top was declared to be female, and having let it spin awhile, he took it up, shook it, and down fell seven distinct tops, all of which whirled merrily round. Another suddenly changed into a lantern, and, after whirling some time, the lamp in the lantern was spontaneously lighted. A piece of sewing thread about five yards long was held extended by two persons; the exhibitor *put a top on this thread*, and it ran from one end to the other, always upright, and constantly revolving. The same feat was performed on the edge of a sword; the top ran from the hilt to the point, and back again to the hilt.[27]

In 1858, following the success of the Americans, the Britisher Lord Elgin also led a mission to Japan to sign a treaty with the Japanese. On August 25, Sherard Osborn, a naval captain on the mission, recorded his impression of a Japanese magician in an article widely reproduced around the world. "The old man performed many tricks of legerdemain," he

A POSSIBLY FANCIFUL SCENE OF ACROBATS PERFORMING AS LONG-NOSED, WINGED TENGU GOBLINS. APPLETON'S JOURNAL OF LITERATURE, SCIENCE AND ART, DECEMBER 4, 1869.

wrote, "in a manner that equaled anything we had ever before seen; but when he proceeded to show the far-famed butterfly trick, all were fairly wonder-stricken." The man deftly created some origami butterflies out of paper, and then set them in motion by gently waving his fan.

> . . . gradually, it seemed to acquire life from the action of his fan—now wheeling and dipping towards it, now tripping along its edge, then hovering over it, as we may see a butterfly do over a flower on a fine summer's day, then in wantonness wheeling away, and again returning to alight, the wings quivering with nervous restlessness! One could have sworn it was a live creature. . . .[28]

Top-spinning and butterfly tricks were some of the most striking and novel acts that early foreigners witnessed, but there were many others, too. Sometimes they fell into the category of *zashiki gei* (parlor tricks) that would be performed at the houses of nobles. But there were also itinerant acrobats and jugglers who would regularly appear at temple fairs, or on street corners, and perform in stalls and tent structures of Edo's Asakusa or Ryōgoku areas, where scenes reminiscent of Western circus were common during religious festivals. Nearly all of them fell into the broad category of what were called *misemono* (literally, "things to show" or "exhibitions"), which were hugely popular in the first part of the nineteenth century. *Misemono* included examples of elaborate craftsmanship, acrobatics, juggling, tightrope walking, intricate pole-balancing acts, and even exotic animals. Japanese were fascinated by exotic things, especially because they were largely cut off from the outside world for over two hundred years. Townspeople went wild with enthusiasm in the 1820s, for example, when camels from Asia were imported and displayed, or when, in 1862, after Japan was opened to the world, an American ship brought an elephant to be exhibited. As *misemono* historian Kawazoe Yū has noted, there was often a folk religion overlay to exhibitions of animals, with people believing that seeing, or touching them, might help ward off illnesses such as smallpox. When rendered in popular woodblock illustrations, the animals were often described, like

Necromancers, prestidigitators, top spinners, and butterfly tricksters of old Japan. AIMÉ HUMBERT, *LE JAPON ILLUSTRÉ* (PARIS: LIBRAIRIE L. HACHETTE, 1870).

Risley's circus, as being from *tenjiku*, or "India," a verbal representation of the exotic land to the west of Japan, from which Buddhism had also been imported.[29]

In Risley's era, it was hard to ignore *misemono*. Francis Hall, an early American businessman and correspondent for the *New York Tribune*, lived in Yokohama from 1859 to 1866. In his diary, he describes numerous entertainments, including *matsuri* festivals, Kabuki plays, sleight-of-hand tricks, balancers, and acrobats and jugglers—all with surprising regularity and a reporter's eye. From what he saw of ordinary Japanese (as opposed to nobility), he concluded that "there is not another nation I believe in the world where so large a portion of the popular earnings are expended for pleasures."[30] Hall was good friends with Joseph Heco (the rescued castaway mentioned in Chapter 1 who became the first Japanese American citizen and later returned to Yokohama to start a newspaper), and the pair even attended what Hall describes as a Japanese "circus," or

Acrobats performing for Japanese nobility. AIMÉ HUBERT, *LE JAPON ILLUSTRÉ* (PARIS: LIBRAIRIE L. HACHETTE, 1870).

"horse theatre." Of this Japanese show—which took place in an arena, and included a drama and the swooping of one man off his horse and the carrying of him to the ceiling by a "rat" character—Hall was not impressed, writing that "the riding was nothing, although the horses showed great docility."[31] His reaction illustrates why Japanese audiences were so stunned when Risley's circus in Yokohama showcased how Americans and Europeans had taken equestrian skills to a new, globally unmatched level.

Yet in Hall's diary entries, we can see how Japanese acts had become all the rage among the foreign community in Yokohama when Risley was there. On November 14, 1864, Hall attended a special exhibition of Japanese top-spinning, given by General Robert H. Pruyn at his Yokohama residence and attended by other diplomats and dignitaries. Pruyn—the American minister to Japan appointed by Abraham Lincoln to succeed Townsend Harris—had brought some of the best top-spinners from Edo, imitating what J. R. Black had done at his residence only a few months earlier. Hall's lengthy entry in his diary shows how impressed he was at General Pruyn's, for the spinners spun tops on the tips of their folding fans, on the sharp blades of swords, on the curved surface of an egg, and even in a cup of water (creating a jet of water through the top of the spindle). To his astonishment, the Japanese performers also set up an elaborate course for their tops, sending them up parallel bars into a miniature shrine, exiting into a miniature garden, crossing a miniature drawbridge, jumping up into a little tower, then another little house, down another drawbridge, into another little house, and so forth, for a "circuitous travel of thirty or forty feet." Some of the tops were also enormous, "weighing forty or fifty pounds, spun by a loose cotton cable as large as my arm." Hall also saw the butterfly trick, but like Townsend Harris he was far more impressed by the top-spinning.[32]

In this environment it is not hard to imagine how Risley, with his ever-sizzling entrepreneurial spirit, came up with the idea of taking a Japanese troupe to America and Europe. He wasn't the first person to consider the possibility. As early as 1858, the American consul general, Townsend Harris, wrote that "the top-spinners would produce a sensation in New York." When Sir Rutherford Alcock, the British minister to Japan, arrived shortly thereafter, he, too, reported extensively about similar performances, leading *Blackwood's Edinburgh Magazine* in Britain to editorialize in 1863 (referring both to Japanese prohibitions on traveling abroad and to the notorious practice of *seppuku,* or *hara-kiri*):

> Certainly an importation of Japanese top-spinners would make the fortune of any Barnum who could induce them to leave their country with the certainty of their being obliged to rip themselves up on their return. Let us hope that the discontinuance of this last trick may be one of the first-fruits of the introduction of Western civilisation into Japan.[33]

Beginnings of the Imperial Japanese Troupe

Assembling a troupe of top Japanese performers and taking them overseas required Japanese connections, and little more than a year after arriving in Japan Risley had clearly established them. He had successfully brought all sorts of performers to Yokohama and hosted them at a variety of venues. Illustrating this, J. W. Smith—another impresario on the Australasian circuit, traveling with the Lenton troupe—wrote Risley from Shanghai in the fall of 1866, asking if he could get hold of some Japanese performers. Risley, Smith said, had "secured a troupe of Japanese gymnasts and acrobats for me, and if they are all as good as he has written, then, indeed, they are wonders."[34] Indeed, Risley had also secured the services of a Japanese agent, or procurer, in the form of Takano Hirohachi, mentioned in Chapter 1, whose journal sheds much light on the eventual travels of the Imperial Japanese Troupe.

Taking a troupe overseas also required money, investors, and connections with influential people in the Yokohama community. The basic outlines of what Risley put together were widely introduced in the newspapers of the day, but in 1994, after some extraordinary sleuthing, modern Japanese performing-arts historian Mihara Aya unearthed

The November 1866 Great Fire of Yokohama. *THE ILLUSTRATED LONDON NEWS*, FEBRU-
ARY 9, 1867.

handwritten records of an 1867 New York lawsuit that also revealed the
troupe's financial structure. The lawsuit (handled in the Supreme Court
of New York) was between George S. Fisher, the American consul in
Yokohama, and San Francisco showman Thomas Maguire, who became
an investor-manager in the Imperial Japanese after their arrival in the
United States. The court records contain a copy of the original and
remarkable contract for the formation of the troupe, which is transcribed
in its entirety in Mihara's 2008 opus on early entertainers, *Enter Japanese:
A Night in Japan at the Opera House.*

The contract shows that four people—De Witt C. Brower, Edward
Banks, William F. Schiedt, and Richard R. Risley—entered into an
agreement on November 1, 1866, before George S. Fisher in Yokohama.
Fisher, as noted previously, was the acting U.S. consul, but he also bought
shares in the operation from Brower and thus became another investor. Brower was a Yokohama merchant and partner in the company that

National Museum of Japanese

The Tetsuwari family of performers before leaving Japan. Also see color pages for the Hamaikari family. COURTESY, NATIONAL MUSEUM OF JAPANESE HISTORY.

chartered the ship for the troupe to sail to America. Banks, as noted in Chapter 1, accompanied the group as its interpreter. One of the few foreigners who could speak Japanese, he was also the former U.S. Marshal in the Yokohama/Kanagawa settlement (appointed by Abraham Lincoln in January 7, 1864, at a salary of $1,371.26). Of William F. Schiedt little is known, except that he worked for a famous merchant company, Glover & Co., in Yokohama, was only twenty-seven, had tattoos, and could speak some Japanese. By investing in the venture, Fisher, an active U.S. government employee, put himself in a serious conflict of interest that would contribute to his eventually losing the lawsuit. But as Mihara has noted, Fisher was only one of many early diplomats in Japan to invest in acrobatic troupes venturing overseas (and thus to moonlight as impresarios).[35]

The contract names the primary Japanese performers in the Imperial Troupe, the ship they were to sail on (the *Archibald*), the division of labor and responsibility, the allocation of profits, and the term of the contract (two years). To take a troupe of Japanese performers around the world, the venture was capitalized at the then-huge sum of $100,000, which was divided into thirty-two shares.

Risley's impoverished state precluded him from making the largest investment. As a result, perhaps, Brower received sixteen shares, Risley six, Banks five, and Schiedt three, with two shares equally shared. Brower had full control of the financial business and disbursements of monies. Banks and Schiedt, under the written instructions of Brower, were to handle all the income received from performances (Schiedt effectively serving as "cashier"), but Banks was to serve as interpreter and directly manage the Japanese. Risley was to be the general manager, in charge of scheduling, booking, traveling, and so forth. However, perhaps reflecting his limited investment, as well as his chaotic and spectacular failures in the past, he would "have no control over the said shares or any of the financial receipts or disbursements." In effect, he would have no financial responsibility. His expenses would be paid for, and he would of course share in the ultimate profits of the venture (if there were any). But unlike Banks and Schiedt (who were to be paid a salary), his salary would be contingent on the box office take, and he would receive $300 a month if net receipts were $5,000, or $200 per month if $3,000. On the other hand, he would be allowed to take potentially lucrative complimentary benefits for himself in San Francisco, New York, Philadelphia, London, and Paris, as long as he paid all expenses.[36]

There was also the issue of securing passports for the Japanese performers, since the Japanese government had for nearly 250 years prohibited any Japanese from going abroad, on pain of death. One can only speculate, but perhaps because of the indirect involvement of U.S. consular officials in the venture, the group determined to abide by the law—to go through the arduous process of navigating the bureaucracy of a soon-to-collapse feudal government and to boldly apply for the first passports ever granted to ordinary Japanese civilians. As a reporter in New York later explained it:

> The Japs are a curious people and don't permit any great
> amount of foreign interference; very naturally, then, the

Professor's proposition to carry off their expert jumpers and balances made them wroth. But, no ways daunted, Risley stuck to it. He . . . had many interviews with the hicockalorums of lofty degree, and finally, after four years incessant argument, disappointment and devilment, obtained the kind permission of the imperial Tycoon to bring away the nimble japs, giving bonds in $100,000 for their certain return.[37]

And this, as noted in Chapter 1, is one of the main reasons for the delay in departure of the *Archibald* from Japan. The other was surely the devastating fire that broke out in Yokohama on November 26, destroying not only much of the town, including the U.S. consulate, but also Edward Banks's collection of Japanese curios. A competing troupe—the Tetsuwari family managed by Smith and Burgess, which left Yokohama and arrived in San Francisco before Risley's group—did not bother to apply for passports.

Risley's Imperial Japanese Troupe had plenty of competition. The idea of taking Japanese performers abroad was so popular among foreigners in Yokohama that, by the fall of 1866, three acrobatic groups (and eventually more than five) were being organized to go abroad. In fact, out of the very first seventy-one "passports" granted to ordinary citizens by the feudal government in a two-month period that fall, most were issued to the members of acrobatic troupes. Two groups, including Risley's, would travel east, via the United States, hoping to make the 1867 Exposition Universelle in Paris. Yet another group was to travel to the same Exposition in the opposite direction, via India. As the *Japan Times*, trying to be impartial, would note on October 31, 1866, "The world is wide enough for all, and we wish each of the enterprises the utmost success."[38]

Japanese acrobats and jugglers were swarming to Yokohama in the fall of 1866. While out on an excursion, two officers in the British regiment stationed in the town (who later wrote an entire book based on a stay of a few months), happened to run into a merry band of some of them—of "conjurers and top-spinners"—on their way to the settlement.

Whether these same performers later worked for Risley is unclear, but according to the officers, they later appeared in Yokohama and eventually "made their debut before American and British audiences." When the officers gave them a little money, they were delighted to put on an impromptu performance of top-spinning, the butterfly trick, and tumbling. Except for the music, which the officers found "hideous with discordant notes," the performance hinted at the acclaim the Japanese would soon meet overseas.

> We have seen in crowded assembly rooms, in gorgeous
> theatres, in drawing-rooms amongst friends, wizards of
> the north, wizards of the south, wizards of every point
> of the compass, "caressed of crowned heads," *et hoc genus
> homne*; but never have we enjoyed anything of the sort as
> much as we did that half-hour with these top-spinners,
> in that shady, quiet little glade, with its soft, grassy bank
> whereon to recline and smoke the fragrant cheroot, and
> its clear limpid stream, at which to slake our thirst.[39]

ACT 6
Taking America

Everybody remembers the furore that was created in this country by the first troupe of Japanese acrobats and jugglers which came here.[1]

—Olive Logan, *Before the Footlights and Behind the Scenes*, 1870

After their resoundingly successful reception in San Francisco in January 1867, Risley and the Imperial Japanese Troupe headed to the east coast of the United States, where they would cement their reputation. Under the wing of the flamboyant and powerful West Coast showman, Thomas Maguire, who had invested in both Risley's troupe and that of Thomas F. Smith's Tetsuwari family, the entire group of over thirty Japanese embarked for New York on the steamer *Constitution* on the 30th. They headed south along the California and Mexico coast for the Isthmus of Panama, where they would cross over and board another ship for New York. It would be a long and hard journey, but in the days before the transcontinental railroad, it was still far easier than crossing the continent by land or sailing through the treacherous Straits of Magellan at the tip of South America.

Heading for the East Coast

The two Japanese troupes had never been on a steamship before, so it was both a novel experience and a chance for the otherwise-rivals to socialize and compare notes. Unlike Risley, Maguire, and the Smiths, they were traveling in the ship's steerage class, famous in the nineteenth century for being horribly crowded and stuffy, with poor sanitation and food, and usually reserved for the poor. Nonetheless, they marveled at the ship. It was huge (it could carry over six hundred people), and it had fancy furnishings, lights, and many "businesses" on board (including multiple saloons, barber shops, and dining rooms). Hirohachi, the overseer of the Imperial Japanese Troupe, faithfully recorded the trip in his diary, including the spouting whales he saw along the way, a stop for coal at what was presumably Acapulco, and their arrival at the Isthmus of Panama, where they boarded a train to Aspinwall (today's Colón), on the other side. It was an alien, oppressively hot tropical environment, and he carefully noted the strange and perhaps dangerous foods, and the presence of so many different "black" people who looked like animals to him. On the eastern side of the isthmus, the Japanese boarded another, smaller steamship, the *Rising Star*, which carried three hundred and fifty passengers. When the weather worsened, it rocked violently and made them seasick. Wending their way through the West Indies, Hirohachi noted that the inhabitants of some of the islands ate meat and sometimes their own friends—or at least that is what someone told him. Finally, on February 23, after a journey of over three weeks, they arrived in New York harbor safe and sound and traveled through the city by four large horse-drawn carriages to their lodgings. It was terribly cold, the ground was covered with a foot and a half of snow, and they were tired, but they had all made it alive. The journey via the isthmus might be safer than other routes, but it was still dangerous. Only a month earlier, when Mark Twain made the same trip from San Francisco, eight passengers on his ship from Nicaragua had died, six of them from cholera, one of the most dreaded diseases of the mid-nineteenth century.[2]

The next day the Japanese went to see a local play. Afterward they were taken to a bath house and able to clean up, which must have overjoyed them, since back home bathing was an important daily ritual. Maguire had hoped to showcase the group at the city's Academy of Music, but this was not to be, as it had burned down in a fire. While he and Risley searched for other venues, the Japanese had time to rest, engage in sightseeing, and practice their acts. On February 24, however, it was discovered that one of the young women of the Imperials, called Tō (a twenty-year-old samisen player who was Hamaikari's "woman"), and a man from the Tetsuwari group had struck up some sort of inappropriate relationship. This so enraged the Imperials that they threatened violence on the other party. They were only pacified when Hirohachi made the Tetsuwari members write an apology.[3]

As noted in Chapter 1, Maguire considered Smith's Tetsuwari group to be his "left wing" and Risley's Imperials to be his "right wing," and he had resolved to focus on the latter, superior group. He therefore spun the left wing off to tour the cities of the Northeast. They eventually traveled out west as far as Milwaukee, Wisconsin, not far from the then still-wild American frontier, and even visited Cuba. For fans of the Japanese acrobats (not to mention historians) it was all very confusing, because in newspaper advertisements the left wing (the Tetsuwari group) was sometimes referred to as "Maguire's Imperials," and later "Smith's Imperials," while the right wing was usually referred to in the press as "Maguire & Risley's Imperials," "the Imperial Japanese," or even simply the "Imperials." But no matter what the nomenclature, Risley's Imperials were always given top billing and attention, and ultimately they were the only ones who would go on to Europe.

Philadelphia

Unable to book the Imperials in a suitable venue in New York, Maguire and Risley made the smart decision to tour other cities on the Eastern seaboard first and return to the metropolis later. That way, the acts could be refined, and a crescendo of publicity and anticipation could be orchestrated in advance of their official New York debut. So at the end of February the group went to Philadelphia by a train gaily flying both Japanese and American flags. As in San Francisco, the first days of their stay on the East Coast were like a surreal dream. Hirohachi's diary reflects his continuing amazement with Western technology. He marvels at the construction of the New York harbor, the fact that faucets in the baths allowed one to mix hot and cold water together to get just the right temperature, and, in Philadelphia, the sight of a horse-pulled fire engine with a steam-powered water pump and an eight-story building with an elevator.

For Philadelphia, Risley had plotted his publicity strategy carefully, and it unfolded in classic Risley fashion, taking into account all the points that he needed to stress about the exoticism, refinement, and originality of his troupe. Advertisements began to appear in the city almost immediately. On February 26, right before the troupe left New York, a large ad appeared in the *Philadelphia North American and United States Gazette*, highlighting what Risley believed would build excitement and serving as the prototype for subsequent publicity. Both Maguire's and Risley's names were in bold upper-case letters. The advertisement stressed that the Imperials had just arrived from California after a huge success, and that they would appear in Philadelphia on March 4. It stated that the Japanese government had prohibited its citizens from leaving the country for over two hundred years, but that as soon as the policy changed, Risley had engaged the Imperial Troupe and, with the help of some gentlemen financiers, had put up a $100,000 bond for them. This ensured their safe return and guaranteed them a collective salary of a similar amount. The advertisement further stated that after sixty appearances in San Francisco, the troupe had been unanimously declared by the city's press and inhabitants "the most unprecedented performers ever yet seen in this country."

In San Francisco, Risley had duly noted the particular appeal of the female performers, and of Hamaikari and his nephew, Umekichi, or "Little All Right" (who was usually billed as Hamaikari's son). He did the same in the Philadelphia:

> This Troupe is composed of the most celebrated of all
> the Extraordinary Performers, Males and Female.
> ACROBATS,

TOP SPINNERS,
POETRY OF MOTION,
BUTTERFLYING,
&c.,&c., &c.,&c.,
And the Daimio's favorite, the greatest performer in the
world,
HAMAIKARI SADAKITCHI,
And his beautiful and most wonderful son,
ALL RIGHT.[4]

Risley in typical fashion emphasized the troupe's credentials, stressing that they had appeared before the Tycoon of Japan, the United States
ministers, the British ministers, foreign plenipotentiaries, consuls, vice
consuls, officers naval, military, and civil, and the elite of the society
in the foreign settlement of Yokohama. As if that were not enough, on
the front page of the same issue of the paper Risley had persuaded the
editors to run a testimonial by George S. Fisher, the U.S. Consul in
Yokohama. Dated December 1, 1866, and addressed to Risley on the eve
of his departure from Japan, it did not mention that Fisher himself was
an investor in the production but had him proclaim the Imperials to be:

> the only genuine troupe of artists that has left, or is likely
> to leave Japan, and it gives me pleasure to feel assured
> you will not only astonish but afford unusual delight to
> a discerning public wherever you may perform. I do
> cheerfully state that the most of your artists are known
> to be not only the best in Japan, but the ones who have
> frequently afforded the public of this settlement, under
> your management and at your theatre, the privilege of
> witnessing their remarkable feats and powers, always so
> interesting, extraordinary and novel.[5]

On February 28, another mention of the troupe appeared in the
Philadelphia newspapers, along with the standard advertisement. As if
to cover any residual concerns Risley might have, it emphasized that

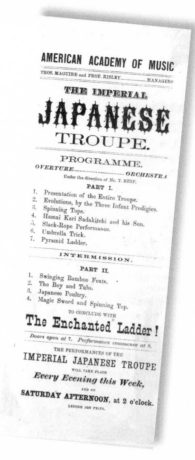

AMERICAN ACADEMY OF MUSIC

THOS. MAGUIRE and PROF. RISLEY..............MANAGERS

THE IMPERIAL

JAPANESE
TROUPE.

PROGRAMME.

OVERTURE...........................ORCHESTRA

Under the direction of Mr. T. REIF.

PART I.

1. Presentation of the Entire Troupe.
2. Evolutions, by the Three Infant Prodigies.
3. Spinning Tops.
4. Hamai Kari Sadakitchi and his Son.
5. Slack-Rope Performance.
6. Umbrella Trick.
7. Pyramid Ladder.

INTERMISSION.

PART II.

1. Swinging Bamboo Feats.
2. The Boy and Tubs.
3. Japanese Poultry.
4. Magic Sword and Spinning Top.

TO CONCLUDE WITH

The Enchanted Ladder !

Doors open at 7. Performance commence at 8.

THE PERFORMANCES OF THE

IMPERIAL JAPANESE TROUPE

WILL TAKE PLACE

Every Evening this Week,

AND ON

SATURDAY AFTERNOON, at 2 o'clock.

LEDGER JOB PRINT.

Playbill from Philadelphia's American Academy of Music, March 1867.
COURTESY, THE LIBRARY COMPANY OF PHILADELPHIA.

while Asian jugglers and acrobats were generally superior to the Western version, this troupe of Japanese "far exceeded" even a group of Chinese acrobats and jugglers who had been in the city some years previous, and that they had cleared $33,000 in only a few weeks in San Francisco. It also stressed that three of the group members were female.

On March 5, a day later than originally advertised, the Imperials finally opened in Philadelphia, at the local American Academy of Music on the corner of Broad and Locust Streets. This was one of the larger and more prestigious performance halls on the East Coast. As Japanese historian Miyanaga Takashi discovered in the 1990s (when he meticulously retraced Hirohachi and the Imperials' journey), the old but grand and opulent opera building still stands today. With hundreds of gas lights and gold trim, it delighted visitors in the latter half of the nineteenth century, and it could hold three thousand people in its main hall. Today it is a registered National Historic Landmark.

Despite a big snowfall, the opening night was a wild success, with tickets sold out early and Standing Room Only signs posted. The next day, local newspapers were unanimous in their approval. The *North American and United States Gazette* noted that the Academy of Music had seldom been so crowded, and it complimented Risley on his success. Race was always on the minds of Americans in the mid-nineteenth century, so the reviewer claimed they were "better-looking" than the Chinese and noted with particular interest the habit the Japanese had of squatting on the stage, bowing their heads to the floor each time a performer came onstage, addressing the audience in a language that no one understood, and playing odd-and-not-always-musical lutes or banjo-like instruments (*samisen*). Of the performances, Hamaikari's son Umekichi came in for special notice.

> Some of their feats of dexterity are really wonderful. Among these we may mention the strangely interesting features of top-spinning, which baffles all imagination. These Japanese tops are great curiosities in themselves, but the feats executed with them are amazing. The concluding scene, with the descent of the inclined wire by the wonderful boy above mentioned, must be seen to be appreciated.[6]

As in San Francisco, Umekichi frequently exclaimed "All Right!" at times varying it with the "All Right! You Bet!" he had learned in California. This further boosted his, and the troupe's, popularity, so that the rave reviews continued. On March 8, *The Public Ledger* gushed that "their performances are truly wonderful and go far ahead of anything ever witnessed in this city." A week later, the *Philadelphia Inquirer* noted how "their incomparable feats of balancing astonished and delighted everybody," how "All Right You Bet" and his father were "perfect wonders," and that the slackrope walker was a "remarkable performer," that the

21. Hamaikari Sadakichi.

HAMAIKARI SADAKICHI.

22.

HAMAIKARI MIKICHI.

23.

24.

CARTES DE VISITE, 21–25

Taken of the Imperials in Philadelphia in March 1867 at the F. S. Keeler Studio, Philadelphia, in a Victorian setting.

21. Hamaikari Sadakichi.

22. Sumidagawa Koman, with book in hand.

23. Hamaikari Umekichi, or "Little All Right."

24. Sumidagawa Koman (center), with what is presumed to be Tō, the troupe shamisen player and "musical directress," on her left, and the top-spinning wonder-girl, Matsui Tsune, on her right. They are all wearing Japanese *geta*, or wooden clogs. The adults have Victorian-style collar pins, or brooches.

25. From left to right: Denkichi, with the brothers Sentarō and Yonekichi and their father, Rinzō, of the Hamaikari family.

CREDITS. CDV 21, 23: TCS 20, HARVARD THE-ATRE COLLECTION, HOUGHTON LIBRARY, HARVARD UNIVERSITY. CDV 22: LIBRARY COMPANY OF PHILADELPHIA. CDV 24: COUR-TESY DR. ROBERT H. SAYERS. CDV 25: LIBRARY COMPANY OF PHILADELPHIA.

25.

great ladder feat was "incomprehensible, and acts at defiance of the laws of gravitation and all other natural laws," and that "everybody should see the 'Japs,' it is the popular and fashionable idea just now."[7]

There was also great interest in the Japanese outside of their professional appearances, for few Americans yet knew much about far away and still mysterious Japan. The first official Japanese government mission had visited Philadelphia on its way to Washington to ratify a treaty with the United States in 1860, but it had merely stimulated curiosity about the country. The Imperials were part of a foreign land's popular culture, not a bunch of stiff, government officials. As would be true of the populations of other cities, Philadelphians found the Japanese to be odd, exotic creatures yet were mostly unable to imagine how odd and exotic they themselves might seem to the Japanese. "They are a very queer people, these oriental athletes," the *North American and United States Gazette* editorialized, obliquely alluding to their potential profitability:

> They decline utterly to partake of hotel fare—they regard wine and seasoned meats as kindred abominations. They look upon beds with contempt, and upon luxuries as so many hindrances to their professional agility. They subsist upon tea, rice, beans and potatoes, eschewing stimulants of every kind, whether solid or fluid. . . . More than this they abjure the use of furniture in their dormitories. They are a jocund, merry party, and in the way of muscle will be very difficult to excel. Their maintenance here will cost them but one dollar per day each, a matter that is slightly in contrast with the diurnal expenses of our Italian operatic performers.[8]

After failing to secure a venue in New York, there was a reason Risley had chosen to take the Imperials to Philadelphia for their East Coast debut. Philadelphia was his official hometown in the United States. It was where he had once owned considerable property, where his wife (Rebecca) and his sons John and Henry still lived, and where he could exploit a wide variety of contacts. In the 1850 United States census,

Risley had miraculously (given his travels) been recorded as a Philadelphia resident, and he had presumably visited there in 1854–55, before heading West. Risley left us no personal records, but when visiting with the Imperials in 1867 after being absent for over a decade, one would assume that he visited his family again. In the 1870 census, his son Henry Risley is listed as having two children, five and three years old, so in 1867 the Professor was already a grandfather. That year both John and Henry were also working in the elite Continental Hotel, as the proprietor of the local news and ticket stand, and as a clerk, respectively.[9] Not coincidentally, in Philadelphia the Continental was the first place that the Imperials were taken. And John Risley's ticket stand was also one of the main places to buy tickets for local shows, including those for the Imperials at the Academy of Music.

We know in surprising detail what the Japanese did in Philadelphia. Hirohachi's journal records that the Imperials spent around a month in the city, performing nearly every day to sold-out crowds, despite the fiercely cold weather and occasional snow. During rare breaks in performances, they enjoyed sightseeing, including (as in San Francisco) a visit to the local mint. They were also wined and dined by the city's high and mighty, who found the exotic Japanese fascinating and wanted to be associated with them. Perhaps as a reward for their hard work, after a difficult but successful day of performances on March 11, someone also took the males in the troupe to visit Philadelphia's red light district. In his journal, Hirohachi diligently recorded his first experience with a "foreigner" prostitute, and he apparently enjoyed the experience a great deal. It henceforth became a regular part of his life on the road.[10]

At the end of March, Risley took the Imperials to Baltimore, Maryland. On April 2, they opened for only a few days at the Maryland Institute, again playing to sell-out crowds. Then, on April 7, they moved to Washington, D.C., which Hirohachi referred to as the "capital of America and the place of its king." There, in preparation for a series of performances at Wall's New Opera House, they checked into the National Hotel. Wall's Opera House was on the corner of Pennsylvania Avenue and 9th Street. It was far smaller than the Academy of Music in Philadelphia, but it had been newly refurbished and it was in the nation's capital. The Imperials' move to Washington would generate an enormous amount of national publicity in the United States, garner Risley more of the powerful testimonials he cherished, and set the stage for the Imperials to completely win over the American public.

Washington, D.C.

There was plenty of competition for attention in the nation's capital. There was of course the usual overheated political theatre provided by always-jousting senators and congressmen. But that week, the residents of the capital were also riveted by the trial of John Surratt, the recently apprehended adult son of Mary Surratt (who had been executed two years earlier along with three other Confederate sympathizers for having conspired to assassinate President Abraham Lincoln). And in Washington, D.C., there was plenty of ordinary entertainment, too, in the form of plays and musical events. Forepaugh's Circus and Menagerie was also in town, with over two hundred "living animals and birds," including elephants.

Risley's advertising strategy nonetheless worked well. The local newspapers ran notices for the troupe, again highlighting both Maguire's and Risley's names and stressing, as usual, that the Imperials were the first group of "Japanese Artists ever allowed to leave Japan." The wonderfulness of the young "Little All Right" was duly proclaimed. The local *National Republican*, in a short article, noted that Risley was one of the "sharpest and most enterprising showmen" the country had ever produced. It declared that he had "brought a set of those Japanese genii, whose manipulations are so astonishing as to inspire a distrust of the reliability of the senses, while they amuse the mind to a wonderful degree." At the National Hotel, gawkers gathered when the Japanese checked in, including many Native Americans who also happened to be in town.[11]

Citizens of the nation's capital were used to, if not numb to, visits by foreign dignitaries. And they were not entirely ignorant of Japan. The famous Japanese castaway, Joseph Heco (Hamada Hikozō), had met with Presidents Franklin Pierce, James Buchanan, and even, during the

Civil War, Abraham Lincoln. Japan's first official government mission to the United States had also paid its respects to the capital in 1860, met Buchanan, and been attended by extraordinary public and private hoopla. After that, the Civil War had dominated people's attention for years, until it finally ended in a type of exhaustion in 1865. When the Imperials arrived two years later, there was a renewed opportunity to interest people in something as exotic as a troupe of Japanese acrobats.

As had happened in Philadelphia, when the Imperials opened on April 8 the response was overwhelmingly good, and they continued to pack their cozy but comfortable venue. "The exhibition of these wonderful acrobats and Eastern magicians at Wall's Opera House is no humbug," reported the *National Intelligencer* on April 10. The reporter on the scene from New York's *Commercial Advertiser* wrote, "The Japanese acrobats and jugglers have taken the town by storm. . . . Nothing in any way approaching them has ever been witnessed here." The next day, the *National Republican* stated that the "Japanese are the attraction of the town just now. . . . It is truly astonishing to witness their numerous pranks and various feats of gymnastic exercises, deceptions and clever cheaters. This place is bound to be crowded every night while these people remain." On April 12, the same paper proclaimed, "It would seem that the Japanese can never fail to draw full and overflowing houses; and the audiences are composed, in a large degree, of many of our most intelligent and respectable citizens."[12]

At the performances in Washington, Risley was able to collect several prized testimonials from some of these very important people, including diplomats from the British and French legations, Postmaster General Alexander Randall, and former Civil War hero and soon-to-become-president Ulysses S. Grant. General Grant penned in Risley's book, "I have had the pleasure of witnessing the performance of the Japanese troupe, now exhibiting under the direction of Professor Risley, and think some of their performances truly wonderful." But the best testimonial of all would come from U.S. President Andrew Johnson. Known for his pithiness and uninspired comments, Johnson wrote simply, "I was much pleased with your troupe."[13]

Johnson was not feeling well that spring. On April 11, the newspapers reported that he had a severe cold as well as pain in the back and side. His physician diagnosed it as a liver complaint and said he must be kept as quiet as possible, but he was also under a great deal of stress.[14] In 1865, while serving as vice president under Abraham Lincoln, he, too, had been targeted in the assassination attempt led by John Wilkes Booth. Because he had survived, he had automatically assumed the office of president. But during the difficult post–Civil War years of Reconstruction, his rule was increasingly unpopular. In 1867 he narrowly missed (by one vote) becoming the first sitting president to be removed by impeachment.

On April 17, Johnson nonetheless found time to meet with the Imperials in the White House, thus generating a gold mine of publicity for Risley and some for himself, too. Dozens of articles and mentions were published in newspapers all across the United States. Sometimes they were edited and tailored, but they were mostly reprints of two articles that first appeared in either the Washington, D.C. *National Intelligencer* or the *New York Herald*. The *Intelligencer*, in a straightforward fashion, described how the Imperial Japanese, accompanied by Risley and Edward Banks, their interpreter, were received by Johnson in his official reception room. Because of Johnson's indisposition, the meeting was short. Banks introduced the group's leader, Hamaikari Sadakichi, who asked to make a few remarks and was allowed to do so. Hamaikari, presumably speaking through Banks, thanked the president for the meeting, which was an "honor and a privilege they did not enjoy in their own country, which they would ever gratefully remember." Johnson in turn expressed his appreciation of the visit by the Japanese and hoped their visit to the United States would be pleasant and profitable. He apologized for not yet having seen their performance, but gave them a tour of the Executive Mansion, including the State Dining Room, the Blue, Red, and Green rooms, and ending in the celebrated East Room. When it was all over, he shook hands with each Japanese performer individually.[15]

The *New York Herald* either had a reporter on the scene or did extensive interviews with the participants, because it ran a lengthy, fairly colloquial article, giving more details and cultural information. The

Japanese, the paper said, had taken off their sandals to go into the office where the president was standing to meet them, and

> advanced slowly, in a low stooping posture, with their arms folded over their heads, and manifested the most marked reverence and humility. . . .[T]hey seated themselves in a row upon the floor cross-legged, but did not venture to look towards the President, except by sidelong glances, until informed by the interpreter that they might rise and look upon the President, whereupon they rose respectfully and gazed at the chief magistrate long and earnestly.[16]

Each member was introduced by name and greeted by the President in a cordial manner, but the President was "especially attentive" to the young star, All Right, taking him by the hand several times and talking with him through Banks, the interpreter. All Right, true to form, was self-possessed and bold. When the President led them through the White House, explaining as they went along, one of the women noticed a Japan-made punch bowl, as well as other articles of furniture from Japan, which delighted the group. At the end of the article, the reporter provocatively posed the question: "Has President Johnson gone into the show business?"[17]

In 1867, most Americans, if they knew anything about Japan, were often sympathetic to it. Japan was not yet a threat, and it was still seen as an exotic and mysterious place. And it was also a land that some thought the United States had a certain responsibility for, because the United States had forced Japan to end its isolation and dragged it unwillingly into the modern world. Perhaps because of this, almost all the reports of the Imperials' visit to the White House were favorable. In Texas, however, the visit provided Galveston's *Flakes Bulletin* an occasion to heap some more scorn on the already unpopular Johnson and to indirectly criticize Risley, too. The visit had turned "our Chief Magistrate into a gigantic advertisement for all kinds of enterprising mountebanks [*sic*]." Risley, the writer claimed, was a well-known circus athlete managing the troupe, and the visit to the White House had provided "an advertisement worth thousands of dollars to their adroit manager."[18]

As for the Japanese, despite having Banks to interpret for them, they saw much of Washington, D.C. and the organizational workings of the United States through a dense linguistic and cultural fog. On April 15, they visited Brady's Gym and saw demonstrations by Mr. Brady and his pupils of American gymnastic prowess, which the local papers reported the Japanese "hugely enjoyed."[19] But Hirohachi does not mention this in his diary at all. Of their visit to the imposing U.S. Capitol and Senate chamber, he writes that he was awestruck by the building, but he obviously comprehended little of what he was told, for he notes the height and "countless other fathomless things." A local newspaper corroborates his confusion, reporting that the Japanese "seemed thunderstruck when the Senators roared, and looked at each other dubiously, apparently uncertain whether they ought not to draw their swords and make the nearest doorkeeper commit Hari Kari. [They] evidently are not used to such curious sounds in their own country."[20]

Hirohachi described the troupe's encounter with President Johnson in his diary: "On this day we went to the castle on the invitation of the king of the country, had an audience with him in his room, and did what is called a handshake, where people grab hold of each other's hands in what is regarded as a type of formal greeting . . . "[21] Back in Japan, bowing, rather than handshaking, was the rule, and for Japanese commoners, even looking directly at samurai or nobility could be a very risky act.

After visiting the president, the troupe all went to see the U.S. Treasury, where bills were printed. Then, perhaps in a spirit of celebration, Hirohachi visited a local prostitute. In fact, in his diary he expends more lines describing the prostitutes of Washington, D.C. than anything else. The next day, he went back again to visit another one whom he found particularly beautiful, and his diary describes not only her almost translucent skin but also the layout of her room, including its beautiful décor, mirrors, furniture, and bed. The woman made him view her genitals, slapped the inside of her thighs, and made him show her his, to his discomfort, apparently to check for venereal disease. Both also washed themselves. Yet Hirohachi commented disapprovingly that after sex

American women seemed to clean themselves with washcloths—unlike Japanese who used disposable paper tissues—and that they also used the same cloths the next morning to wipe their faces.[22]

New York and the Imperials' Acts

After their publicity coup in the nation's capital, the troupe returned to Baltimore, performed at the Maryland Institute again for a few nights, and then moved on to the entertainment capital of nineteenth-century America—New York. With a then-huge population of nearly one million, New York was not only the largest city in North America but the most sophisticated and the most connected to the cultural centers of Europe. Like the citizens of Philadelphia and Washington, New Yorkers had been previously exposed to official Japanese culture. When the first government mission from Tokyo had arrived in 1860, the city had nearly swooned. There had been elaborate parades and receptions for the samurai officials; otherwise-respectable Caucasian women had fallen scandalously in love with their young interpreter, nicknamed "Tommy"; and Walt Whitman had even written a poem about the visit. But this time, as commoners and entertainers, the visitors seemed even more exotic.

As had been true in Washington, there was no lack of competition in New York in May. There was P. T. Barnum's museum and menagerie, and there were operas, minstrel shows, plays, panoramas, and even the New York Circus. But this time the Imperials had finally secured one of the city's more coveted venues—the newly renovated and huge Academy of Music on 14th and Irving. And now Risley was also able to advertise in local papers that the Imperials had been declared "The Wonder of the World" based on their reception not just in San Francisco, but in Philadelphia and Washington, D.C. In Washington, he could proclaim, they had created "A Perfect Furore" and "been witnessed with marked demonstrations of approbation and delight by the President and family, Gen. Grant, the foreign Ministers, heads of Departments and overwhelming audiences."[23]

When the Imperials debuted on May 6, they did not disappoint. As a *New York Times* reviewer put it the next day:

> People came here with great expectations, predicated upon wonderful reports that had come to them from San Francisco and other places that had witnessed the marvelous works of the Imperial Japanese Troupe, whom Prof. Risley has kindly persuaded to tarry with us for a few weeks *en route* to the Paris Exhibition; but we risk nothing in asserting that of all that vast assemblage (there must have been at least 3,000 persons in the house,) if there was one individual who went away unwilling to confess that the promises made in the small bills were not more than redeemed, he ought to emigrate from this to some other sphere, where, possibly, there is something left to astonish him.[24]

The Imperials had a nearly two-month run in New York, where they were sold out nearly every night and crowds had to be turned away. In the process they became a national phenomenon in a still young and recently divided nation. But what sort of acts did the Japanese introduce that so drove the Americans wild? The *New York Post* ran one of the best summaries of the performances at the Academy, with a long article titled "An Evening with the Jugglers." It declared the Japanese "wonderful," and said that the show had lasted two and a half hours, with a succession of acrobatic and gymnastic feats "which defied the laws of gravity and made every spectator catch his breath." When the curtain rose, twenty Japanese men, women, and children "simultaneously knocked their heads against the floor," in bows of respect. A short oration, in Japanese, was then delivered by the master of ceremonies, "but not generally understood."

First three children came out and engaged in contortions and acrobatics, with panache and humor. Then the head of the troupe, Hamaikari Sadakichi, lying on his back, juggled his son, Umekichi (otherwise known as "All Right") with his feet in a Japanese version of the Risley

Act. In this case, however, a series of up to twelve wooden tubs were gradually inserted between Sadakichi and All Right, stacking up gradually, and eventually revolving while All Right kept his footing on the precarious stack, shouting "All Right" and grinning with delight. Then the tubs were pulled away and All Right did a pin-point landing on his father's upturned feet.

The tub balancing was followed by top-spinning, performed by Matsui Kikujirō and his daughter. They threw tops into the air, jerked them down, made them travel up inclines, into miniature pagodas, spin around and come out, then spun them on a man's shoulder and back and arms, threw them twenty feet into the air and caught them on a samurai sword blade where they spun back and forth. If a top fell off, Kikujirō "abased himself before the people, and rose from his knees to do still more wonderful things."

Following the top-spinning was the famous butterfly trick, usually performed by Sumidagawa Namigorō, but in this case by his son, Matsugorō, who made paper butterflies and launched them into the air with his fan. "A bouquet of flowers held in the hand of one of the performers attracts the butterfly; presently other butterflies appear, and soon a swarm hovers around the nosegay. This trick is simple, but very graceful and beautiful."

Then two women appeared, a juggler and a musician, accompanied by a drummer, and they performed some magic tricks, including pulling a huge amount of silk ribbon from a lacquer box; when lit, "it exploded like a piece of fireworks and changed into a huge Japanese umbrella, gorgeously colored."

Later in the evening, the acts included Little All Right performing at the end of a twenty-foot-long bamboo pole, supported vertically on the shoulder of his father. He posed and shouted his "All right, you bet!" while the other Japanese performers below chimed in with *kakegoe*, or yells of encouragement. The highlight of the evening was the death-defying "ladder trick" in which one adult performer, lying on the ground, with his feet balanced a huge ladder to which a smaller ladder was attached at a right angle. All Right scrambled up to the top, posed and performed, and then sprang up a rope to the roof of the building. A tightrope and a pulley then allowed him to zoom down to the floor at high speed, where he was caught by two adult performers and dramatically announced "All Right!" again. As the *New York Post* reporter commented, "The perfect grace of these performers is noteworthy. All they do is to destroy our faith in the laws of nature by the calm performance of feats apparently impossible."[25]

Even after watching a show, exactly how the Japanese were able to accomplish their feats remained a mystery to many. "Everybody who goes to see Prof. Risley's *Japanese* is puzzled to know how those dusky jugglers do their 'tricks,'" wrote the *New York Evening Express*, which then proceeded to quote a letter from a humorous but anonymous correspondent who claimed to have uncovered the "secret." Since the Japanese were always nonchalantly fanning themselves during the most difficult and dangerous acts, this man surmised, the secret obviously lay in the fans themselves, and that if he could have "a fan and perhaps a pair of *Japan-knees*, I could perform all the tricks they do."[26]

In the mid-nineteenth century, photographs were not yet widely used in the media, and cameras were not yet capable of capturing movement well, so there are only a few visual images of what the Imperials' performance might have looked like. One of the best was a full-page lithograph illustration that appeared along with a long article in *Harper's Weekly*. One of the most popular illustrated magazines in the United States at the time, *Harper's* helped seal the Imperials' national fame, for it detailed each of the individual acts in a type of creative montage and showed the paraphernalia used as well as the more cultural aspects of kimono-clad women and exotic musicians. In an accompanying article, the reviewer had nothing but glowing praise for the troupe's performances, adding that they "reveal to us a phase of the interior life of Japan which can not be otherwise gained in this country, and which no one should miss seeing."[27]

With their shows in New York, the Japanese were showered with praise both direct and indirect. The famous nineteenth-century preacher

"Maguire and Risley's Japanese Troupe in their marvelous feats at the Academy of Music, New York." *HARPER'S WEEKLY*, JUNE 15, 1867.

MAGUIRE & RISLEY'S JAPANESE TROUPE IN THEIR MARVELOUS FEATS AT THE ACADEMY OF MUSIC, NEW YORK.—[See First Page.]

Carte de visite showing the Imperial Japanese Troupe performing at the Academy of Music, New York. F MS THR 828, HARVARD THEATRE COLLECTION, HOUGHTON LIBRARY, HARVARD UNIVERSITY.

Rev. Henry Ward Beecher, a man not normally thought of as a circus or drama fan, saw them at the academy and incorporated laudatory references to their remarkable athleticism in his sermons that week. In the ultimate tribute, some local entertainers staged burlesque acts, parodying the Japanese, just as they had in other American cities (later, one such show would be titled "Hernandez Jap-on Knees"). On May 17, author and humorist Mark Twain was in town, and he had a complaint. He had a considerable following of his own as a lecturer, but the Japanese were stealing his thunder.

> [The] Japanese jugglers have taken New York by storm.
> . . . It has to be a colossal sensation that is able to set
> every body talking in New York, but the Japs did it.
> And I got precious tired of it for the first few days. No
> matter where I went, they were the first subject men-
> tioned; if I stopped a moment in a hotel, I heard people
> talking about them; if I lunched in a Dutch restaurant,
> there was one constantly recurring phrase which I
> understood, and only one, "*das Japs;*" in French restau-
> rants, it was "*les Jap;*" in Irish restaurants, it was "thim
> Japans;" after church the sermon was discussed five min-
> utes, and then the Japs for half an hour. . . . The Japs are
> a prodigious success.[28]

Success brought excitement, and opened up new worlds for the Japanese. There were jaunts outside Manhattan in flag-flying carriages to perform in Brooklyn and Newark, New Jersey, and even a train trip up north to Boston, where the Imperials had another short but spectacularly successful run. For performers who were of low social status back home, fame opened new doors. In early June, the second official Japanese government mission to the United States happened to be in New York at the same time as the Imperials were performing, and three samurai came to see their show. They delighted in talking with their fellow country-men so much that the next day they invited Hirohachi and others to their hotel and treated them to a meal. Remarkably, Hirohachi was even

THE CHILDREN HAVE BEEN TO SEE THE JAPANESE.

"The Children have been to see the Japanese." *HARPER'S WEEKLY*, JUNE 15, 1867.

able to ask the samurai to take some letters back to Japan for him. It was a type of familiarity that would have been unthinkable back in Japan, and an interaction made more poignant today because we now know that one of the young samurai was none other than Fukuzawa Yukichi, who later became a famous intellectual and philosopher. Along on the mission as a translator, he is known today as one of the founders of modern Japan (and at the time of this writing his countenance still graces most ten thousand yen notes). But Fukuzawa wasn't the only exalted visitor the Imperials met. In Boston, Hirohachi notes in his journal, they again ran into the "Washington King" (President Andrew Johnson). He was in town for a rare presidential visit, having been invited by the local Masons, and as Hirohachi described it in his journal, he spotted them when passing before about "ten thousand people," and "put his fingers to his mouth," apparently blowing them a kiss. They were sad to part with him.[29]

The Imperials had become media celebrities in the United States. They were idolized by Americans and, as Mark Twain noted, referred to in conversation regularly. Children across the land delighted in imitating the washtub and other tricks of the Japanese. Much as "Risley" had become a household word twenty years earlier, so, too, did little "All Right." There were poems written about him. The blind composer, Edward Mack, wrote the "All Right Polka," which was "respectfully dedicated to Hamai Kari Sadakitchi" and copyrighted. A Massachusetts firearms manufacture later created the "smallest and most perfect revolver in the world" and of course called it the "Little All Right." There were even matchboxes and cigar boxes with his image and name on the cover. In 1867, in faraway Fort Riley, Kansas, on the Western frontier, nearly ten years before he met his inglorious and bloody end at the Battle of Little Big Horn, General Custer went riding with his wife, Elizabeth, and she awkwardly fell off her horse, exclaiming "All Right!" As Elizabeth later described in her book, *Tenting on the Plains*, the cavalry soldiers accompanying them delighted in mercilessly ribbing her: "They brought little All Right, the then famous Japanese acrobat, into every conversation. . . . "[30]

Overexposure and an Identity Crisis

Fame also brought unwelcome attention and confusion. Americans wanted to know more about the off-stage lives of the Japanese, and newspapers responded. And when they did, as usual in mid-nineteenth-century America, the issue of race and alien-ness was never far away. The Japanese were regularly referred to as saffron-colored, copper-colored, swarthy, oily, ugly, and small, and the children as "little monkeys." Even when they were referred to positively, it was often with a condescending type of cultural humor. Reporters reflected their readers' fears of and disdain for many aspects of Asian culture, including food, dress, fashion, and music. Lodged at the corner of Fourth Avenue and 14th Street in New York, the Imperials were regularly subjected to crowds of gawkers. When a *New York Times* reporter visited them on May 11, he described in detail for readers the way they lived, looked, and the foods they ate. He concluded his long article by saying:

> On the whole, it can't be nice to be a Jap. Setting aside
> the hari-kari business, and the color and the hair and the
> grease and the prevailing notions in regard to clothing,
> there are insuperable objections connected with their
> ideas of privacy—brother, sister, another man and wife,
> a third man and two boys, all sleeping in a little box
> of a room—their tastes in food, their habits of squat-
> ting, their infernal music, and all that sort of thing . . .
> which would forever interfere with the naturalization of
> a genuine Yankee into a regular-built Jap. These speci-
> mens are civil, quiet, orderly, kind and peaceable—they
> certainly are wonderful in their line of art, but beyond
> that nothing.[31]

Early Japanese performers abroad faced huge cultural barriers in the form of language, food, and lifestyle. And sometimes the American media seemed to anticipate problems occurring, almost hoping to witness the exotic "hari-kari" they had heard so much about. After a white woman fell in love with a young member of the Tetsuwari faction in Chicago, a scandal ensued. One American writer, tongue-in-cheek, envisioned the shogun of Japan commanding all Japanese in America to commit suicide, so that of the Imperials, "Zumidangawa Matsimgoro [*sic*] springs from the slackrope to impale himself upon his umbrella [and] little All Right dexterously rips himself open on the summit of a revolv-ing tub." And some of these imaginings later did become reality. After the leader of another Japanese troupe in America (Hayatake Torakichi, leader of the renowned Osaka-based Ha-Yah-Ta-Kee Troupe) died of natural causes in March 1868, two performers reportedly threatened to hang themselves. And a member of yet another troupe, upon learning that he could not go back to Japan in time to meet the conditions of his Japan-issued travel permit, was said to have committed *seppuku*.[32]

The Imperials generally held up quite well, but they were not immune to stress. Denkichi, the tightrope-walking member of the Hamaikari family who had taken a terrible fall in San Francisco, in private life had some trouble adapting. Like Hirohachi, he had taken to frequenting prostitutes. In early June, along with Kikujirō (the thirty-year-old Matsui family top-spinner), he was robbed of his money by New York prostitutes known as "Greene Street" ladies. He created a bit of a commotion by reporting them to the police. On June 8, Denkichi was himself hauled into court on an assault-and-battery charge, after a dispute arose between him and a neighbor who complained of his scanty dress, which a *New York Times* reporter described as "the primitive costume of Adam after the Fall."[33] Then, on June 18, after the Imperials had arrived in Boston and were performing at the Boston Theater on the night of a huge rainstorm, a burglar entered the Imperials' quarters with a duplicate key. When the Imperials returned to their quarters, Hirohachi and Hamaikari discovered they had been robbed of $180 in gold, which they had brought with them from Japan. The troupe members were shocked and reported the theft to the authorities, but the money was never recovered.[34]

Even the always cool and collected star, Hamaikari Umekichi, or All Right, had difficulty. During their time off in New York, the Japanese were able to indulge in sightseeing, and wander around the city, admiring the buildings and scenery as well as gadgetry like sewing machines and the animals in the zoo in Central Park. Yet wherever they went crowds tended to form. And as the darling of the troupe, Umekichi was followed everywhere. People wanted to fete him, wine him, dine him, and show him off to friends. Others teased and stared. He was, as a result, "troubled very much by the attentions he receives from all parties with whom he meets, and the handshaking to which he is subjected from everybody on appearing in the street evidently bewilders and annoys the boy."[35]

The stresses culminated on June 12, at the Academy of Music, when a much-feared accident happened. At the climax of All Right's performance—just when he was to have swooped dramatically down to the floor from high up on the theatre's proscenium, hanging from a pulley on a rope—the rope broke. All Right plunged into the audience from an altitude of what some papers described as forty feet, and others fifty. As the *New York World* described it:

> Those in the parquette were really paralyzed with terror, while the ladies in the elde and front boxes gave expression to their feelings by screams and moans, and many of them were noticed to faint. The Japanese rushed from the stage to help and convey away their little countryman, and the band stopped playing. All Right, insensible and bleeding, was taken away, and the stage curtain dropped on a scene unexpected and regretted. . . .[36]

The audience left the academy believing that the much-loved Little All Right was dead. As news of his accident spread like wildfire across America through telegraph and newspaper, his name was further burned into the public consciousness. Some papers declared him dead. When it seemed that he had survived, others ran playfully affectionate headlines declaring "Little All Right, All Right still," while writers lamented his injuries and prayed for his speedy recovery. Yet rumors of All Right's death persisted, amplified by reports that he had really died in Chicago, where the Tetsuwari troupe was performing. The rumors became so entrenched that Thomas Maguire, ever the showman, later "authorized a wage of $10,000 to $500 to any of the eager parties who, eager to annoy him, are willing to bet that the little Jap is dead—the winner to hand the sum to an Orphan Asylum of this city."[37] Of course, the more All Right was reported to be alive and once more performing, the more the arc of his life's story also began to resemble that of Lazarus and a near miracle.

By July 4, All Right was back to performing in New York, to great acclaim, in a new death-defying act at the Academy of Music. But things were about to become even more confusing. Risley's Imperials and All Right had become so popular that the inevitable was happen-

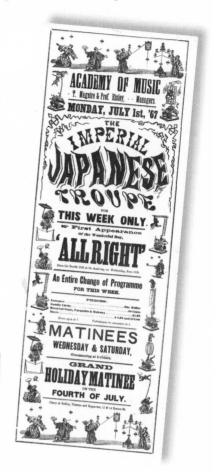

Broadside for the Imperial Japanese Troupe's July 1, 1867, performance at the Academy of Music, New York. BPF TCS 65, HARVARD THEATRE COLLECTION, HOUGHTON LIBRARY, HARVARD UNIVERSITY.

ing. A great deal of money was also now being made off them, and true imitators—the constant curse of Risley—were also beginning to spring up. Maguire's left wing, the Tetsuwari troupe touring out West, had not only begun calling themselves "Maguire's Imperial Troupe," but also "The Imperial Troupe." Moreover, in advertisements for the Tetsuwari shows, Rinkichi—the young boy lead performer originally nicknamed "Tommy" in San Francisco—was increasingly being referred to as "All Right." In far-away Milwaukee, when the left wing appeared, the local paper even ran a preposterous article about the Japanese and Maguire. It claimed that Maguire had gone to Japan to get the Japanese, that he was fluent in Japanese, and that to secure the Japanese services he had "disguised himself as a Japanese and penetrated the country farther than any white man before him."[38] Whether Risley knew that his role in history was being usurped by his biggest investor is unclear, but if he did, it surely would have galled him.

It became increasingly necessary to distinguish between the two groups, especially when their paths started to cross, either in real time or sequentially. In March, Maguire's left wing had appeared in Boston, so when his right wing—Risley's Imperials—had a short run there in the second half of June, the *Boston Journal* had to announce that they were "*not* the company which appeared at the Tremont Temple last spring." Plus, the left wing was also headed toward New York, where other American promoters were bringing yet other groups of Japanese acrobats, such as the Mikado and Red Dragon troupes. By mid-July these newer groups were in New York, in effect piggy-backing on the popularity of the Imperials. Only four days after the Imperials vacated New York's prestigious Academy of Music, the Imperials would be replaced by the Mikado troupe. Soon after that, New Yorkers could choose between going to see either the Mikado *or* the Red Dragon troupe.

The confusion that Maguire had helped sow with his two "wings" of similarly named Japanese soon came back to bite him. On August 11, in New York City, Maguire heatedly accused Fukumatsu, the head of the Tetsuwari faction, of stealing $3,500 from him and had him arrested. As papers far and wide reported it, Maguire believed he had paid to have the troupe perform until February 1868, but the Japanese wanted to go home, and Fukumatsu believed the contract to be valid only up to the end of August 1867. Through interpreters, the judge tried mightily to interrogate the Japanese, the newspaper reporters delighting in their unpronounceable names. Ultimately, Fukumatsu was released, and it then became clear that Maguire's real dispute was with the Smiths (the American couple who had originally brought the Tetsuwari faction from Japan and accompanied it through the West as part of Maguire's left wing). The Smiths were claiming custody of the young star the paper referred to as both Little All Right and Fukumatsu's nephew, but Maguire believed the boy to be directly contracted to him.[39] In late August, instead of Fukumatsu, Maguire managed to get the Smiths temporarily

ALL RIGHT POLKA

BY

E. MACK.

Philadelphia, **LEE & WALKER** 722 Chestnut St.

W.H.BONER & C.º 1102 Chestnut St.   Troy, N. York, CHAS. W. HARRIS.

The All Right Polka, by E. Mack. COURTESY, LAURENCE SENELICK COLLECTION.

jailed. A real scene in the courtroom ensued, with epithets freely bandied about, and a physical struggle taking place over Little All Right. As the newspapers reported it, Little All Right was so sympathetic to the Smiths, and not Maguire, that he accompanied the former to jail and later had to be physically dragged out by Maguire and his agents.[40]

If nothing else, the lawsuits seemed to confirm that the oft-rumored-dead All Right was truly alive, but in reality they only exposed a tangled mess and the more sordid side of nineteenth-century entertainment, especially as it involved exotic foreigners and child actors. As the *New York Evening Post* astutely noted on August 26, "The facts thus far made public would go to prove that the Japanese performers receive but a small portion of the money which their performances draw from the people."[41] Rumors continued to spread that perhaps All Right had really died in his fall, and that Maguire had merely foisted a look-alike substitute upon the unsuspecting public.

It was no wonder that the rumors would not die. It was hard for European Americans to tell the difference between Japanese. And the real story was even more confusing than the reported one. The Little All Right who the papers had described as having accompanied the Smiths to jail was not even the real Little All Right, but Rinkichi, of the Tetsuwari faction, who had been increasingly referred to as All Right in ads for Tetsuwari performances. The real Little All Right—Hamaikari Umekichi—was already gone, having left America over a month earlier with Risley and the Imperials on July 10, on the steamer *Tripoli*, for Liverpool, England, and eventually Paris.

By September, news of what was happening back home reached Risley, and he knew it was time for him to step in and set the record straight. From Paris, he wrote directly to the editor of the entertainment-oriented *New York Clipper*. His entire letter was published. In it, he restated the fact that the real Imperial Japanese troupe had been selected, organized, and brought from Japan by himself, Banks, and Schiedt; that he, Risley, had found and named Little All Right in Japan; and:

> The report circulated in America that he died in Chicago was untrue, and the further report, by denigrating

CARTES DE VISITE, 26–27

26. "Little All Right," in a very American pose, in a New York studio. COURTESY, LAURENCE SENELICK COLLECTION.

27. Along with many others, Rinkichi of the Tetsuwari group—the "left-wing" of Maguire's Imperial Japanese Troupe—also became known as "Little All Right." Photographed in Chicago in 1867. TCS 20, HARVARD THEATRE COLLECTION, HOUGHTON LIBRARY, HARVARD UNIVERSITY.

27.

26.

and unscrupulous parties, that the boy "Tommy," as he was named and only known by in Japan, and who was brought from Japan by Mr. Thomas Smith and wife (now in New York and in litigation with Mr. Maguire) is the little "All Right," is untrue. . . . By kindly inserting this note you will do an act of kindness to one whose life has been devoted to endeavoring to please the public, as well as an act of justice to artists who fame has not yet by any means [reached] its zenith, and disabuse the minds of all persons who so truly . . . sympathized with my heroic and unrivalled *protégé,* 'All Right,' when in the United States.[42]

ACT 7
At the Exposition

"Everyone was going to the famous Paris Exposition—
I, too, was going to the Paris Exposition. . . . If I met
a dozen individuals . . . who were not going to Europe
shortly, I have no distinct remembrance of it now." [1]
                                        —*Mark Twain, 1867*

In the summer of 1867, the Exposition Universelle was the place to be. Held on the site of the vast, former military parade ground of the Champs de Mars in Paris, it was a watershed event in the latter half of the nineteenth century. Between April and October, it attracted over ten million curious people from around the world—ranging from kings and queens to common citizens—who flocked to see the latest technology, manufactured goods, and art of over forty-two countries. A showcase for international progress, it also ushered in a new, temporary sense of global unity and symbolized Japan's shy debut on the world stage. This was the first time that Japan was officially invited, with space allotted for a pavilion. Japanese arts and crafts on display helped to stimulate the Japonisme craze among Europeans and Americans and inspire the Impressionists. Professor Risley's Imperials and other groups of Japanese jugglers and acrobats—while not an official part of the Exposition—had traveled halfway around the world to perform for its crowds. They helped usher in a temporary craze for Japanese acrobats and jugglers throughout Europe.

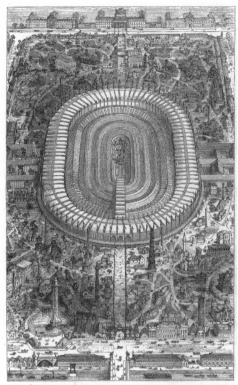

A bird's-eye view of the Paris Exposition. RECOLLECTIONS OF THE PARIS EXPOSITION OF 1867, BY EUGENE RIMMEL (PHILADELPHIA: LIPPINCOTT, 1868).

Bird's-Eye View of the Paris Exhibition.

That year, France was able to bask in the glory of its recent accomplishments, and nowhere more so than in the capital, Paris, and at the Exposition. International exhibitions had been held before, but nothing as grand and as global as this one. It was initiated by Emperor Napoleon III, nephew of the famous Napoleon I, and designed in part to broadcast France's re-ascendance on the world stage. After serving as an elected president for four years, in 1852 Napoleon III—or "Louis Napoleon," as he is often called—had become emperor and dictator through a coup d'état. Determined to resurrect the glories of his uncle's era, Louis Napoleon had pursued a dramatic policy of modernization and expansionism. Under his leadership, Paris had been modernized for the new age with broad boulevards, parks, and a new sewage system. France was somewhat of a late-comer to the Industrial Revolution, but he had stressed the importance of developing science and industry, as well as the arts, building up a massive army, promoting international trade, and cementing France's position as a global empire rivaling Britain, with colonies throughout the world. But Louis Napoleon's empire combined over-expansion and a theatricality bordering on farce. During the American Civil War, he had hoped for a Confederate victory and made an abortive attempt to expand into Mexico. On July 10, 1867, only two weeks before Risley's arrival, while attending to award ceremonies at the Paris Exposition, he was horrified to learn that Maximilian—the proxy emperor he had helped install in Mexico—had been executed by a Republican firing squad. From then on it was all downhill. Only three years later, in 1870, Napoleon III would reluctantly lead France into a disastrous war with Prussia. His own countrymen would turn on him, his empire would collapse internally, and he would be forced to take refuge in France's arch rival, Britain.

Still, in the summer of 1867 things seemed to be going marvelously, especially at the Exposition. Even the usually cynical Mark Twain remarked of Louis Napoleon, after seeing him pass by, that there was "no element of true greatness which he does not possess."[2] Paris was packed with visitors, and Twain spent only a couple of hours at the Exposition itself before giving up. He was overwhelmed by the fair's size and the number of things to see, for it consisted of a giant, elliptical exhibition hall (with a circumference of nearly a mile) in the middle of the nearly one-hundred-acre Champs de Mars, which had been reworked with artificial hills, lakes, and chalets. At the Exposition, one could see each nation's manufactured goods, newfangled technologies, elaborate artwork, exotic grottos, rare animals, aquariums, factories, trains, deadly new weapons, examples of architecture, and even model villages populated with real people. Twain found himself particularly amazed by the diversity of the people. France, Britain, the nations of Europe, and the United States were of course represented. But there were also exhibitions by Africa, the Middle East, and Asia, or what were sometimes then called the "Mohametan and Pagan" nations. The Egyptians were there with camels. The Turks were there. The Siamese were there. And so, too, were the Chinese and the Japanese. The Chinese,

Japanese geisha on view at the Japanese teahouse of the Paris Exposition. *ILLUSTRATED LONDON NEWS*, PARIS INTERNATIONAL EXPOSITION SUPPLEMENT, NOVEMBER 16, 1867.

in addition to an official exhibit, had a less official theatre in the Exposition grounds where one could watch a conjuror named Ling Loup swallow "a long sword, rammed down by a 30-lb shot, and followed by any number of eggs, with their shells, [who] really seems to thrive on this indigestible diet."[3]

The shogun of Japan, invited but unable to attend, instead sent his fourteen-year-old younger brother, Tokugawa Akitake, with a retinue of over twenty people. Japanese arts and manufactured goods—including ceramics and lacquerware and life-size mannequins wearing samurai armor—were on display. In what proved enormously popular among the French, there was even an entire Japanese teahouse built on the Exposition site, where visitors could watch three playful young Japanese geisha, dressed in kimono, serve tea and act just as they might in Japan.

In addition to the shogun's younger brother and his entourage, there were numerous other Japanese present at the Exposition. Japan still had a feudal system, with the Shogunate ruling over domains, and at the Exposition, in addition to the Shogunate, both the Saga and Satsuma domains had exhibits. In fact, in a development that confused the French enormously, the southern Satsuma domain presented itself independently of the Shogunate, in association with the Ryukyuan Kingdom, thus leading some to think that it was equal in status to the Shogunate. At the end of 1866 the Shogunate had also begun granting passports to citizens (the first one having been issued to a member of Risley's Imperial Troupe). Japanese who could afford the trip and obtain permission could legally visit the Exposition without fear of being executed on return; in the summer of 1867, in addition to government officials, there were therefore also Japanese students, businessmen, and entertainers present. The Imperial Japanese Troupe had already faced formidable competition in the major cities of the United States, but in Paris they would face even more.

Competition in Paris

The Imperials left New York by steamship on July 10, sailing across the Atlantic and docking first in Queenstown, Ireland, then Liverpool, England. After resting briefly, they crossed the English Channel to L'Havre, France, and took a train to Paris, arriving on July 26. It had taken slightly more than two weeks. But one of Risley's partners from Yokohama, W. F. Schiedt, had journeyed to Europe as early as May, and advance agents for the troupe had already blanketed Paris with beautiful, colored handbills advertising the troupe's arrival and building anticipation.[4] Maguire, upon arrival, also made advance rounds of local editors, explaining the superiority of the Imperials and countering rumors that the star, All Right, could no longer perform because of his accident in New York.[5]

The advance advertising backfired because it led people to think that the Imperials would open at the Cirque Napoleon on July 15, then on July 24, and eventually at the end of the month. This led the Paris correspondent of San Francisco's *Daily Dramatic Chronicle* (and the *New*

York Clipper) to write home on July 29, grumbling of the troupe, "I have not seen anything of them, although they should be here now, if they expect to open tomorrow." In this and another piece filed a week later, he fed fans back home gloomy news; that there were already "Japanese performers of every kind in the gardens of the Exhibition," and that "another genuine Imperial Japanese troupe of the Tycoon, 'the only troupe ever permitted to leave Japan,'" had already opened a week earlier in Paris at the Theatre du Prince Imperial (which he declared larger and superior to the Cirque Napoleon). Moreover, he wrote, the rival troupe of twelve performers, who had already toured London, had been visited by the brother of the Tycoon and the Japanese Embassy in Paris and must therefore be the genuine one. But even this competing troupe had had difficulty financially, and on the arrival of Risley and Maguire's Imperials, it had been forced to join with an American circus in Paris at the Prince Imperial and reduce admission fees by half. "Japanese performers in Europe have been hitherto a complete failure," the correspondent declared, predicting a similar fate for Risley and Maguire's troupe.[6] Yet he was writing for a San Francisco paper that had been sued for slander the previous year by Maguire. He was certainly influenced, if not rewritten, by his editors, and they were not inclined to be nice. The reality in Paris was quite different.

The competing troupe in Paris went by various and confusing names. Since it had had no competition in Britain, it had often been referred to there simply as the "Japanese Troupe" or the "Japanese Jugglers." Later, it was often referred to as "St. Martin's Japanese" (after the name of the hall in which it had debuted in London). In Paris, perhaps as a pre-emptive strike against Risley's Imperials, it began to call itself the "Troupe Japonaise du Taicoun," or the "Tycoon's Japanese Troupe." Today, in Japan, it is usually referred as the "Gensui Troupe," after Matsui Gensui, the troupe's headman.

The Gensui Troupe was actually composed of twelve members from three performing families—Matsui, Yanagawa, and Yamamoto. The Matsuis were famous for their top-spinning, the Yanagawas for the butterfly trick, and the Yamamotos for acrobatics and slack- or tight-rope walking. The Gensui Troupe's shows were exceedingly similar to that of the Imperials, and Risley was well acquainted with many of the members. Yanagawa Asakichi and others had performed in the foreign community at Yokohama in 1864 and 1865, at the evening home performances of Risley's good friend, J. R. Black (editor of the *Japan Herald*), and probably even at Risley's own events. Put together by two men named Prior and Grant, with the help of Sir Harry Parkes, the British minister in Japan at the time, the Gensui Troupe had left Yokohama at almost the same time as the Imperials. Instead of sailing east to Paris via North America, however, they had gone west, on the *Nepaul*. After an arduous journey halfway around the globe—one that required crossing the Indian Ocean, navigating the Red Sea, and going over the Isthmus of the Suez by land—they had finally arrived in London and made their debut at St. Martin's Hall on February 11. While Risley's Imperials had been creating a sensation in the United States, the Gensui Troupe had thus been doing the same in Britain. Japanese were still an extreme novelty in Britain, and people had flocked to see the exotic troupe perform. All the major newspapers reviewed them and generally showered them with praise.

Yet when the Gensui Troupe debuted in Paris in July, the French critics were not as kind as their British counterparts. The troupe appeared at the cavernous Prince Imperial Theatre on February 21 and shared billing with the American Circus, which was also in town (it had not only famous American equestrians and clowns, but "real Indians"). The next day, the famous Parisian daily *Le Figaro* reviewed the performance by the Japanese and noted that they had benefited from curiosity generated by the advertising blitz conducted by their soon-to-arrive competitor, the Imperials. The reviewer was impressed by the performances and the costumes, but noted that some of the conjuring acts would have benefited from a smaller space. He was especially critical of the long-winded speeches, presumably given in Japanese. While these may have been especially long that day because the shogun's young brother was in attendance, they caused the reviewer to write in an almost scolding fashion, "We are not in a parliament." He was also maddeningly irritated by the long preparation time for the acts, and suggested that the Japanese should have preceded the more exciting American Circus, instead of fol-

The Cirque Napoleon, in Paris. Renamed the Cirque d'Hiver, the exterior of this venerable structure looks otherwise exactly as it did in 1867, and it is still used today for circuses. © 2012 FIAMMETTA HSU.

lowing them. The French, he noted, were not known for being polite to foreigners, and there had been whistles of derision mingled amid the applause. Even more damning, he implied that the troupe might not really be the Tycoon's officially sanctioned entertainers, and that they might in fact be "counterfeit."[7]

On July 30, *Le Figaro* featured advertisements for both the Gensui Troupe and the Imperials on the same page. The first ad, in the middle of the page, had text and an illustration for the American Circus, showing a "real Indian" hanging upside down from his galloping pony and firing a rifle; below that the ad proclaimed the concurrent appearance of the "true and wonderful troupe of the Tycoon," with individual member names listed. The second advertisement, further down the page, was a bold announcement for the Risley-Maguire production, confusingly called the "Imperial Japanese Troupe of the Tycoon." The Imperials, it stated, were to "definitely" appear that same day—July 30—at the Cirque Napoleon and provide performances of "extraordinary skill, balance, strength, and suppleness."[8]

Performing in Paris

Multiple records survive of the actual debut of the Imperials in Paris. In his diary, Hirohachi, the overseer of the Imperials, describes arriving in Paris on July 26, being amazed by the "seven or eight" story buildings, and doing some sightseeing (including visiting what was presumably a zoo). But on the day after their arrival, one of the first things the Imperials did was to go check out their competitor, the Gensui Troupe, led by the forty-three-year-old Matsui Gensui. It is easy to imagine their mixture of great pleasure and jealousy, for in the small world of performing arts they had more than a professional connection: Matsui Gensui was actually the older brother of Matsui Kikujirō, the Imperials' top-spinner. In his diary, Hirohachi notes that the Gensui Troupe had already been performing in Paris for a week. Reading between the lines of his diary entry, his disappointment at arriving late is palpable. But he also notes that on July 27, the audience for the Gensui Troupe was sparse, implying that the Imperials could do much better.

On July 29, the Imperials busied themselves spreading playbills around town and setting up their stage up at the Cirque Napoleon. Located on the Boulevard des Filles-du-Calvaire, outside of the main Exposition grounds, the building was a twenty-sided polygon with no central pillars and steeply angled seats, allowing a good view of performances. It could hold four thousand spectators, but, as Hirohachi noted in his diary, at the time it was mainly used for equestrian acts. The Imperials also gave a preview show to some Paris officials that day. Hirohachi's confidence is revealed in a colloquial phrase he regularly employed in his diary to express great success. The officials, he wrote, were amazed beyond belief, using the expression *kimo wo tsubusu*, which literally means that their "innards were crushed" or, in more modern English parlance, that their "minds were blown."[9]

Prince Akitake and retainers in Paris. *ILLUSTRATION*, APRIL, 27 1867.

The Imperials opened on July 30. It was good weather, and luck was with them. Hirohachi notes in his diary that there was a huge crowd and that the doors had to be shut and people turned away. Moreover, Banks (presumably operating on Risley's suggestion) had specifically invited the shogun's representative and younger brother, Akitake, who came specially to see the performance with his retinue. Hirohachi's diary entry is short and pithy as usual, but in the formal honorific Japanese he uses, the thrill the visit gave the Imperials—who were ordinary commoners, after all—is quite obvious. They were, he wrote, "infinitely happy." And their happiness was presumably amplified by the fact that Akitake and his men left 2,500 francs in tips and appeared willing, after an entreaty, to see the members again on a following day.[10]

It is not clear how the fourteen-year-old Akitake (or his retinue) felt about having two Japanese troupes of acrobats in Paris with similar names, both claiming to be official performers for his brother, the shogun, whom Westerners then called the "Tycoon." For the young boy, it probably was simply all good fun. He had been sent to represent Japan, but he was also charged with furthering Japan's relations with European nations, and, after the Exposition concluded, he was supposed to spend a year or two studying European ways before returning home. He still represented a feudal state, and he arrived in France with all the pomp and circumstance of royalty, surrounded by samurai wearing robes and top-knots and two swords. He was treated like a true crown prince (which he wasn't), but history would not be kind to him. While in Europe he would run out of money, the Shogunate back home would collapse, his exalted position would evaporate, and the feudal world into which he had been born would vanish in a tidal wave of modernization.

As Japanese historian Miyanaga Takashi has noted, the officials around Japan's then shogun—Tokugawa Yoshinobu (the fifteenth and last in the Tokugawa line)—probably had a poor understanding of what the invitation from Emperor Napoleon meant and what the Exposition really represented. Indeed, they may have thought it was simply a large Japanese-style *misemono*, or carnival event.[11] Had they known, they might have dispatched a more exalted emissary, for Akitake was sixteen years younger than Yoshinobu, only his half-brother, and only one of Yoshinobu's estimated thirty-plus siblings.

At the time, the Tokugawa Shogunate had lots of other things to worry about. They were a hereditary family of feudal dictators. They had kept the emperor powerless in seclusion and ruled over dozens of semi-autonomous domains in Japan for nearly 250 years. Yet in the wake of Perry's visit, Japan had been rocked by political instability. The conservative *sonnō jōi* factions hoped to drive all foreigners out of Japan and restore the emperor to power. The southern domain of Satsuma— which had its own pavilion at the Exposition and created great confusion among the French—was a particularly thorny problem for the Shogunate; it was one of the most rebellious domains in Japan at the time and would eventually play a major role in the overthrow of the Shogunate and the entire feudal system.

Perhaps because of his tender age, young Akitake's diary entries are even pithier than Hirohachi's. In them, he makes no direct mention of visiting the Imperials in Paris. In the latter half of July, he was spending a great deal of time visiting the Exposition, sightseeing, meeting with notables, and taking horse-riding lessons. On the evening of July 21, he notes merely that it was cloudy, everything was all right, and that he had gone to see the top-spinning of Matsui Gensui of the Gensui Troupe. There is another brief notation on August 5, indicating that it was good weather and that he had visited the Cirque Napoleon, where the Imperials were performing.[12]

Among the notables accompanying Akitake was a young samurai named Shibusawa Eiichi. Shibusawa is known today as a prominent financier and major contributor to the modernizing of Japan, yet less than a decade before his trip with Akitake he had been a passionate member of the *sonnō jōi* faction, even plotting to attack and burn the foreign settlement at Yokohama and overthrow the Shogunate. After a political conversion, in 1867 he had decided to serve the Shogunate by accompanying the teenage Akitake to Europe. He kept a diary slightly more detailed than that of his young charge, and in it he mentions that on August 30 he went to see the Imperials' Hamaikari Sadakichi after receiving an invitation from Banks. He also includes a translation of an August 1 review from *Le Figaro* of the Imperials' July 30 debut at the Cirque Napoleon.[13]

The *Figaro* review begins with the statement, "The new Japanese troupe, which debuted yesterday at the Cirque Napoleon, is definitely the official troupe of the Tycoon." This had been proven, the reviewer noted, by the fact that the young brother of Japan's "Tycoon" had personally visited the performers and showered them with an enormous tip of 2,500 francs. Moreover, the Imperials had far more agility, dexterity, and suppleness than the rival Gensui Troupe, and their costumes were even more sophisticated than those of European acrobats. "Their program resembles that of the Japanese acrobats appearing with the American Circus, but it is more varied, and it leaves out the magic tricks. . . . They also have less of a parliamentary style; they all describe their acts, but they do not make boring speeches. . . ." Little All Right of course came in for the most praise for his poise and élan, but he wasn't the only one. "Everything was warmly applauded," the writer concluded, "because it was executed to perfection, and the munificence of the young brother of the tycoon became a mere token of the public's admiration."[14]

In his diary, Hirohachi normally described each day's attendance at the Imperials' shows with the Chinese characters for "big," "medium," or "small." For nearly their entire run at the Cirque Napoleon in Paris he wrote down "big." But in between practices and performances, there was time for other things. Other Japanese in Paris, such as members of the Saga domain, occasionally came to see them and exchanged information. And there was lots of sightseeing to do. The day after the shogun's younger brother visited again on August 5, Hirohachi visited the Exposition and recorded at length his amazement at not only the size of the fair and its buildings but at seeing seven real elephants, some enormous horses, and a variety of other wonderfully big and novel animals and fishes, including some skeletal displays of giant whales. Of the fair, he wrote, "It is a huge place for sightseeing, and there is no way one could see all this in one or two days."[15] Along with other members of the troupe, he would go back again and again.

For the next ten days, Hirohachi was either too busy or too excited to make any entries in his diary. But on August 14, he had a chance to see a passenger-bearing balloon, and his entry for that day describes its structure and workings in great detail. He does not appear to have ridden in one, for his entry simply reflects his astonishment and joy at seeing it and observing it closely through a telescope. Balloons were not unusual in Europe in 1867 (Risley having gone for a ride on one in England twenty years earlier). At the Exposition site, the famous photographer Felix Nadar offered rides on a balloon tethered to the ground. But other than a kite, most Japanese had never seen anything manmade fly.

By the middle of August, the Imperials had settled into a successful routine in Paris. In addition to tourists, the city that year was filled with more prostitutes than usual, and Hirohachi began visiting them with remarkable regularity. But he also visited the new and vast underground sewer system of Paris (one of the proud accomplishments of Emperor Napoleon III and still a popular sightseeing item today), and what he calls a "castle" (which may have been Versailles, or simply a grand palace or cathedral).

By mid-August, the Imperials had vanquished their main competition in Paris, the Gensui Troupe. It was an act that the Parisian press treated almost as a type of military victory. On August 24, the weekly *L'Indépendance Dramatique* noted that the Imperials were "decidedly in vogue" at the Cirque Napoleon. Of the Gensui Troupe that had been playing at the Prince Imperial, it rather cruelly said, they had been "put to flight by the authentic Japanese at the Cirque Napoleon and taken refuge in Brussels. Belgium is the home of counterfeiters!"[16] In fact, while the Imperials probably did have superior performers, their success also depended greatly on Risley's rich experience and vast network of connections, as well as his superior choreography, sense of presentation, and shrewd marketing.

On August 29, a review of the Imperials appeared in the *Le Moniteur Universel*, authored by Théophile Gautier, the famous Parisian poet and art and dance critic. Twenty-three years earlier, the influential Gautier had helped cement Risley's reputation, describing his act with his sons as a new type of ballet. This time, he had already seen the Gensui Troupe perform and been quite impressed, but he was even more enchanted with the Imperials at the Cirque Napoleon. The Imperials were "all the vogue" in Paris, he declared, describing the scene in the theatre that was densely packed with crowds each night:

> Never, in fact, has a more amazing show been offered
> to the curious people of Paris—or perhaps I should say
> cosmopolitan people of Paris, because there are now in
> our capital, thanks to the Exposition, as many foreigners
> as natives. How quickly what was once unimaginable
> becomes so simple. That the Tycoon's son [*sic*]—the
> mysterious prince of a formerly impenetrable empire—
> was applauding the gymnasts from Japan, his own sub-
> jects, [at the Cirque Napoleon] on the Boulevard des

LES JAPONAIS DU CIRQUE NAPOLEON, par Crafty

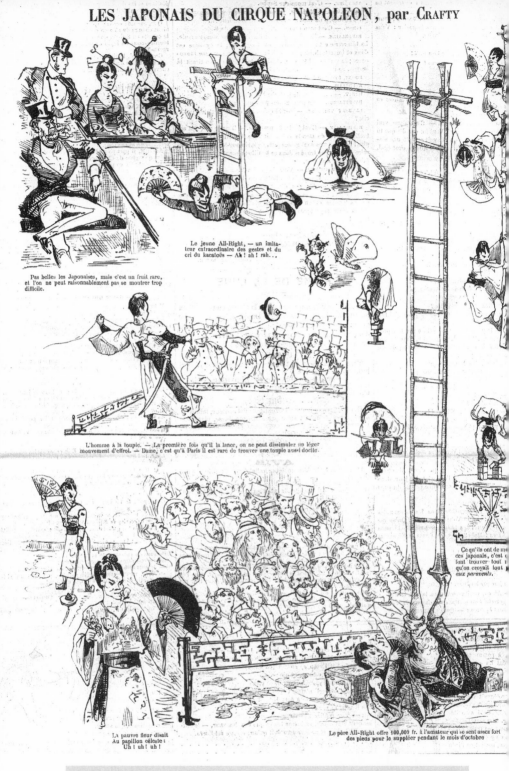

"Les Japonais du Cirque Napoleon," by Crafty. *LA LUNE,* SEPTEMBER 22, 1867.

"Les exercices de l'échelle"—
The Imperials and their
amazing ladder act at Cirque
Napoleon. *LE MONDE ILLUSTRÉ*,
OCTOBER 26, 1867.

Les exercices de l'échelle.

Filles-du-Calvaire, in front of a crowd assembled from
all corners of the world, who were speaking every different language created in the wake of the collapse of
the tower of Babel—surprised no one. The most distant
lands, the most eccentric lands, the most fabulous lands,
were represented.[17]

Gautier went on to describe the costumes, music, and individual
acts of the Imperials. He did not mention Risley, but he did indirectly
refer to his old act of years ago, describing one of the Japanese gymnasts
(presumably Hamaikari) as preparing for a ladder stunt by "plopping
down on a mattress upside down, feet in the air, in the style of the American acropedestrians." Gautier was particularly impressed, as were most
people, by Little All Right, who during the most daring and difficult
acts showed nary a bead of sweat and nothing but the utmost panache
and grace.[18]

From August through October, crowds continued to visit the Imperials, and Risley made sure the Japanese varied their routines to keep audience interest high. Parisian newspapers did not usually advertise the troupe's programs for the evening, but at the end of September, *L'Orchestre*, a daily devoted to entertainment listings, printed the following, with a reminder that shows started at eight o'clock in the evening (translated from the French):

Part I:
Presentation of the Troupe
Dance of the drum
New balancing acts by Little All Right and his father
Top-spinning
The living pyramid
Rope dancing
New Perch pole act by All Right, on his father's
shoulder

Part II:
Folding fox screens, by young All Right and father
The pyramid of tubs
The promenade of tops
Three suspended bamboos
Demonstrations of balancing and agility
The grand game of seven ladders, by Little All Right
and father[19]

On October 20, *La Sylphide* declared that "it is impossible to imagine anything more curious, clever, and marvelous than the performances of the Japanese."[20] Around the same time, in publications such as *Le Pantheon des Industries et des Arts*, the Imperials could be seen boasting of success in their own advertisements, saying, "It is impossible to compete with these performances due to their superiority, and the Cirque Napoleon has been turning over a thousand people away at the doors from the start."[21]

A Few Difficulties

Of course, the troupe was never completely without problems while in Paris. Risley generally stayed out of the news, but unbeknownst to him because of the lag in communications, back home in San Francisco he had lost his lawsuit with former employee Louisa Gordon, who had won a judgment of $5,200.[22] His partner and investor, Maguire, was in even worse straits. The lawsuit back in the States with the managers of the Tetsuwari troupe and their "All Right" doppelganger was such a headache that Maguire returned to New York. But on October 3, he was assaulted and wounded by two men in the streets, who tried to relieve him of "$4,500, a gold watch, and jewelry."[23] Around the same time, Maguire also relinquished his control in the Tetsuwari faction. There were problems among the Imperials' partners in Paris, too, so much so that they had to appeal to a French court. As *Le Figaro* quipped on September 9, a French tribunal had been asked "to reestablish a sense of balance" among the Japanese acrobats. Risley, Banks, and W. F. Schiedt had apparently petitioned the tribunal to ask that a new provisional financial administrator be nominated for them and that Maguire be denied the right to cash the receipts the Japanese were making in Paris. The tribunal rejected their claim.[24]

As for the Japanese, they had something to complain about, too. At the end of September, Hirohachi notes in his diary that one of the "foreigners" he served (presumably Risley or one of the partners in the venture) had told them to wear Japanese clothes when moving about in town as a way to advertise their presence. To the Japanese, however, this created a problem: Whenever they went out, they drew huge, unwelcomed crowds of gawkers that made it difficult to do anything.[25] At this point in history, Japanese men and women still wore traditional dress such as the kimono, and the men shaved the front of their heads and wore their hair in a *chonmage* top-knot style. But as Japanese were increasingly exposed to foreign fashions, they also began to feel the need to modernize, and they felt increasingly embarrassed by their traditional, native dress, which made them so conspicuous. Photographs that survive of the shogun's younger brother and his retinue in Paris, for example, usually show them in traditional samurai outfits with shaved heads and *chonmage*. As one observer at the Exposition had quipped, the young boy emissary had attracted great attention not only because of his "dark complexion," but because of "the assortment of huge sabres under which he [was] almost buried."[26] Yet a photograph of Akitake's aforementioned retainer, Shibusawa Eiichi, also shows him proudly dressed in Western-style top hat and tails, holding a fancy walking stick. Even Little All Right was often photographed around this time fashionably attired in European clothes. Only four years later, the Japanese government would ban swords and top-knots for men.

Modern Japanese writer Yasuoka Shōtarō authored the first book on Hirohachi and the Imperials. He has noted that racial issues which the Japanese likely experienced when they went out on their own probably increased their desire to blend in. Mid-nineteenth-century Paris was a very cosmopolitan place for its day and mercifully free of the charged racial atmosphere that so poisoned the United States at this time. Still, the situation was particularly complicated for both the performers and the American partners because French audiences loved the Japanese for their exoticism, and for their "otherness."

In his review of the Imperials on August 19, Paul de Saint-Victor wrote in *La Presse*:

> All Paris is running to the shows given each night by the Japanese troupe at the Cirque Napoleon, almost as if taking a pleasure train to the Antipodes. The mere sight of these yellow men—with their shaven temples, slanted eyes, flat noses between two protruding cheekbones, and blue-black hair rolled in a top-knot on top of the skull—transports us into a world as eccentric as that of another planet.[27]

There was also the ever-present danger of accidents. Around October 21, when eighteen-year-old Sumidagawa Matsugorō was in the middle of his slackrope act, the rope broke and he fell, injuring his leg and terrifying his father, Namigorō. As *L'Independance Dramatique* reported it,

Namigorō does the butterfly trick. *LE MONDE ILLUSTRÉ*, NO-VEMBER 23, 1867.

he fell backward from a height of nearly fifteen feet after performing a variety of routines.

> Seriously injured in various places, he still managed to smile to the public with the contempt of pain that characterizes his nation, until he was taken behind stage where a doctor on duty administered first aid. The accident was attributed to the dangers of rope walking, but it is hoped that it will not prove fatal to him. Afterwards, several newspapers again started circulating old clichés about how barbaric trapeze work is, and how cruel it is to enjoy watching acrobats on ropes. . . . If people are afraid, however, they shouldn't go to the circus.[28]

Even after the accident, crowds kept coming, right up until the troupe left Paris on October 29 and moved to Lyon, France's second largest city, some three hundred miles to the south.

South to Lyon

At Lyon, the Imperials had a month-long run. They got off to a good start on the opening day, but Hirohachi's diary indicates that attendance thereafter was often "medium." Still, there was time for sightseeing, to watch European-style wrestling, and to have a delightful boating session on a lake (presumably the famous Parc de la Tête d'Or), where they made some French friends. For Hirohachi, one of the highlights of his stay in the city was a visit to a silk-weaving factory, since he was from a silk-producing area of Japan and probably knew a great deal about it. But he also had the chance to sample the local women. Lyon had numerous professional women of different nationalities, including an Italian, working in a popular brothel. As he carefully noted, they were beautiful, talented, hard-working, and, compared to other cities, quite a bargain. He especially liked the Italian, and went back to see her three more times while in Lyon.[29]

Little All Right, or Umekichi, became a truly global pop star in Lyon. On November 17, 1867, half a world away, the *Daily Alta California* in San Francisco ran a report of a poem by someone who had seen him in New York. One of the verses went as follows:

> *A Japanese,*
> *A comic, vaulting boy,*
> *With his attempts to please,*
> *Uses two words that hold more joy*
> *Than chapters novelists indite:*
> *Those words,* All Right.[30]

Purely by coincidence, in Lyon on the same day, the local *La Marionnette* ran a poem composed by "Pivoine." Dedicated to the Imperials, but misleadingly titled "La Troupe Japonaise du Taicoun," it contained the following verse (loosely translated into English):

> *Twenty feet above the ground, on the tip*
> *Of a trembling and fragile bamboo pole*
> *All Right gives his shrill yells;*
> *Supporting him below with his spindly legs*
> *Hamaikari never once bends under the weight.*[31]

At the end of November, the Imperials returned to Paris, spent two nights, and then on December 5 traveled by train through a heavy snowfall to Calais, where the next day they boarded a ship. They arrived in Dover, England in the evening, after a stormy passage across the English Channel with sleet and heavy rain during which everyone threw up. From Dover, they made their way by train to London.

ACT 8

The Long Way to London

*"The Emperor of Japan, on a steady white horse stenciled
with black spots, was twirling five wash-hand basins
at once, as it is the favourite recreation of that monarch
to do."*[1]

–from *Hard Times*, by Charles Dickens, 1854

It was the height of the Victorian Age. Britain—strengthened by a powerful navy, early participation in the Industrial Revolution, and a global network of colonies—was the imperial giant of the mid-nineteenth century, effectively controlling much of the globe. London—the capital—was one of the world's largest, richest, and most exciting cities, with an increasing demand for sophisticated entertainment.

Starting in late November 1867, Risley and Maguire began promoting the Imperials in local London papers. They would appear, advertisements announced, in Her Majesty's Theatre in Haymarket, with performances scheduled to start on Monday, December 16, replacing an Italian opera. It was quite a coup, for they had secured one of London's largest and most prestigious theatres. But in London, as had been the case in Paris, they faced a highly competitive landscape.

London was filled with museums and musicals, plays, panoramas, and circuses, and the usual panoply of entertainment popular in the nineteenth century. Not just London, but nearly all Britain was already used to Japanese acrobats and jugglers. Interest in Japanese popular entertainment had been spurred by accounts sent back from Japan right after it was opened to the outside world, so much so that in 1854, in his novel *Hard Times*, Charles Dickens even described a Japan-themed circus act in a fictional industrial British town. But by the end of 1867 many people had seen real Japanese acts, too. The Great Dragon Troupe, which left Japan after Risley and the Imperials, had already toured Ireland, Wales, and Scotland in the summer of 1867, billing itself as the "Largest and only Complete Troupe of First-class Male and Female Artistes that has ever been permitted to leave Japan."[2] The Gensui Troupe (which had opened over a week before the Imperials in Paris in June) had gone directly to Britain even earlier, arriving from Yokohama in early February 1867. It had spent over five months performing in London and other British cities. At the time, the British people had never seen any sort of real Japanese popular entertainment before, so the Gensui Troupe, in particular, had been treated as an extraordinary novelty, attracting both devoted fans and laudatory press reviews.

Directed by Andrew Nimmo, the Gensui Troupe, like the Imperials, had advertised their "Japanese-ness," dressed in native costumes, spoken Japanese in performances, and used Japanese music. The British public had been especially awed by the top-spinning and the butterfly tricks, the likes of which they had never seen. There had been some typical sniping in the press over the quality of the Gensui Troupe's acrobatics, and disappointment over the fact that the forty-three-year-old elder of the group—Matsui Gensui, a renowned top-spinner and older brother of one of the Imperials' stars—had injured himself and was thus unable to perform properly. As had been the case with the Imperials in the United States, people made fun of the incomprehensible Japanese language in the show and especially complained about the music.

> There is now and then some native music (so called) written, one would imagine, in the key of Z minor, in comparison with which the marrow-bones and cleavers

THE BUTTERFLY TRICK.

THE TOP-SPINNER.

THE JAPANESE JUGGLERS AT ST. MARTIN'S HALL.

Prior competition in London: Asakichi does the butterfly trick and Gensui spins tops, at St. Martin's Hall, London. *ILLUSTRATED LONDON NEWS*, FEBRUARY 23, 1867.

are melodious, and which, combined with the natural somberness of St. Martin's Hall, creates a disposition to fall upon your neighbor's neck and weep.[3]

Still, in Britain the Gensui Troupe had been a sensation, and in April it had even been retained by Queen Victoria to perform at Windsor Castle for the birthday party of Princess Beatrice and other children of the royal family. The general consensus among even the most jaded Londoners seemed to be as summed up by the *Weekly Times* on February 17, 1867:

We have had Indians, Bosjesmen, Chinese, Turks, New Zealanders, Aztecs, "niggers," Arabs, and various other representatives of nationalities or peculiar localities, and the world has been ransacked from time to time to find a new sensation. The difficulty of procuring a novelty has, however, been overcome by the appearance at St. Martin's hall of a troupe of twelve Japanese.[4]

A Rough Start

The Imperials finally arrived in London on December 6, but the very day they arrived, they ran into extraordinary bad luck. *Lloyd's Weekly* reported:

> On Friday night one of the handsomest, certainly, if not the finest, theatre in London went the way of all theatres, and was burnt to the ground in less than two hours. The fire while it raged was one of the fiercest ever known in London, and though the main building, the beautiful theatre, quickly burnt itself out and crumbled away in a towering pyramid of flame, yet its surroundings continued to blaze as house after house in the colonnade caught fire and were burnt from roof to basement.[5]

As a result of the theatre fire, the Imperials lost many of the beautiful and colorful playbills they had prepared and were idled for nearly two weeks with little to do. It was typically bad London winter weather, with occasional snow and sleet. Hirohachi's diary entry on December 10 simply states, "Because there are no theatres available, we are taking it easy every day." His entries are pithier than usual, and other than a comment about how London seemed to him "big enough to fit three Edos in," he says little about his environs because their sightseeing was kept to a minimum and they stayed mainly in the hotel. Reflecting his personal boredom, in one four-day period he visited London prostitutes three times. Risley and his partners, on the other hand, busied themselves trying to secure an appropriate venue, but they eventually gave up. Instead of starting in London, they decided that they would tour the "provin-

The Burning of Her Majesty's Theatre, Haymarket. *ILLUSTRATED LONDON NEWS*, DE-
CEMBER 14, 1867.

cial" towns and cities first and return to London later. And they would
start with England's second largest city, Birmingham.[6]

In Birmingham, Risley booked them into the famed Curzon Exhibition Hall, which had been rapidly refitted for them. The hall was normally used for panoramas and even circuses, but the Imperials had been
immediately preceded by the popular annual dog show, then in its ninth
year. On Christmas Day, the *Birmingham Daily Post* ran a preview article,
describing the hall as 103' by 91' in size, with a handsome new proscenium laden with gaudy gold and color ornamentation, and a roomy,
43'-deep stage fitted up with new curtains and scenic wings—more than
tall enough to accommodate the Imperials and their tallest ladder tricks.
For the benefit of British readers, the article also introduced many of the
performers by name and described their roles both on and off the stage.
Twenty-one-year-old female *samisen* player Tō was described as someone "musical, in the Japanese sense of the word." Edward Banks, the

group's interpreter, presumably supplied the reporter with information on an idiosyncrasy of the Japanese language; Kanekichi (referred to as the "stage manager") was said to have a particularly difficult job:

> It is actually impossible to swear in Japanese. To curse a man up hill and down dale is a feat the accomplishment of which, by a subject of the Tycoon, would necessitate the study of foreign languages. The vocabulary of Japanese objurgation is limited to a few terms, the strongest of which, perhaps, is "beast."[7]

On the day after Christmas, or Boxing Day in England, the Imperials opened to a packed house. The next day, in an article titled "The Japanese Jugglers," the same *Birmingham Daily Post* gave the Imperials a glowing review. It noted that they were appearing in Birmingham because they had been burned out of their theatre in London. It covered Risley's great difficulties in bringing the troupe out of Japan, and the group's great success in the United States and France. It attempted to introduce the names of each member of the troupe (there being no standard Romanization of Japanese yet, this was always a treacherous proposition). And it gave readers a positive but racially tilted description of their program:

> While "top-spinning" and "balancing" and "butterflies" and "tight-rope dancing," &c., formed part of the programme, the actual performances were absolutely novel and startling, and entirely different from those of the smaller company of Japanese who appeared here some months ago. When the curtain rose, twenty quaintly dressed figures, in many varieties of costume, with sallow skins, almond-shaped eyes, close-laid hair, curiously shaped foreheads and simial profiles, appeared, and prostrated themselves to make their national "kow-tow" to the barbarians of the West.[8]

From the review, it is clear that the troupe was performing many of the same routines it had worked on in Paris. The acts included the "Dance of the Drum," the "Living Pyramid," the "Perche on the Shoulder," the "Transformation Fox Screen," the "Butterfly Trick," and the grand finale of the "Ladder Trick." The last act usually involved Little All Right doing evolutions on top of a precariously balanced contraption of multiple ladders, which was in turn perched on the soles of the reclining Hamaikari's upturned feet. The original troupe members only numbered eighteen, so the mention of "twenty quaintly dressed figures" in the review was either due to error, clever marketing on Risley's part, or the near-miraculous procurement of two unattached Japanese (or Asians) somewhere. The review indirectly compared the Imperials not only to Risley's act with his boys two decades earlier, but also to the performances of the Gensui Troupe (who had previously appeared in the same city). All in all, it was more than Risley or the performers could have wished for.

> Not only on the power of muscle, but in mobility of limb, nearly all the performers surpassed all ever seen in "Professor Risley's" school. In the art of balancing the Japanese seem to have outwitted nature, and to set at defiance all ordinary laws. . . . When their nationality is remembered, the novelty of their feats, the gorgeousness of their dresses, the Oriental originality of their stage arrangements, and the strange music and still stranger language associated with their proceedings, the whole performances afford unrivalled attractions, and must attract crowded houses to witness the wonders of the East.[9]

From the start in Britain, Risley faced a bit of an advertising dilemma. Since the Gensui Troupe had already entertained in areas the Imperials planned to tour, he had to explain what made the Imperials different, and also why they had gone to Paris first instead of going directly to England. As a defense, advertisements for the Imperials in

Lloyd's Weekly stressed that the Imperials "have never appeared in Europe, except at Paris, where their success has been extraordinarily great," that "they have nothing in common with any company which has previously visited England," and were "unequalled in their own land."[10] The *Era*, on the other hand, proclaimed that the Imperials had left Japan intending to come to England via the United States, but that "hearing of their projected trip, another company of less distinguished artistes endeavoured to forestall them, and came to England last summer [*sic*]."[11] It was a clear dig at the Gensui Troupe.

The Imperials also had to contend with the fact that audiences were already familiar with several of their basic acts, such as top-spinning and the butterfly trick. In fact, the people of Britain were so familiar with Japanese acts that parodies of them had been incorporated into minstrel shows, as had been done in other regions. Imitators also abounded. There was the minstrel named "Japanese Tommy" (actually Thomas Dilward, an African American dwarf) appearing at the London Pavilion. In early 1868 there was an unnamed "Japanese" performer (who may have been a real Japanese, but may also have been a British impersonator) listed in an equestrian and acrobatic act put on by Messrs. J. and G. Sanger at the Agricultural Hall in London. And at the Pavilion Theatre there was a young British woman named Miss Lizzie Anderson, daughter of the famous magician, John Henry Anderson, who was said to excel "the Japanese artistes in the elegance and perfection of her Great Butterfly trick."[12]

Still, Risley had a big advantage. The Imperials were far better than anything the British public had ever seen before. And, even more than in Paris, Risley was regarded as a returning hero, still remembered because of his numerous performances with his sons in England a quarter of a century earlier. Risley had legions of allies in the media, and they were at times willing to describe his competitors in less than flattering language, to promote the Imperials' superiority, and to hype the idea that they were actually the first troupe to have left Japan. Prior and Grant had brought the Gensui Troupe to England nearly a year before, and when Prior found out that his troupe was being described retroactively in the British media as "clumsy imposters," he wrote an angry letter of com-

PRICES OF ADMISSION, 2s., 1s., and 6d.

CURZON EXHIBITION HALL,
TOP OF SUFFOLK STREET, PARADISE STREET,
BIRMINGHAM.
OPEN EVERY EVENING.

THE
IMPERIAL JAPANESE COMPANY
OF HIS MAJESTY THE TYCOON,
FROM THE COURT OF JEDDO, JAPAN.
POSITIVELY THE LAST FIVE NIGHTS.

Directors of the Troupe,
Messrs. THOMAS MAGUIRE and Professor RISLEY.

This is the most extraordinary assemblage of Oriental Artistes who
have at any time visited European Shores. The Company number
TWENTY PERFORMERS.

ON THURSDAY, AT TWO O'CLOCK,
Doors open at half-past One.
LEADER OF BAND....Mr. D. FFRENCH DAVIS.

Admission : Side Seats and Promenade, 6d. ; Centre Seats, 1s.;
Stalls, 2s.
The Doors will open at Seven, and the Performance begin at
Eight p.m.
Refreshments supplied by the Eminent Firm of SPIERS and
POND.   139

Advertisement for the Imperials' appearance in Curzon Hall. *BIRMINGHAM DAILY POST*, JANUARY 14, 1868.

plaint to the *Illustrated Times*. In it, he stated that, in fact, the females in his—not Risley's—troupe had indeed been the first to leave Japan. To which the editor responded with sharp British wit:

> Let me assure Mr. Prior that nothing was farther from my intentions than to reflect on the genuineness of his troupe as actual natives of Japan. I simply meant to imply that, representing themselves to be remarkably clever conjurors and acrobats, they were, in point of fact, conjurors and acrobats of insignificant talent.[13]

In general, Risley seems to have had the trust of the British media. In the world of the circus, hyperbolic advertising and exaggeration were (and still are) often taken for granted, even expected, but Risley was careful to adhere to a semblance of the truth in both his publicity statements and his advertising. He was, in nineteenth-century American parlance, relatively free of "humbug." This helped give him a special aura in his industry and position his acts as "art" as well as entertainment. There was, however, the minor issue of nomenclature, which was in itself a contradiction in terms. In newspaper advertisements the "Imperial

Japanese Troupe" was sometimes said to be the Tycoon's official troupe, but there is little evidence to suggest that any of the acrobatic troupes that emerged from Japan in 1867-68 ever had official Imperial or Shogunate backing. Moreover, back in Japan, the Tycoon (the shogun) and the emperor were entirely different political entities, their forces about to embark on a war with each other in which the Tycoon would come out the loser.

The Imperials remained in Birmingham for a month of chilly midwinter weather with occasional snow. Attendance was only moderate most days, but the press continued to be highly favorable. On January 20, the *Birmingham Daily Post* ran another review of the Imperials' show, declaring that the theatre had been "overflowing" during the week, that the troupe had been an "unrivalled attraction" in the city, and that their upcoming departure would "involve a loss not likely to be made up some years hence." The article was novel in that it contained information on Edward Banks, one of Risley's partners, and the interpreter (as well as the main interface between the Japanese troupe and the foreign world in which they had to move). Banks was described as having lived in Yokohama for seven years, having mastered the diabolically difficult Japanese language, and having negotiated with the Japanese government to obtain permission for the acrobats to leave—which may all have been correct—but he was also said to have been the vice-consul there, when he had only been the U.S. Marshal. The writer also visited the Japanese in their local lodging and included a rare description of their private lives:

> Their little community has not adopted Western habits, but for the most part live in a purely Oriental style. Fruit and vegetables form their principal food, tea their constant beverage, wine, spirits, or liquors being very rarely used. The troupe forms quite a "happy family," retiring about eleven, rising at six, breakfasting at eight, dining at one, supping at six, and taking a lunch or tea after the evening's work is done. None of the professional jealousy, common to European artists, is found, and each artist . . . is always ready to take another's place

and do the best he can, if any necessity arises for such a course. The Japanese are remarkably intelligent, industrious, and inventive. Much of their time is occupied in reading and writing, and one of the party, Iwa Kai Chi [Iwakichi, another name of Hirohachi], is the historian who in his long notebook of silky paper, and his brush and Indian ink, scrawls down in vertical lines the incidents of the tour. All are very fond of pictures, photographs, and stereographs especially.[14]

The writer then went on to describe the dress of the Japanese, which contrary to their rich appearance on stage, was "of simple and often scanty kind." Also unlike their energetic stage presence, he found them as a rule very quiet, often sitting cross-legged on the mattresses, smoking, chatting, and amusing themselves "in a quiet way." Off stage, he remarked, the tailor and barber among them were always busy, the former sitting cross-legged and repairing or making costumes, and the latter—to the writer's obvious amazement—shaving the foreheads of the men with "a dry razor of very keen edge, no lather ever being used."[15]

After Birmingham, the Imperials were on a quick roll, their schedule tightening into a tour of the north of England, where they performed in packed halls in the new factory and mill towns of the industrial era. On January 27 the Imperials opened in Leeds; on February 3 in Bradford; on February 8 in Manchester; on the eleventh in Blackburn; on the fourteenth again in Manchester; on the twentieth in Wakefield; and the twenty-second in Hull.

But big changes were occurring around the Imperials, some of which were apparent to them, and some of which were not. The most momentous change was hinted at in reports in the British press—relayed from San Francisco and New York—of a revolution in faraway Japan, and the collapse of the Shogunate. For whatever reason, the Japanese members of the Imperials—at least as indicated by Hirohachi's diary—either did not learn of the reports or did not understand their implications.

More directly, Thomas Maguire, Risley's partner and investor since San Francisco, was facing a tsunami of lawsuits. One in February, in

Britain, was with a Mr. Wittgenstein, who had purchased a share of Maguire's profits from the Imperials and wanted to be paid. Another, coming up in May in New York, was related to infringement of a theatrical copyright issue unrelated to the Imperials. But the most serious suit of all, also in New York, involved George S. Fisher, who had been the U.S. consul in Yokohama when Risley and his other partners formed their contract to take the Imperials to the West. Fisher claimed he had been given some of the shares for his help in making it possible to take the Japanese out of their country, and he was suing Maguire for his share of the presumed profits. One of Maguire's defenses was that Fisher had been a U.S. government official at the time and was therefore not supposed to have been investing in business ventures that would create such a conflict of interest.[16]

Presumably because Maguire was so preoccupied with lawsuits and had to return to the United States to deal with them, a man named Van Gieson was brought on board the Imperials' management team. Starting in mid-February, instead of "Maguire and Risley's Imperial Japanese," advertisements in British newspapers were crowned with the phrase, "Risley and Van Gieson's Imperial Japanese."

Holland and Belgium

Little is known about Van Gieson. He may have been Dutch or at least had good contacts on the Continent, for soon after he joined the Imperials they boarded a steamer and crossed the English Channel. They arrived in Rotterdam, Holland, on March 1, and performed there the very next day. On February 7, they opened in Amsterdam. They would spend nearly a month in Holland, billed in the press as the "*Keizerlijk Japanschgezelschap*," or the "Imperial Japanese Troupe." And wherever possible they trumpeted their prior accomplishments. The first advertisement that appeared in the March 1 edition of the *Nieuwe Rotterdamsche Courant* boasted of their success in California and of having attracted audiences of three thousand nightly at the New York Academy of Music and four thousand nightly at the Cirque Napoleon in Paris. In what had rarely

RISLEY & VAN GIESON'S
Keizerlijk
JAPANSCH
GEZELSCHAP.

(5894)

KUNSTMIN, DORDRECHT
Zaturdag 28 Maart 1868.

1e rang ƒ1.49, 2e rang ƒ0 99. Kinderen beneden de 12 jaar betalen voor den 1en rang half geld. Aanvang half 8 uur.

Advertisement for the Imperial Japanese Troupe in Rotterdam. *NIEUWE ROTTERDAM-SCHE COURANT*, MARCH 28, 1868.

been done in newspapers before, it also introduced the Imperials' full program, giving the names of the individual Japanese performers next to their acts, such as the "*tolspelen, door MATSUIKIKUJIRU en zijne Dochter OZUNE*" [Top-spinning, by Matsui Kikujirō and his daughter Tsune].[17] In Amsterdam, in the *Algemeen Handelsblad*, advertisements also included little illustrations of kimono-clad Japanese top-spinning and other acts. And the reviews were good. On March 26, after appearing at the Royal Holland Theatre in The Hague, the Imperials were praised for the novelty of their derring-do performances, and for their speed, suppleness, and bravado. The calm manner with which their acts were executed was also praised because it helped allay audience fears that they might injure themselves. The "yellow children of the East," the writer declared, had performed to great acclaim and were unequalled.[18]

Yet if Hirohachi is to be believed, the Japanese performers were not happy in Holland. He describes the lowlands and the windmills, but he didn't much like the place, calling the Dutch "very bad people" and criticizing everything from the way their homes were built to the "gold-plated" coins they used. Some of his information seems wrong, leading one to speculate that he may have been reporting gossip he had overheard from others, filtering it through the fog of a language barrier. But why he was so profoundly unhappy with the Dutch is something of a mystery. In addition to Rotterdam and Amsterdam, the Imperials performed in Utrecht, Leiden, and The Hague, and attendance was great at most performances. Japanese people also had a long history of friendship with the Dutch. In fact, for the nearly 250 years of the Tokugawa Shogunate, Holland had been the only European nation officially allowed to trade with Japan, and a small contingent of Dutch merchants had been permitted to reside on a tiny trading post on a mini-island off Nagasaki, the port city at the southern tip of Japan. The Imperials even met several young Japanese who had been sent to study in Holland as part of a first wave of exchange students. Perhaps after a year on the road in foreign lands, eating strange food and listening to strange languages, the Imperial Japanese Troupe members, or at least Hirohachi, may simply have been experiencing a type of cultural fatigue. Or perhaps his entries on Holland were added later, after he had had some unpleasant experiences.

On March 16, the Imperials opened in Utrecht. The next day the four Japanese exchange students came to see their performance and later trade gossip with the troupe. At night, on the way home, there was such a crowd of "foreigners" gawking at them that they could not pass. A fight broke out between the Imperials and the local Dutch, causing a huge commotion. Fearing the crowd might take the official passports they carried—their key to one day returning to Japan—Hirohachi drew his "long-sword" and "waved it about wildly, showing them what Japanese were made of, whereupon the foreigners were all shocked, and fled in all directions. . . . " His samurai sword was presumably a prop, but they nonetheless lost two days of performances due to interrogations by the local police.[19]

On March 29, the Imperials left Holland and went by steamship to Antwerp, Belgium, where they performed in the Royal Theatre. And then, on April 3, they traveled to Brussels and performed at the Theatre du Boulevard and also the Theatre National du Cirque. The local paper declared of the performance at the latter venue, obliquely referring to competitors named the Dragon Troupe:

> On Thursday, the first performance of the Japanese Troupe under the direction of Messrs. Risley and Van Gieson drew a large audience. Their success exceeded all expectations. This troupe, not to be confused with the one which last year passed through Brussels, is made up of acrobats and tightrope walkers who all greatly surpass their European counterparts. In particular, they have a very unique ladder act. Most of their performances have a novel charm; moreover, all are extremely remarkable.[20]

The Japanese were professionals, and they kept one of their biggest problems hidden from their audience. Matsui Kikujirō, who normally performed the top-spinning acts with his pupil Matsugorō and daughter Tsune, had long been complaining of ill health. In his April 4 diary entry, Hirohachi describes him as being too "thin and weak." He notes that they had decided to send him ahead to London, accompanied by Umekichi (not All Right, but the tailor in the group) and an interpreter (who Hirohachi implies was Chinese), while the rest of the troupe completed their run in Brussels.

On April 8, the remainder of the troupe crossed the channel and arrived in London, where they checked into their lodgings at Upper Stamford Street, in preparation for their long-awaited debut at the prestigious Royal Lyceum Theatre. To their shock, the elder Matsui had already succumbed to his illness. He was only thirty-one years old.[21]

The presence of Japanese people in Britain was still a novelty, and the death of a Japanese even more so. Kikujirō's death was widely reported in the press, not only in London, but also in towns where the Imperials had previously performed, such as Manchester and Leeds. For the Japanese, adrift in a foreign land, the death of their comrade presented unique problems: they could not perform normal Japanese Buddhist funerary rituals such as cremation and had to improvise a service on their own. Nonetheless, with the help of Risley and Banks, they buried their comrade in a grave in Brookwood Cemetery, some thirty miles south of London. It was a better sendoff than a commoner in Japan would have received, wrote Hirohachi. And even if everything were not perfect, they could at least console themselves with the fact that they had been able to carve Kikujirō's post-death Buddhist name (*kaimyō*) into the headstone in Japanese. Two other Japanese who had died in Britain earlier had already been buried in Brookwood, so after offering incense to Matsui Kikujirō's soul, the troupe members also offered incense to the souls of their fellow countrymen.[22]

By coincidence, back in New York, the leader of another Japanese group of acrobats—the Hayatake Troupe, also billed as the "Imperial Troupe"—had died less than two months earlier. Hayatake's exotic funeral ceremonies had been widely reported and exaggerated in the American press, even lavishly depicted with lithographs in *Frank Leslie's Illustrated Newspaper*.[23] Perhaps in an effort to ward off too much sensationalism in the British press over Kikujirō's death, Risley appears to have convinced editors of some London newspapers to run a disclaimer:

> In order that our readers may not form erroneous impressions from having read a paragraph published last week, we hasten to explain that the top spinner whose death was recorded was not an important member of the extraordinary *troupe* now performing at the Lyceum. The company is in no degree weakened by the death of this artist, for he had taken no share in the performance for twelve months past. The cause of death was consumption.[24]

"Consumption," was the catch-all label in the mid-nineteenth century for tuberculosis and many wasting diseases, especially of the lungs. The disclaimer itself was disingenuous and rather cruel, and hopefully none of the Japanese ever learned about it, for in Holland, Matsui had been given top billing in the newspapers.

Hamaikari Denkichi (lying) and Umekichi (flying) perform the tub trick at the Lyceum, in front of fanciful Japanese background scenes painted by Grieves & Son. *ILLUSTRATED LONDON NEWS*, MAY 2, 1868.

London at Last

The show had to go on. On Easter Monday, April 13, the Imperials finally opened at London's Royal Lyceum on Wellington Street. It was one of the most prestigious theatres in the city and could accommodate over two thousand people. The Japanese were a huge success, with people turned away at the doors. Advertisements placed in London newspapers, even before they had left Belgium, explained to readers that they had been prevented from appearing earlier in London because of the fire at Her Majesty's Theatre:

> It is absolutely necessary the English public should, in justice to themselves as well as to this remarkable Com-

pany of Artists, know that this is the first and greatest troupe of Japanese that ever left Japan. They were
personally selected by the world-renowned Professor
RISLEY, during his four years residence in Japan, from
the most talented and celebrated artistes of the Imperial Court of Jeddo, with the personal influence of ED-
WARD BANKS, Esq, Deputy-Consul to Japan from
the United States, now interpreter and stage-director to
the company.[25]

Shows at the Lyceum usually started at eight o'clock in the evening
and ran until half past ten, but there were matinees on Wednesdays and
Saturdays. Even without their master top-spinner, at London's Lyceum
the Imperials arguably reached a pinnacle of success. In London, they
faced jaded and sometimes cynical theatregoers and had to go up against
some of the world's best entertainers. There was a highly popular "Oriental Troupe" (of Indian acrobats) at the Crystal Palace. Charles Dickens's beloved story, *Oliver Twist*, was being staged over at the Queen's
Theatre. And many Londoners had already seen similar Japanese acts
performed by the Gensui Troupe. But the Imperials' detour to the provinces and the Continent had paid off. Their fame by now had preceded
them. And in the nearly two years since leaving Japan they had had time
to hone their acts in front of audiences in both the New and Old worlds,
to synchronize their efforts, and to learn to tailor performances to people
of different classes and cultures. And it certainly did not hurt that in London they were also represented by a new agency, the well-known team
of Parravicini and Corbyn.

Reynold's Newspaper complained of a Japanese troupe traveling "several thousands of miles to exhibit feats that English street and music hall
tumblers can just as well perform"[26] The *Illustrated Times* grumbled that
the ladder trick was too dangerous.[27] But the reaction of the British
press was generally one of astonishment, and even surprise at its own
astonishment. *Lloyd's* declared, "Nothing like their performances have
been previously seen, and they cannot fail to excite the utmost astonishment."[28] The *Examiner* marveled, "Although the fame of this company

The Imperials at work, advertising the British humor magazine, *The Mask*. OPPOSITE PAGE: The Imperials at work. BOTH IMAGES FROM *THE MASK*, VOL. I, FEBRUARY—DECEMBER, 1868.

had reached us long since, we were unprepared for the grace and daring skill which marks their performance."[29] And surely for Risley one of the most gratifying reviews of all came from the *Era*, the London paper famed for its coverage of theatres and entertainment. In a lengthy piece, the reviewer waxed ecstatically about the troupe:

> Some of the most astounding feats of agility and con-
> tortion that London has, we will venture to say, in the
> whole course of its existence as a city witnessed have
> been introduced. . . . The extraordinary feats which are
> represented by the illustrations on the broadsides which
> have for some short time adorned our streets are in no
> degree exaggerated; on the contrary, they give but a
> faint idea of what the performance really is. . . . It is
> beyond our power to speak with sufficient approval of
> these performers.[30]

The *Era* reviewer then went on to heap praise on the individual acts, which were divided into two parts, each with seven subdivisions. He was amazed by the posturing, gymnastics, and contortions of Yone-kichi and Sentarō; the dancing drum and flying tub act of Denkichi; the *perch* act performed by Hamaikari and Little All Right; the top-spinning done by Sumidagawa Koman and poor Kikujirō's daughter, Tsune; the slackrope walking of Matsugorō (whom he mistakenly describes as a fe-male); the butterfly trick of Namigorō; and the climactic ladder trick of Hamaikari Sadakichi and All Right.

From this and other reviews we can also see both how the troupe had filled in for the loss of Kikujirō, and also how Risley had tightly tailored his performances to his audiences. The evening's act in London was billed as a "Night in Japan." For atmospherics Risley had commis-sioned background scene paintings by Mr. Thomas Grieve and son, fa-mous scene painters whose mere participation would help ensure atten-dance. In this case, the artists worked from sketches by Japanese artists, with the result that "the curtain rises on a drop scene of Japanese land-scape. In the middle distance is the magnificent snow-crowned sacred mountain of Fusiyama, and in the foreground a tea-garden on the banks of a stream, crossed by a wooden bridge of most unenviable gradient."[31] Compared to the Gensui Troupe, Risley made sure that there was not too much extraneous patter to slow down the show. And in a concession to his audiences, he had also hired the Lyceum Theatre's orchestra to provide a musical accompaniment between the acts and to accompany performances. As the *Daily News* reviewer sighed, alluding to the Gensui Troupe of the previous year, "Those who remember what Japanese music was at St. Martin's hall will be thankful for this mercy on the part of Professor Risley."[32] As for Risley, his reception in London must have been extraordinarily gratifying, for in the first week, at the end of the performances, the entire troupe was called upon the stage to receive the acclaim of the audience, whereupon "a cry was also raised for 'Professor Risley' himself, the founder of a clever and distinct school of acrobatic evolution, who selected the Japanese troupe during a four years' residence in Japan, and under whose auspices they have since performed with great success."[33]

Drama Onstage and Off

In London the Imperials did not have much time to savor their success on the stage. They were still recovering from the death of Kikujirō, and around half-past four in the afternoon of April 18, while giving a performance at the Lyceum, a terrible fire broke out in the six-story stone building where they were lodging, at 47 Gerard Street. It started in the room that Hirohachi and three of the Japanese males occupied, when a piece of coal spilled out of the room's stove grate, rolled onto a blanket or carpet, and went on to gut the upper three stories of the building. While the local firemen were able to save some of the performers' effects, they lost many, including souvenirs, a tidy sum in gold and silver coins, and a pet dog—the favorite of All Right—who burned to death while guarding his master's property. To Hirohachi's relief, because the building had been made out of stone, it survived, as did their passports, which had been stored in a safe.[34]

THE IMPERIAL JAPANESE TROUPE OF ACROBATS AT THE LYCEUM THEATRE : THE TRANSFORMATION FOX SCENE.—SEE PAGE *

The "Transformation Fox Scene," as performed in London's Lyceum theatre. *THE PENNY ILLUSTRATED PAPER, MAY 9, 1868.*

The show again had to go on. Imperials would continue their run at the Lyceum in London until the end of June. Risley—ever mindful of the need for good community relations—at the end of April staged free performances for 185 children of the prestigious local "Licensed Victuallers' School." In May, the Imperials also gave occasional performances at London's Crystal Palace, traveling there in carriages gaily flying Japanese flags to promote themselves. In his diary, Hirohachi struggled heroically to phoneticize the name of this new venue in Japanese (which lacks an "L" sound) rendering it as "*keshitaru harishi.*"

The Lyceum was full nearly every night, and the Imperials were the talk of London during their run. Captain Applin, former secretary to the British minister in Japan, had recently returned from Yokohama, where several years earlier he had seen Sumidagawa Namigorō's butterfly tricks performed at the residence of Sir Rutherford Alcock. He sent Risley, to give to the performers, the gifts of a Japanese umbrella and a *koi-nobori*, or carp-fish shaped flag, usually flown for good luck in May.[35] A writer at *The Era* gushed in early May, two weeks into the Imperials' run at the Lyceum, "The performances of the Japanese troupe are the most talented and wonderful ever seen in this country, and they are now performing to numerous and fashionable audiences. . . . When the unqualified approbation of the whole of the Press has been bestowed on the performers, there can be no dispute about the quality of the entertainment." The same review also carried a rare first-hand description of the transformation fox trick.

> I came in as one man was balancing on his feet a large square of wood covered over with white paper. This man was lying on his back, turning his back to the audience, or rather the back of his head. His feet, which had all the intelligence of hands, supported this frame, about the height of two ordinary street-doors. Up this frame springs the little Japanese child, breaking through the paper, and thus disclosing small transparent squares of woodwork, throws down some of them, and disappears through the hole, clings to the back, and there undresses, to reappear the most foxy of foxes with a sweeping brush—the most perfect personification of a Reynard, climbing down with all the movements—nay, with the very expression of the animal.[36]

On May 17, *Lloyd's* again favorably reviewed the Imperials' performance, but the same issue of the newspaper also gave them publicity in

London that they did not want, courtesy of court proceedings involving Hirohachi. According to the paper's report, a little after eleven pm on May 4, "Ha Ha Swakicke" [sic] had been picked up by two women near the Lyceum and driven in a cab with them to a "house of bad repute" in Granby Street, Waterloo Road. He had in his purse eleven pounds and, after giving the females ten shillings, had placed it on the table. One of the women sat on his knee in a way that he couldn't see the purse, and after a few minutes she had jumped up and tried to rush from the room, but he stopped her and realized that "nine of the sovereigns" in his purse were missing. A struggle ensued, and the landlady of the building and a man had come and helped the woman escape. After notifying the police, Hirohachi had been able to identify the woman later in custody, in a police lineup. She admitted having been with him and said that she had given him back his money as soon as he had taken off his hat because she had been frightened, but that he had tried to hit her with a candle-stick. In court, Hirohachi was assisted by the interpreter Edward Banks. According to the newspapers, when he testified, he was not put under sworn oath. Instead, he merely subscribed to a declaration to speak the truth, because they "had no oath or bad words in the Japanese vocabu-lary." The woman, a "nymph of the pavé" named Sara Malyon, was sen-tenced to four months of hard labor after pleading guilty.[37]

In his entire diary, Hirohachi devotes more space to describing this incident than almost anything else. His account gives far more detail than that of the newspapers and reveals how he was tormented by his inability to communicate, feared the foreigners were making a fool of him, and was deeply embarrassed as well. In the initial stages, he felt he was be-ing ignored, and he tried to enlist the help of a young samurai from the Chōshū domain (who happened to be one of the few other Japanese in the country, studying in London) to write a letter in English for him. Banks may have been exasperated by Hirohachi's behavior at this point, but eventually Hirohachi did get Banks to help him out. Still, even go-ing through an interpreter, the British legal system was often a mystery to him. He had difficulty picking the woman out of a lineup of suspects (and probably had difficulty in telling the difference between Cauca-sians). He was impressed by the attention the British gave to protecting the rights of people charged. But when the judge explained to him (through Banks) that the woman was from the country, with no home or family in London, and that his money was already gone and would not come back, he was dumbfounded. The authorities should have made more effort to recover the money, he believed. As he wrote sarcastically, "In Japan the woman would have lost her head for stealing ten *ryō*," meaning three pounds, or a third of the actual amount he had lost. Given the light sentence, he also suggested, when he went back to Japan he just might tell all his friends to visit England and engage in a little stealing.[38]

It would be the last time in his diary that Hirohachi ever mentioned buying prostitutes, but not the last rough patch for the Imperials in London. Foreigner fatigue seems to have been setting in. On June 19, Matsugorō, the tightrope walker, also got into a fight with a "foreigner." According to Hirohachi, "the troupe members jumped in to help, bashing the foreigner's head and as a result losing only twenty five dollars."[39]

There were nonetheless some very happy events. Shortly after the trial, on May 27, the Imperials were graced by a royal visit to the Lyceum. Hirohachi describes "the king of England" as having attended, but in reality it was the Prince and Princess of Wales in a party that included the Crown Prince of Denmark. The Prince of Wales met with Risley after the performance "and spoke in high terms of praise and astonishment of the daring, graceful, and original feats of the Japanese."[40] On June 7, Hamaikari Sadakichi's wife, Tō, the samisen player, gave birth to a baby girl, delivered by a Mr. O. Pearson (listed in the press as an "accoucheur," or male midwife). The mother had been suspected a year and a half earlier, during the voyage to New York from San Francisco, of an inappropriate relationship with a member of the Tetsuwari faction, but this time she hopefully pleased her husband. It was also a chance for more publicity, and the London press delighted in proclaiming the baby "the first child of pure Japanese blood ever born outside of Japan." Risley induced the parents to give the baby girl, in addition to her Japanese names, the English name of "Victoria," and in the age of Queen Victoria this was a guarantee of favorable press. Umekichi, or Little All Right, it was also reported, had exclaimed "All right!" upon seeing her. Hirohachi never mentions the baby's birth in his diary.[41]

As the Imperials wound down their London run and got ready to leave, it became clear that whatever problems they might have had, they had grown to like the city and its people. And the feeling was mutual. At the end of June, they had time for some more sightseeing and toured the city by carriage. This time, Hirohachi felt that London was even bigger than when he had first seen it, writing that it seemed to him that "four Edos could fit in London." They made an excursion out to the gravesite of poor Kikujirō, held an impromptu ceremony for his soul, and on June 27 held their last performance in a packed house. They were next headed to Spain. When they packed up their possessions and headed off by carriages to the waterfront on June 29, they were seen off by a huge crowd that extended several blocks, all London fans sad to see them go.[42]

ACT 9

The Matter of the Contract

The said parties . . . have entered into contract with for
the term of two years or more [the performers] to perform,
play and exhibit for hire before the people of the United
States and Europe in their several lines and to the best of
their ability. . . .[1]
　　　　　　—Signed in Yokohama, November 14, 1866

Professor Risley, his partners, and the Imperial Japanese Troupe still had
time left on their original contract. The troupe had reached new heights
of perfection in their performances, but in their itinerary and lives the
members were encountering increasing turbulence. Now, nearing the
end of the term of their agreement, they were headed for the Iberian
Peninsula, where things would get dramatically worse.

Spain

On June 29, the Imperials crossed the English Channel by steamer. They
spent a night in Paris celebrating with old friends and fans, and then
on "trains that seemed to fly day and night," made the long trip all the

Map of Europe

way down to Madrid, the capital of Spain. After arriving tired on July 3, the troupe members bathed, did their hair up, and rested.[2] Risley had booked them into the Prince Alfonso, also known as the Circo Rivas, starting on July 7. It was one of Madrid's most prestigious entertainment venues for circuses and other acts. They would spend more time in Madrid than any other place in southern Europe, not departing until the end of August.

Reports of the "Gran Compañia Imperial Japonesa" had begun running in Madrid papers several days before they arrived, stoking interest. On June 30, the *Boletín de Loterías y Toros* ("Bulletin of Lotteries and Bulls") noted that they would be providing "extraordinary and amazing performances."[3] The *Diario Oficial de Avisos de Madrid* ("Daily Official News of Madrid"), in its column on upcoming performances, ran a more detailed announcement, presumably based on information supplied by Risley. It emphasized that the troupe had performed to acclaim during the Paris Exposition, and that it consisted of "twenty artists of both sexes of such extraordinary merit that their acts border on the impossible and have never been performed or even imitated by the most celebrated artists of Europe's principal circuses." It further announced that the troupe would, at great sacrifice, be charging a third of the ticket price it charged in England, where it had also met great acclaim, and that it would be appearing—not alone, as usual, but jointly—with the principal circus artists of the Prince Alfonso.[4] While one could interpret this as a generous service to Madrid audiences, it conversely may also have reflected Risley's fear that, compared to northern Europe, the average Madrid citizen would have less spending money and less interest in Japanese entertainment.

In Madrid, the Imperials had a few days to prepare and do a little sightseeing. It was a new city and a new culture. Even though Spanish pronunciation sounds far more similar to Japanese than English, by this time the Japanese were more used to the sound of English and probably even capable of simple communication in it. On their first day, Hirohachi noted that "in this country, we don't have any idea what people are saying, so we are in a real fix, and feel like deaf-mutes." Still, on the second day, he observed after sightseeing that "the people of this country look like Japanese. Their hair is black, their eyes are black, and they have a similar disposition to us."[5]

Hirohachi's sense of familiarity had historical roots, for Japan had a deeper relationship with both Spain and Portugal than any other European nation. After 1542, when a Portuguese ship was shipwrecked in Japan, Franciscan and Jesuit missionaries had arrived and begun to convert large swaths of southern Japan to Catholicism. In 1584, the Tenshō mission of young Japanese converts, dispatched from Japan on Spanish galleons, had even stopped in Spain and met King Philip II before proceeding on to Rome and an audience with the Pope. In 1613, another mission to Europe had left behind several members near Seville (where

Saltábamos ya al bote para tomar tierra, cuando
el aviso *Chismografía* nos comunica el enrolamiento
hecho en Lóndres por la direccion del Príncipe Alfonso, de la gran compañia imperial japonesa, capitan
Risley, que iniciará muy luego sus estraordinarios y
sorprendentes ejercicios.

One of the first, excited mentions to appear in a Madrid paper of Risley having
signed a contract to appear with the Imperial Japanese Troupe at the Alfonso. BOLETIN
DE LOTERIAS Y DE TOROS, JUNE 30, 1868.

hundreds of descendants today use the surname "*Japón*").[6] Fearing foreign encroachment and subversion, the rulers of Japan had soon thereafter banned almost all contact with foreigners, all travel abroad, and
Christianity. Catholic priests were banished or put to death in a myriad
of gruesome executions, and so were multitudes of Japanese Christian
converts. In 1640, when the Portuguese sent a ship to Japan to beg that
the ban on contact be lifted, the ship was burned and the crew all executed.[7] Reflecting this raw history, when the Imperials were in Spain,
local Madrid bookshops were still selling a popular illustrated history of
the "martyrs of Japan."[8] What the troupe members thought of all this is
unclear, but to them Christianity was still a prohibited foreign religion.
In his entire diary, Hirohachi never once mentions Christianity, in the
United States, northern Europe, or even the heavily Catholic Iberian
Peninsula.

What did fascinate Hirohachi in Spain was bull-fighting. His
descriptions of it take up more space than anything else. On July 5,
with wide-eyed wonder, he witnessed a bull-fight and described it as a
"battle" for life and death in a flat, round ring surrounded by spectators.
In great detail, he writes of how the bulls were killed by the cape-waving
men (the toreadors) and by lance-carrying men on horses (the picadors,
who goad the animals into attacking). He astutely notes, however, that
one of the additional highlights of bull-fighting was to see horses and
humans badly gored and sometimes killed by the bulls.[9]

Hirohachi's fascination with bull-fighting likely reflected the fact that, in the Japan of his era, while fish were part of the regular diet, most people never ate meat, and killing animals was generally taboo. There is a limited tradition of bull-fighting in Japan in the Oki and Okinawan islands, but this would be more correctly described as "bull *sumo*," for there is no matador, and the bulls instead vie to push each other out of a small ring. Of the Spanish variant, Hirohachi writes, "Spain is the only country in the world where this bull-killing, where humans also lose their lives, is done."[10]

On July 7, the Imperials opened at the Prince Alfonso, performing with a circus, including an equestrian act. The Imperials were also competing locally with yet another equestrian-acrobatic act at the Circo de Price (newly formed by Britisher Thomas Price), and the regular bull-fights at the Plaza de Toros. Despite this, at the Prince Alfonso the Imperials proved hugely popular, and people had to be turned away at the doors. Reviews were also glowing, the *Diario Oficial de Avisos de Madrid* describing the Imperials' show as having an "extraordinary turn-out" and praising their daring and feats of balance but of course finding their music a bit odd. The ladder trick and Matsugorō's slackrope walking came in for particular approval, Matsugorō being described as nearly as flexible and lithe as a monkey, even though the reviewer could not resist comparing him to the "gorillas exhibited every day at the anthropological museum in Alcala." Another paper, *La Nueva Iberia*, described the balancing acts as "leaving behind all that we have understood about this type of performance."[11]

The mentions outside of Spain were even more laudatory, presumably because Risley fed his friends in the English-language media some irresistible tidbits. In both England and the United States, reports soon appeared that prominently mentioned Risley and variously declared that either (1) the Imperials had specially appeared by royal order before her Majesty Queen Isabella II and her court at the palace, or, (2) that the queen and her court had graced the Imperials with their presence at the circus, with over five thousand people in attendance.[12] Oddly, in his diary Hirohachi never mentions the queen's presence at a show, nor does there seem to have been much mention of her in the local Madrid media, but perhaps that was because she was so unpopular. She had only two months left on her throne. In September, she would be deposed in what came to be known as The Glorious Revolution—one of the seemingly endless insurrections and revolts that convulsed Spain at this volatile period of its history.

From Hirohachi's diary, we know that attendance at the Imperial Troupe's performances was "big" until around July 28. Then, perhaps because of the intense summer heat, it started to tail off. His entries thereafter describe more and more days with the annotation, "medium." In Madrid, as with nearly every other city where they had performed, the Imperials had to contend with the existing local entertainment, but at least audiences had not been exposed to other Japanese competitors. There were soon imitators, however, in the form of a burlesque, or parody, of their performances that appeared at the local Circo de Price.

Even if shows did not always sell out in Madrid and other Spanish cities, the Imperials occasionally made the news in entirely novel ways. In the press, for example, they were written about not just for their performances and exoticism, but for their extraordinarily successful entrepreneurship in retailing souvenirs at events. They had done this in other countries, too, but in Spain it attracted particular attention. As one Madrid newspaper noted, in addition to steep entrance fees, the Japanese were making "great profits" from selling prints that displayed their performances as well as small gold fans adorned with photographs of themselves.[13] Sumidagawa Namigorō, the butterfly-trick master, created a sensation beyond the circus ring. As another paper humorously noted (valiantly trying to reproduce his name properly), because of the "incomparable Zumindangarao Wamingaraoo . . . paper butterflies have become all the rage. . . . The arrival of the Japanese company has created a domestic revolution. Houses are filled with paper butterflies; artists, employees, merchants, all are ignoring their more pressing work and passing their idle moments trying to fan life into a new species of Hymenoptera [butterfly] from the pages of paper books. . . . "[14]

The major exception to the days with so-so attendance was a grand finale held in Madrid on August 30 and 31. The Imperials then performed at the Prince Alfonso and at the Plaza de Toros, where an extraordinary extravaganza was staged. Fifteen different events were advertised. There

RECUERDOS DEL AÑO DE 1868.

compañia imperial japonesa ó sea la compañia imperial de los demonios.

As a cartoon in an 1869 Madrid almanac suggests, the Japanese made a big impression on the locals: "Record of the year 1868—'The Imperial Japanese Troupe was an Imperial Troupe of Demons.'" *L'ALMANAQUE DE EL CASCABEL*, 1869.

was a regular equestrian circus complete with clowns and acrobats and a real lion act. The Imperials appeared in the middle of the show. (The program printed in the local newspapers listed both the individual Japanese performers' names and their acts.) The Japanese were followed by the grand spectacle of a balloon ascension by Alexandre Braquet,

COMPAÑÍA IMPERIAL JAPONESA.

Cartoon lampooning the Imperial Japanese Troupe, including their music and fashion, in a popular Madrid periodical of satire. From left to right: (1) The view of the Japanese presentation from the roof. (2) "La Senorita" (3) One way to get fresh air (4) The Japanese orchestra: Like a concert of mice (5) The artists, up to a point. GIL BLAS, NO. 80, AUGUST 9, 1868.

with music provided by the band of the Mallorcan regiment. Hirohachi wrote, "There were over ten thousand spectators, and we had to shut the doors, many foreigners going home unable to see the show." His use of the phrase "ten thousand" may have been inflated and figurative, but on August 31, he annotated his entry for the attendance of the day using the ideograms for "big" twice in a row, which was exceedingly rare.[15]

On September 2, the Imperials traveled by train over the mountains to Barcelona, a city that Hirohachi describes as bigger, prettier, and more prosperous than Madrid. Compared to northern Europe, Spain was late to the Industrial Revolution and a bit of a backwater, but Barcelona, the center of Catalonia and a bustling port city on the coast, was in the forefront of developing light industries such as textiles and crafts. It was also in the forefront of incorporating the cultural and intellectual changes occurring in the outside world.

The Imperials stayed in Barcelona only two weeks, but they were able to perform there in what Hirohachi describes as Spain's "most beautiful theatre"—the famously ornate and still-beloved opera house, the Gran Teatre del Liceu—where they opened on September 3. Hirohachi liked Barcelona a great deal, and his diary indicates that the attendance was big, except for three days where it was medium. His entries on Barcelona are notably brief, however, as he was not feeling well and had developed a problem with his eyes, for which he began seeing a doctor. At this point, it is hard not to speculate that Hirohachi may have been suffering from some sort of venereal disease, but other than affecting his vision and making it difficult for him to savor the local nightlife, it appears not to have put much of a crimp on his ability to function. He did manage to do some sightseeing and even to buy some inexpensive coral souvenirs. His mind was slowly starting to focus on his return to Japan.

As they had in Madrid, before departing Barcelona the Imperials moved from the Liceu to the local bullring, allowing them to accommodate an even bigger crowd. They performed there in another extravaganza similar to that of the Madrid finale, complete with the same acrobat-balloonist, who performed another grand ascent in a hot-air balloon named the "Prince Alfonso."

In a remarkable conclusion to the Imperials' stay in Barcelona, Hamaikari Sadakichi, the unofficial leader of the troupe, did something very unusual. He delivered a message to the public that was reprinted in the local newspaper, the *El Principado*, on September 17. Hamaikari could neither speak nor write Spanish (nor Catalan, the language of Barcelona, nor English, for that matter) and no one in Barcelona at the time could likely understand Japanese, so the message presumably was first translated by Edward Banks into English, and then—unless Banks himself was also fluent in Spanish—translated into Spanish. Or it may have been written by Banks or Risley in English to reflect Hamaikari's sentiments and then translated into Spanish and reworked by the newspaper editor. Process aside, the final version, translated back into English, reveals a distinctly non-Japanese sentiment in the last line, for Japanese normally do not invoke higher deities in speeches, and they never invoke the name of the Hindu creator, Brahma.

Gran Teatre del Liceu, restored today and still in use. © 2012 RICARD BRU I TURULL.

To the Public: It has been only three months since our Troupe first set foot on the beautiful soil of Spain. In that time our hearts have been touched, and we are filled with gratitude and appreciation for the extremely

warm welcome we have received from the respected citizens of this cultured and industrious city. As a humble token of our gratitude we offer to the public our combined farewell performance. And may the Great Brahma protect and shine his light upon us all.
—Hamaikari, the Director[16]

The Imperials had originally planned to stay in Spain only one month and then return to England and tour the provinces again, but they wound up staying nearly three months, giving the troupe what seems to have been a disproportional local influence.

Aside from Hirohachi's diary, much of what we know about the details of the Imperials' visit to Spain comes from Dr. Ricard Bru i Turull of Barcelona. An art historian and curator, he specializes in the history of *Japonisme* in Spain, especially in Barcelona. In 2011 he published a 1,134-page book on the subject (in Catalan), and in it he concludes that the Imperials helped to trigger a later boom in interest in Japanese arts and entertainment in both Madrid and Barcelona, and especially the latter.

In both North America and northern Europe, after Commodore Perry's 1853 mission to Japan, there had been a boom in all things Japanese. But not so in Spain. Japan concluded treaties of some sort (usually amity and commerce) with the United States starting in 1854, and with Britain, Holland, Russia, France, in 1858, but not with Spain until after the Imperials left, in November 1868. The Imperials were thus the first direct exposure Spaniards had to Japanese, and especially to Japanese popular culture, after having been cut off for nearly 250 years. They thus helped bring about a new view of a country until then remembered mainly for its persecution and martyrdom of Christians in the seventeenth century. As Bru i Turull notes, the Imperials were long remembered and talked about in Barcelona in particular, where they served as a frame of reference for later acts. The interest they generated sparked a new diversity in spectacles in the 1870s and 1880s, with theatres and circuses scheduling more and more Japanese and Japan-themed shows. And as the years went by, in the theatre this "Japonisme" manifested itself more and more in operas, operettas, plays, parodies of Japanese, and even masked balls.[17]

The Imperials still had other Spanish cities on their agenda after Barcelona, but their influence there would be diluted, for they were about to be swept into a political maelstrom. They quickly packed up after their Barcelona finale and, on September 18, took the train to the coastal city of Valencia. Some tunnels they passed through were so narrow it seemed to Hirohachi as though "there wasn't even room to fit a fingernail" between the train and the walls. They arrived in Valencia in the evening, and were put up in a "cheap lodging house" where the conditions were so bad the troupe members became angry. But when they opened the next day, a Saturday, they had a big turnout. On Sunday, Hirohachi went to see a bull-fight, but his eyes were getting worse, and he had two physicians treating him. Then, on September 23, the turnout for their performance was only middling, and it continued that way until September 27. That day, Hirohachi wrote in his diary, "A big war has started in this country, and horse carriages, steam trains, and steamships cannot get through; the roads are blocked, and we cannot perform. . . . "[18]

A Republican fleet of warships was shelling the town. With shells and rocks flying outside and crowds surging, the Imperials were in a state of shock. Hirohachi writes forlornly that because of his eye problems he had to stay indoors alone, implying that the other members of the troupe may have gone somewhere else or even been evacuated. As it was, they were forbidden by local officials to perform, and all the shops in the town were shuttered. Finally, on October 1, the fighting calmed down and people began celebrating. Hirohachi notes:

> This is a war of people throughout the land revolting against their ruler, whose governing is bad and interferes in too many things because she is a queen, but it appears that she has realized she has lost and fled to France, where she is under the wing of the French ruler.[19]

Discounting the implied sexism, it was an accurate summary of what had happened, and probably an opinion formed from information fed Hirohachi by Risley and Banks. The queen of Spain, Isabella II, had indeed fled. She had first assumed the throne in 1833 at the age of three, with her mother serving as a regent. She grew into a woman of considerable bulk who was forced to marry her diminutive and effeminate cousin, Francis, the Duke of Cadiz. Highly unpopular, she was regularly accused of meddling in all sorts of things. Her right to be queen was contested even among other Bourbon royal family members, such as the Carlists, who believed that as a female Isabella was not entitled to inherit the throne. Her rule was therefore wracked with intrigues, near-rebellions, revolts, and it ended in what is known today in Spain as the Glorious Revolution. Starting in Cadiz, and led by disaffected military figures such as General Juan Prim and Admiral Juan Bautista Topete, Republican forces sent Isabella fleeing to France and the protection of Emperor Louis Napoleon, who would himself soon be deposed by his own people.

Hirohachi notes in his diary that in witnessing the fighting the Imperials were "shocked," but that was probably an understatement. They had certainly never seen nor heard anything resembling a war in their lifetimes. Although it is true that, since their departure from Yokohama at the end of 1866, fighting had taken place between the shogun and the imperial forces, this was an aberration in recent Japanese history, and they seem to have been unaware of it. Under the shogun's feudal rule, Japan had experienced an almost unprecedented period of peace for nearly 250 years. Save for occasionally hearing about foreign warships lobbing shells into Japanese coastal towns, or samurai cruelly suppressing revolts by starving peasants, ordinary Japanese in the mid-nineteenth century knew nothing of warfare. Guns had been largely banned, swords normally were carried only by samurai, and people were so used to the status quo that the idea of deposing the supreme leader of the land was next to unthinkable.

On October 2, the Imperials resumed performing in Valencia but no one came. This continued for the rest of their stay, except on Sunday, October 4, when attendance was "medium." Then, on Monday, all of the fighting was finally over. No one came on the 5th, and on the 6th the Imperials took a few days off. On the 9th, Hirohachi's diary has a cryptic note about two years being up, going to see Banks, and having some "difficult negotiations." It is not clear exactly what transpired, but modern Japanese writer Yasuoka Shōtarō, among others, believes a dispute may have arisen over when their contract would end, in part because Hirohachi was using the only calendar system he knew—the diabolically difficult lunar calendar of China and Japan, and not the more accurate and modern European, Gregorian one. As even Hirohachi admits later in his own diary, with no frame of reference (beyond his own counting for two years), he had been flummoxed in keeping track of the date. Be that as it may, on October 11 the Imperials finally resumed performing with a bull-fight, and also with a balloon ascension, and enjoyed good attendance. Two days later, they left by train, traveling through the day and night inland to Seville, again passing through mountains and tunnels at which Hirohachi marveled.[20]

The Imperials opened on October 15 in Seville to a large crowd, but for the remainder of their stay in the city the attendance was only middling. On the fifth day, Hirohachi was still suffering from his eye disease, but he notes in his diary that he, Hamaikari Sadakichi, and Sumidagawa Namigorō went to Banks's room and had an argument with him that did not go well. It was again, presumably, about their contract. The Imperials ended their run in Seville on October 21, and for the next few days, until the twenty-sixth, their whereabouts is not entirely clear because there is vagueness in Hirohachi's entries. Japanese historian Mihara Aya believes that the troupe may actually have opened in Malaga, on the coast, but wherever they were, they had rather poor attendance. On at least one day, no one came even though they were on a double-billing with bull-fighting. They continued to perform, but on October 24 troupe members appear to have had another dispute with either Banks or Risley about pay and refused to work.[21]

Portugal

On October 30, the Imperials left Spanish territory and traveled by steamship to Portugal. They stayed one night on Gibraltar (which Hirohachi correctly identifies in his diary as being British territory) and arrived on the morning of November 2 in Lisbon, where they had a two-week run. Attendance was good in Lisbon, with Hirohachi noting "big" in his diary every day except one day when it was "medium," and two days when he wrote the rare annotation of "double big," or "huge." They performed in the evening and in the day went sightseeing, and they bought more and more souvenirs. Their minds were turning to Japan. Hirohachi notes, "We are now basically on our way home."[22]

On November 19, the Imperials traveled about 200 miles north by train to Porto, a picturesque city on the banks of the Douro River estuary on the coast of Portugal. Known for its bridges and its wine (whence comes the name "port wine"), Porto also proved good to them, for they stayed and performed for another two weeks, enjoying a good turnout most days. When not performing, they went sightseeing. On November 24, they appeared as part of a rare triple-billing, along with an equestrian act and some singers.[23]

Hirohachi made few observations of Portugal in his diary, other than to note that Lisbon seemed to be a bustling area and that he found Porto a "pretty place, a big place, and a good place." After what the Imperials had gone through in Spain, they were probably relieved simply to be in a more politically stable area, even if it was a bit backward. Portugal had shed much of its once vast global trading empire and imperial glory, but it was still being ruled by King Louis I and, unlike Spain, its monarchy would survive continuously into the twentieth century. Hirohachi may also have felt a vague affinity with the local people, as he did in Spain.

Like Spain, Portugal had long ago had a brief but rich period of interaction with Japan, but then relations had been violently severed during Japan's period of seclusion. Still, Portugal had resumed relations with Japan much earlier than Spain, in 1860. And because of the early Portuguese influence, even more than in Spain, the Imperials would have heard many familiar words being spoken. Even today, Japanese preserves traces of early Portuguese (and Spanish) influence, in the form of adopted words such as *pan* ("bread," from *pão*), *buranko* (a "swing," from *balanço*), *kyarameru* ("caramel," from *caramelo*), *tabako* (*tabaco*) and *kappa* ("cape," from *capa*).

While still in Porto, on November 29, Hirohachi made an entry in his diary that is typical in its brevity and matter-of-factness, yet hints at what was a profoundly emotional moment for all the Japanese troupe members.

> We gave both matinee and evening shows, and then cel-
> ebrated the conclusion of our run here. We have been
> working for two years, or seven hundred and thirty
> days, and we are now free to do as we please.[24]

As noted earlier, the original contract signed in Yokohama by Ris-ley, Banks, Schiedt, and Brower—the initial partners in the venture to bring the Imperials to the West—was reproduced in an 1868 lawsuit in New York. The contract was clearly signed by the four principals on November 1, 1866, and it notes that the performers were supposed to accompany Banks, Schiedt, and Risley "to the United States and Europe for the term of two years or more from the day and date of their embar-kation from this port [Yokohama] for San Francisco . . . "[25] Exactly when Risley or Banks concluded some sort of initial agreement with the Japa-nese members of the Imperials is less clear, but it was presumably before the contract among the principals was signed. A letter dated October 18, 1866, from Risley to the *Daily Alta California* in San Francisco indicates that he had already reached an agreement with Japanese performers, but we have no idea if this refers to an oral or written agreement.[26] If Hiro-hachi's diary entry is correct, however, we can assume that the formal period of their employ started sometime around the end of November 1866, a week before they left Japan. Yet this is itself only approximate. Hirohachi's dates were occasionally off because of differences between the Gregorian calendar and the Japanese lunar calendar, and the Imperi-als' actual departure had been delayed partly because of a huge fire that broke out in Yokohama while they were still in harbor.

For Hirohachi, their agreement with the Shogunate back home was probably even more important than the dates on their contract with their American producers. Because a copy of the "passport" of Sumidagawa Namigorō—the troupe's juggler and butterfly trick expert—survives, we know not only that the troupe members received Japan's first official passports for ordinary citizens, but that they were issued on November 23, 1866, permitting them to travel abroad for a two-year period, and to tour six countries.[27] Now, over two years had passed, and they already had toured seven countries. And even with these passports, there would always have been an uncertainty and fear lurking in their minds. During the over two centuries of Japan's official seclusion from the outside world, the few Japanese who had left had sometimes not been allowed to return. Shipwrecked sailors who had been successfully repatriated by Americans or Russians occasionally had spent years under house arrest and undergone long interrogations. And there was always the vague threat of execution.

Back to France

On December 2, the Imperials left Portugal on a steamer for Le Havre, the port town in Normandy, facing the English Channel. It took them five days, and most of the time it was stormy, making the troupe terribly seasick. On December 6, three of the troupe—elder representatives Hirohachi, Hamaikari Sadakichi, and Sumidagawa Namigorō—disembarked and traveled to Paris, arriving the following day. In Paris, they apparently hoped to consult with Prince Akitake, whom they had met during the Paris Exposition and who had left them a huge tip of appreciation after seeing their performances. It is hard to imagine Japanese commoners, especially demimonde entertainers, directly approaching the shogun's younger brother in 1868, but they nonetheless tried to do so, desperate for advice and knowing no other Japanese in Europe who could render it. They were crushed to learn that Akitake had already returned to Japan. One of Akitake's samurai retainers had remained behind in Paris, however. While he could not help them, from him they did learn, to their shock, that there had been a "big battle" in Japan and that fighting had even spread to places like Ueno in the capital, Edo (Tokyo). They therefore resolved to hurry back to Le Havre to tell the others.[28]

Back in Japan, after the arrival of Commodore Perry and the U.S. Navy in 1853, many people had felt humiliated and threatened, and calls for radical change had slowly built up. Although Japan had been one of the most stable nations on earth for 250 years, while the Imperials were touring America and Europe a revolution of sorts had indeed occurred. Forces composed mainly of samurai from the southern Chōshū and Satsuma domains (who supported the restoration of the Kyoto emperor to power), had defeated the Shogunate's forces in battle, and on November 9, 1867, the shogun had formally relinquished his power to the emperor, who had for centuries been kept powerless and secluded in Kyoto. Disagreements nonetheless broke out, and fighting continued in Japan between the Imperial forces and die-hard remnants of the Shogunate until the middle of 1869, but the game was up long before that. Once backward and feudal Japan was about to plunge into a frenzy of modernization, and the social changes that would result would be dizzying in their scope.

How Hirohachi did *not* know of the changes occurring in Japan is one of the central mysteries of his otherwise fairly reliable diary. Even allowing for a time lag in communication in the mid-nineteenth century, news of the revolution in Japan arrived in Europe quite quickly, with articles about the shogun having initially given power back to the emperor appearing in the British press in January 1868, and subsequently in other nations throughout the continent. In Paris, the shogun's younger brother, Akitake learned of the change of power on January 26, and on July 4, he had received a summons from the new government ordering him home, where he would be stripped of his royal privileges.[29]

The Imperials spent nearly three weeks performing in Le Havre and its environs. On November 23, they had been advertised in *Le Figaro* in Paris as being directed by Monsieur Risley, with the announcement: "Good news for fans of non-European acrobats. The famous Japanese, the only ones, the true ones, the ones we applauded together with the young brother of the Tycoon, are returning to perform in Paris at the Cirque Napoleon."[30] But whether they actually appeared there is unknown.

New York Again, at Last

At four in the morning on New Year's Day 1869, the Imperials left Le
Havre by the steamer *Ville de Paris* for New York. According to Hirohachi, it was a small ship and a rough two-week voyage in which they were
buffeted by terrible storms and fed awful food. They were seasick, and
the ship rolled so violently that it was all they could do to avoid being
tossed out of their bunks. Hirohachi at one point described the ship
itself as having been "turned upside down." When they pulled into the
harbor in New York on January 14, they "all sighed with relief."[31] The
ship's manifest survives, with the arrival mistakenly dated by the captain
as "January 14, 1868" instead of 1869. The Japanese members were all
individually listed with the surname "Banks."[32]

To the Imperials, New York must have at first seemed like a home-
coming. They had been gone over a year, they were exhausted from their
rough voyage, and it was bitterly cold and snowing, yet they were at last
back in familiar territory. Surprisingly, however, Risley was unable to
find a venue for them to perform. Given that his younger son, Henry,
had become an event organizer of certain renown in Philadelphia and
happened to be organizing a gala masquerade that same week in New
York, one might mistakenly assume that this would have conveyed some
advantages to Risley. The Imperials spent the first few days resting in their
hotel, but from Hirohachi's entries it is clear that they soon found themselves in a double-bind. Risley finally arranged for them to appear in a
vacant slot in The Tammany, a "Monster Place of Amusements," doing
matinee and evening performances starting on January 23. He had already
started running ads for them, but Banks had also not paid the Imperials
what they expected. The fact that the term of contract was up may have
complicated matters and made compensation on more of a per diem basis,
contingent on performing. Since the Imperials had not been performing
during their voyage and idle time in New York, the Americans may have
been reluctant to pay them. But the troupe members were also probably unwilling to perform because they had not been paid. Tensions were
clearly surfacing between the Japanese and their managers, and to resolve
this quandary Banks had to mediate between them and Risley.[33]

The initial advertisements Risley used for the Imperials at Tammany Hall were slightly different from those he usually employed. Perhaps reflecting fatigue, they were less clever, less creative, and contained remarkable, new hyperbole. The one that ran in the *New York Times* on January 22 stated:

THE WORLD-FAMED RISLEY TROUPE OF
JAPANESE
Who were the first to bring among the Caucasian races
the wonderful and mystic arts of CONTORTION
AND EQUIPOISE
In their most finished forms, which startled the
civilized world, and were the immediate occasion
of bringing the insulated Empire of the Pacific into
commercial relations with the great continents, has
returned to this City, after a
TRIUMPHAL TOUR OF THE EUROPEAN
CAPITALS,
And previous to their departure for Japan, commence
a brief
FAREWELL ENGAGEMENT AT THE
TAMMANY.[34]

At the Tammany, the Imperials were only one of many acts. It had been nearly twenty months since their first appearance in New York, and now they faced audiences who had already seen multiple Japanese performing groups. As one *New York Times* writer lamented, "They fail to satisfy the craving for that which is new."[35] Also, the controversy over Little All Right and his accident, which had caused many people to believe him dead, had been inflamed in his absence, partly because of imitators who had appropriated All Right's name. For the initial performances at the Tammany, therefore, Risley felt compelled to not only pull out all the stops in his advertising, but to also prove the genuineness of his troupe and his young prodigy. On January 25, the advertisement in *The New York Times* emphasized:

It should be understood that the WONDERFUL RIS-
LEY JAPANESE TROUPE are the GREAT ORIGI-
NALS. The troupe contains and presents the original
and favorite LITTLE ALL RIGHT, who was errone-
ously reported by several newspapers to have expired
from the SERIOUS ACCIDENT WHICH BEFEL
him during his PERILOUS PERFORMANCE in
this CITY at the ACADEMY OF MUSIC. Upon this,
his first reappearance in this City, he will be accompanied by his father and Prof. Risley, who will READ
TO THE AUDIENCE the certificate of his convales-
cence from the very eminent Doctor Carnochan, who
attended him.[36]

To further boost the Imperials' chances, Risley also advertised what
had miraculously survived their long journey—"A magnificent Scene
illustrative of the peculiarities of the JAPANESE EMPIRE, painted
expressly for Prof. Risley's production at HER MAJESTY'S OPERA
HOUSE, and which escaped the conflagration of that AMUSEMENT
TEMPLE, which will decorate the stage of THE GRAND THEATRE
TAMMANY during the performance of the Japanese."[37] If Risley
seemed somewhat desperate, it immediately lent itself to parody. Sure
enough, a burlesque was soon staged nearby at Bryants, parodying Risley's use of "certificates" to prove that All Right was indeed all right.

On January 27, 1869, disaster struck. Hirohachi's entry for that day
is short, understated, and cryptic, but it hints of astonishment and rage. It
consists of less than fifty Japanese characters, and the first part of it is not
entirely clear. Japanese tends to be vague by nature, with much meaning
implied. Given Hirohachi's poor education and use of dialect, parsing his
notes is especially difficult. The first part seems to say merely that "the
foreigner [Risley] is dumbfounded by Banks; he has absconded from
New York and no one knows where he is." Yet the consensus of modern
Japanese scholars of the diary is that this means Banks absconded with
all the monies due the Japanese troupe. The second part of the entry is
far clearer, for Hirohachi succinctly states: "Banks is a true scoundrel." [38]

A quarter of a century later, butterfly-trick master Namigorō remembered the event in even greater detail. After arriving in New York, Banks had not paid the performers their due, and worse yet, they had woken up one day to find that the water in their hotel didn't work and that the owners were refusing to feed them, per the usual agreement, because they, too, had not been paid. In desperation, Namigorō went to Banks's lodging, only to spot the man's luggage in front of his room, as if about to check out. Fearing Banks was planning to abscond, he barged into the room and caught him there. Namigorō's memory of what then happened evokes an entertainer from another world, where loyalty and humanity sometimes trumped money, at least in the retelling.

> He had his hands together, pleading "Please, have mercy!" I knew it was all up to me. He had come all the way to Japan and been together with us for a long time. Aside from the fact that he hadn't paid us I didn't have much against him, I had enough money to at least eat at that point, and it didn't seem right not to have some compassion for him, so I said, "Don't tell anyone that I saw you, and I won't tell anyone that I let you go; let's leave, pretending nothing ever happened." With that, I left. Banks, begging forgiveness, apparently took off for Philadelphia.[39]

In the world of mid-nineteenth-century circus, it was certainly not unheard of for managers to embezzle or abscond with the monies due their semi-literate demimonde performers. But why Edward Banks—a former U.S. Marshal, a full partner in the Imperials' venture, the interpreter for the Japanese, the manager of their day-to-day needs, and the disburser of their pay—would sully his name with such a dastardly action, is a mystery that may never be solved, for he subsequently disappears from the historical record.

Only a few days later, on February 6, Hirohachi indicates in his diary that the performances at Tammany Hall had ended, that the members had all made their final decision on whether to return to Japan, and that all were happy. Out of the surviving seventeen members of the troupe, eight, led by Hirohachi, had decided to go back to Japan. Nine—including the stars Hamaikari Sadakichi and Umekichi, or Little All Right—elected to take a new, generous offer from Risley and stay to perform longer in the West under his direction.

On February 10, accompanied by the returnees, Hirohachi left New York on the long journey back to Japan. He would travel by steamer down to the Isthmus of Panama, cross over by land, sail on another steamer up to San Francisco, and then transfer to yet another steamer to cross the Pacific for Yokohama, not arriving home until the end of March. Risley would continue to use the name of the Imperial Japanese Troupe, but it was the end of the group as originally constituted, and they would never regain their former glory.

ACT 10
Final Acts

"The stage had an attraction that he could not resist."[1]
—Obituary for Risley in *The Patriot*, May 28, 1874

Of the original Imperial Troupe members, the eight who left for Japan in early 1869 were mainly older male performers in their thirties and forties, especially from the Hamaikari family. They also included a grown female, Tō, of the Sumidagawa family, and Tsune, the young daughter of Matsui Kikujirō who had passed away in London. Whatever happened to "Victoria," born in London, is unknown. Many of the members had official roles as musicians playing the *samisen*, flute, and drums. While Risley might have wanted to continue touring with a full complement, it appears that he had been able to cherry-pick the performers most marketable to Western audiences—the acrobats and top-spinners and tightrope walkers and butterfly tricksters. Japanese music, he had discovered, did not go over very well in either America or Europe.

Hirohachi and the other returnees arrived back in Yokohama on March 31, 1869, forty-nine days after leaving New York and nearly two and a half years after having first left Japan. The first thing Hirohachi did was to report to the Yokohama authorities, probably with considerable nervousness. Luckily for him, the feudal Shogunate—which had initially issued the troupe members' passports and might have been in a position to punish them for their delay in returning—had collapsed in their absence. A new era—that of Emperor Meiji, who would lead Japan into its breathtaking and headlong plunge into the modern world—had begun. At the local offices of the new government, Hirohachi was merely told to return the troupe members' passports and to explain the circumstances under which they had left Japan, the death of poor Matsui Kikujirō in London, and the decision of the other nine members to continue performing abroad. He was asked to provide detailed information on those who still remained overseas, including their names, ages, and appearance. When they returned, he was told, their passports and information would be sent to the new central government in Tokyo, and he might then have to appear again before the authorities. But in the meantime he and the other members were free to go. It was a huge relief, and the last entry in Hirohachi's diary, dated March 31, conjures up a vision of a deliriously happy group, celebrating their miraculous return.[2]

The returnees must have felt a bit like Rip Van Winkle. Because Hirohachi had had no way of correlating his diary entries with the complicated Japanese lunar calendar system, he had rounded off each month as thirty days; on arrival in Japan he found that his entries were nearly two weeks off. Moreover, Japan was still in the midst of a huge transition. Some Shogunate forces were making their last stand, in the far north, on the island of Hokkaido. Everything was still in great flux. In the next twenty years Japan would go from being a feudal nation to Asia's first rapidly industrializing nation. Top-knots would soon be banned for men. Japan's traditional four-tiered class system would be abolished, and samurai would be prohibited from wearing swords and stripped of most of their special privileges. People would start dressing in Western clothes, eating meat, working in factories, traveling freely within Japan and occasionally abroad, and even learning English. The government would be quickly remolded in emulation of Western powers with a modern constitution, army, and navy. Nearly everything traditional would fall out of favor. And in the process, even traditional Japanese entertainments, such as the acrobatics and juggling skills that the Imperial Troupe represented, would fade from popularity, to be replaced by Western-style circus arts.

Most of the initial returnees thereafter vanish into history, but records of Hirohachi survive. He eventually returned to his hometown in what is now Iinomachi, Fukushima Prefecture, where he passed away in 1890 at the then ripe old age of sixty-nine. Stories live on in the area of him having returned in grand style, riding a white horse, with souvenirs of his travels abroad that included his beloved *samisen* and an unusual, octagonal Western-style wall clock. Something of a local eccentric, he is said to have liked to parade in *geta*, or wooden clogs, with a Western-style umbrella. At one point he may have married or lived with a woman who had a daughter, but they both later died of disease, so most of the time he was alone. He may have taught *samisen* and performed, or even acted as a landlord for income. The local children referred to him as "Amerika *jii-san*" (American "Grampa"). Adults, however, cautioned their children, saying, "If you don't work hard you'll wind up with nothing, like Hirohachi."[3]

The Imperials, Streamlined

The nine Japanese who remained with Risley did not find themselves idle. Because they no longer had a diarist and left no written records, save for newspaper accounts we have little information on their daily activities, or Risley's. From the press reports, we know that Risley was able to extend their run at the Tammany in New York, listing the Imperials in advertisements as "In the Full Tide of Success." And by the middle of February, he had moved them to his official hometown in America, Philadelphia, where they performed at the American Variety Theatre. The reduction in number of performers did not seem to have much effect on his advertising, and he either took to exaggerating their number or figured out some way to augment it, for the Imperials were billed as having "eighteen" members. Perhaps he also obtained an interpreter. Risley may have been capable of pidgin Japanese, and the Japanese by this time may have been capable of pidgin English, but without the interpreter Banks and Hirohachi it would have been extraordinarily difficult to discuss matters of critical importance, such as pay, schedules, and the presentation of acts.

In Philadelphia things went swimmingly. By February 27, an advertisement placed in the local *Philadelphia Inquirer* was already boasting:

PROFESSOR RISLEY'S IMPERIAL JAPANESE.
UNPRECEDENTED SUCCESS.
HOUSES CROWDED FROM ORCHESTRA TO
THE REAR OF GALLERY.
18,000! 18,000!! 18,000!!! 18,000!!!!
PEOPLE HAVE VISITED FOX'S AMERICAN
THEATER . . .

By March 8, Risley had moved the troupe to the Theater Comique.
He was advertising the Imperials as the "whole troupe," and also as "Risley's Imperial and Original Japanese Troupe." He began moving his company fast, perhaps reflecting a gradual saturation in audience interest in
Japanese acts and a need to not stay too long in one place. In mid-April
he was in Trenton, New Jersey; then in the third week of April he had
booked them into the New York Circus in New York City, where they
appeared until early May, advertised as not only Risley's "Originals" but
also "The Great Jeddo Group." As usual, their originality and the presence of All Right were highlighted. Later in May, they moved to the
Stadt Theater, then the Academy of Music in Brooklyn. On June 13,
Risley announced to New York papers that he was taking the troupe
to tour Britain, Germany, and Russia before the members returned to
Japan. He was thinking beyond his Japanese production, even planning
to import a group of Spanish dancers whom he held in particularly
high regard.[4]

There were some highlights during this period. According to the
New York Daily Tribune, sometime in the spring the Imperials paid a call
on the president of the United States (presumably Ulysses Grant), and
members of the president's family came to see them. But whether this
took place in New York or Washington, D.C. is unclear.[5] More than
before, the Imperials also had to perform with other groups. On May
19, while still appearing at the New York Circus, they could be found
at Niblo's Gardens, in one of New York's bigger theatrical events of

the year, a grand benefit for the Irish-American actor John Brougham. The Imperials appeared there with 150 other professionals, but with "the chief of the tribe, Hamicari [*sic*] and Little All Right performing their jar trick," an act not previously mentioned in playbills. Around this time, Denkichi was also being referred to as "Count Denkichi," a grand elevation from his low status back in Japan.[6]

Back to Britain

On June 23, the Imperials opened in Liverpool, at the Prince of Wales Theatre, billed as "Professor Risley's Original Imperial Japanese Troupe with the Wonder of the World, 'Little All Right.'" The *Liverpool Mercury* reported that there were twelve performers. They gave a thirteen-act presentation, and even though the audience was already used to Japanese acts such as the butterfly trick and top-spinning, people packed the hall to see the Imperials perform what still seemed novel routines such as the enchanted ladder trick, the transformation fox scene, and slackrope walking. The reporter declared that the Troupe "eclipses any performance of a similar nature which has yet been brought forward, either in the way of home product or of foreign importation." Risley must have felt gratified to read the review, for above and beyond being a famed former acrobat and impresario for the Japanese, he was also described in pioneering terms as being "intimately associated with much of the 'business' which forms the principal attractions of modern entertainments."[7]

Even with a stripped-down version of the Imperials, Risley was on a bit of a roll in Britain, but his momentum would soon come to an abrupt halt. On July 24, the troupe performed at a gala fete and charity benefit at London's Crystal Palace. Along with dozens of other top-rated London entertainers, they appeared before the Prince and Princess of Wales in an event that included plays and fireworks and specially illuminated fountains. In advertisements for this and other performances in London, Risley also started referring to Hamaikari Sadakichi, the elder of the troupe, as "Count Sadakichi." This simple tactic probably resonated well with class-conscious British audiences and may have reas-

Professor Risley's Imperial and Original Japanese Troupe poster, advertising the start of a series of performances at the Old Theatre Royal, in Bristol, at the end of 1869. © THE BRIT-ISH LIBRARY BOARD, EVAN 2806.

sured the hierarchy-sensitive Japanese performers, too, especially since the younger Denkichi had also been similarly promoted. And that same weekend there was great excitement off-stage as well. At Ashburnham Park in East Sussex, several of the Japanese were able to ascend in a captive balloon of the famous French airship pioneer Henry Giffard, accompanied by James Glaisher, a prominent meteorologist and early aeronaut. It was an experience that few of their countrymen, even the best connected, could ever boast.[8]

By mid-August the Imperials faced competition in London from yet another Japanese troupe that opened at the Egyptian Hall. Known as the "Royal Tycoon" group, it was led by Tannaker Buhicrosan, an enigmatic Eurasian character of Dutch and Japanese descent (at a time when such combinations were still exceedingly rare). Like the Imperials, the Royal Tycoon troupe comprised male and female performers who did balancing acts, top-spinning, butterfly tricks, and so on. They claimed the Duke of Edinburgh as patron.[9]

The Imperials moved to the Surrey Theatre and clearly felt it was time to tour the provinces again and make a preemptive strike against any imitators. On August 22 Risley took out the following notice in the entertainment-oriented newspaper *Era*, addressed to the "Directors and Managers of all Provincial theatres and Halls":

> PROFESSOR RISLEY'S IMPERIAL JAPANESE TROUPE, from the Court of Yeddo, with the Wonder of the World, Little All Right.
>
> The public is now quite satisfied that no other person or persons in the World can possess the least vestige of claim to the honourable distinction of the title of Professor Risley's Imperial Japanese Troupe, who have appeared before their R.H. the Prince and Princess of Wales, at the Theatre Royal Lyceum and Crystal Palace.
>
> Professor Risley wishes to caution the Provincial Public against Troupes calling themselves Japanese, and using Professor Risley's Posters and Bills, which have been surreptitiously obtained.[10]

One week later, Buhicrosan took out an advertisement for his group, emphasizing their uniqueness and genuineness, their patronage by the Duke of Edinburgh, and declaring them "the only Troupe now in London." In an apparent dig at Risley, he added, "The Proprietor also begs to inform the public that this *Troupe* is in no way connected with any persons or persons calling themselves Japanese, who are now travelling in the Provinces."[11] Later on, he would shamelessly add another member to his troupe whom he called Little All Right.

A "Dreadful and Humiliating Punishment"

Meanwhile, for Professor Risley, the main problem in 1869 was not imitators, but himself. In the mid-nineteenth century, Risley was far more than a colorful character; he was a global celebrity, known both for his acrobatic feats and for his skills as impresario and entrepreneur. In the media of the day, he had always been able to carefully cultivate and control his own celebrity. Yet on September 1 that all changed when he was arrested and arraigned in a London court. The charges were "unlawfully attempting to take one Maria Ann Mason, a girl under the age of 16, out of the possession of her father. *Third Count*—for soliciting, &c. Four other Counts, for common assaults."[12] During the course of his trial, Risley's name would appear in scores of newspapers in England and around the world, in a scandal of extraordinary proportions.

Detailed records of the trial and its proceedings show that it was a media event but one with legal significance. In the late nineteenth century, and especially in the Dickensian world of Industrial Revolution London, there was growing concern over the treatment of women and children. And there was a particular concern over trafficking in poor young women, who were being abducted and sold into white slavery, or prostitution, on the Continent. Protections for poor females were particularly weak. It was a felony to take a girl under sixteen out of the possession of her parents or guardians, but if she had no property, it was merely a misdemeanor.[13]

On August 17, the Imperials had been in the process of moving from the Surrey Theatre to Nottingham, but while in London, Risley was spotted "accosting" a young girl named Maria Ann Mason near Leicester Square. She was twelve years and eight months old, on her way to visit a sister. He was said to have tried to persuade her to come with him, or at least to enter some coffee shops with him, offering her various enticements such as the ring on his finger, a new dress, and some apples, and at one point taking hold of her cape or jacket. His actual intent was never made entirely clear, but the girl was never harmed in any way, and she later testified that Risley was very kind in his speech to her. Unfortunately for Risley, the interchange was witnessed by a Mr. Henry Hales, who happened to be a budding newspaper reporter with a heightened passion for law enforcement and social justice. Hales followed Risley over an hour and a half and said that Risley had approached several other young children, too, but been rebuffed, and even had dirty water thrown on him by an irritated local resident. When Hales reported Risley to a constable on the beat, Risley was questioned. He first responded that his name was "Ricardo" (a name which he used occasionally, along with "Ristori") and that he was from a nonexistent address of 45 Surrey Street, from the Surrey Theatre. Seemingly unnerved, he eventually wrote his name down as "Ris" and said he was the "professor." Hales, it turned out later, knew of Professor Risley and may even have been to one of his shows; he seems to have been determined that Risley should face some sort of punishment, for he wrote letters to all the London morning newspapers about this incident. He had an extraordinarily detailed memory of everything that had happened, and at the trial he proved to be one of the main witnesses against Risley. A detective from Scotland Yard later found Risley at Nottingham and read him the charges, whereupon Risley replied (in an innocent fashion that could be misinterpreted by today's English speakers) that "If I did touch the girl it was with no bad intention. I am fond of children and I might have spoken to her in a fondling manner."[14]

After being indicted, Risley was released on bail. The actual trial took place in late October at the Central Criminal Court in Marlboro. Maria Ann Mason was represented by a Mr. Besley, on behalf of the Association for the Protection of Women and Children. The defense was conducted by three attorneys, including Montague Williams, who would much later mention in his autobiography that it was one of the more important cases he had ever undertaken.[15] The British legal system was not as developed as it is today, but the trial was postponed once, the proceedings were heavily covered by the media of the day, and a verdict was rendered on October 25.

The trial ultimately hinged on two points. First, the defense had to establish that it could not be proved that Risley had intended to abduct Maria or that he knew she was under the control of her parents. Second, it had to show that what was perceived as an "assault" may simply have been misinterpreted. Working against Risley was the fact that he was associated with the circus, which already had a terrible reputation when it came to treatment of children, and that he was quite the footloose bohemian. Witnesses included Maria, who was prettily dressed and cried much during the trial, her parents, her sister, Mr. Hales, and the arresting constable and detective. Under cross-examination some contradictions in Maria's story were exposed. Fatal to the prosecution's case, it seems, was the revelation that Maria, one of seven children, normally went by the nickname of "Cock Robin," a fact that caused the courtroom to burst into laughter. Also, on the day she met Risley, the sister she had been on her way to meet was not the married sister she had claimed, but a sister who was a prostitute. Particularly helpful to Risley were the large number of character witnesses the defense was able to enlist in his behalf. These were prominent Londoners, many of whom had known Risley for twenty-five, even thirty-five years. Their testimony greatly aided Risley (as well as later historians), for they shed light on the character and eccentricities of the aging impresario, described in the papers as "a stout, gentlemanly dressed man of fifty-six, and married."[16] It was, in nearly thirty years of press reporting about him, one of the few times that Risley's marital status was ever mentioned.

Mr. E.T. Smith, a well-known theatrical figure in Britain, testified that Risley was always kind and proper toward girls and children, but that he had a habit of pulling people by their clothes when conversing with them, and that as a former acrobat he sometimes held their arms so tightly that he made them black and blue. This again made the courtroom audience laugh. A Mr. Johnson also testified to Risley's always proper conduct, but said that he had a habit of nearly pulling people over when addressing them. Mr. Corbyn, a theatre manager who had met Risley in many parts of the world and also worked for him, said that he was in the habit of telling funny stories and was "a regular button-holder." He would "seize a person by the button hole, and, as he proceeded with his story, he would unbutton his coat all down." Another witness testified that Risley "was one of the most kind-hearted men he ever knew in his life. His conduct towards children was exceedingly proper and becoming."[17]

After a brief consultation, the jury returned a verdict of "not guilty," and loud applause broke out in the courtroom. Risley left the dock and was warmly congratulated by his friends, but the damage was great, not only to his name, but to his state of mind. The next week Risley wrote a touching letter that was published in *Lloyd's Weekly London Newspaper*, thanking his friends, counsel, and the press for their support.

> Though the verdict was unanimously and without hesitation given in my favour, there still seems to be a taint of suspicion remaining. Deeply sensible of the terrible degradation intended for me, I address the public with a view to assure all who know me now, and all who may know me hereafter, that I am guiltless, not only in deed, but in thought; not only legally, but morally. The accusation of "unlawfully taking hold" of a young child fell on me like a thunderbolt. It has caused me mental agony indescribable; and the manner in which my name has been held up before the public has been a dreadful and humiliating punishment for a crime not only never committed, but never for a moment contemplated. I may add, that I never meant to compromise the matter, but invited the fullest investigation, despite the exposure. The result has been complete exoneration.[18]

The End of a Long Run

Despite the distraction of the trial, the show had to go on. The stripped-down Imperials continued performing in the provinces. Less than a week after Risley's acquittal they were in Stuart Hall in Cardiff, Wales, to great press acclaim but modest audiences. Then they appeared in Exeter, where they were listed as "twelve male and female artistes, including the Great Little Wonder, 'Little All Right,'" in a production that was titled "A Night in Japan!" The troupe was, as the local paper said:

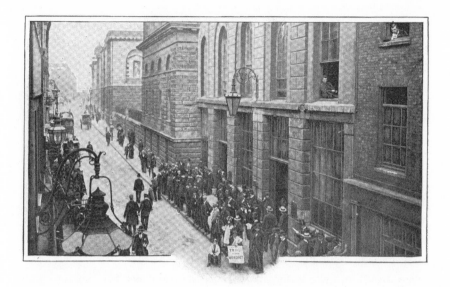

Outside "Old Bailey," or the Central Criminal Court of London, 1902. SIMS, GEORGE ROBERT, *LIVING LONDON; ITS WORK AND ITS PLAY, ITS HUMOUR AND ITS PATHOS, ITS SIGHTS AND ITS SCENES*, VOL.I, NEW YORK: CASSELL AND CO., 1902.

. . . characterized by its atmosphere of Eastern grotesqueness. . . .The halo of the Orient is around them in all their actions. Classical in their own land, they may be rightly accepted in this as the exponents of amusements which have for many centuries delighted the inhabitants of one of the least known but most singular countries of the earth—a country wherein a civilisation of its own has attained great development, and where the arts and sciences flourish under phases not unfamiliar to us, nor readily recognizable from our point of view.[19]

On December 27, in a special treat for the holidays, the Imperials appeared at the Olde Theatre Royale in Bristol for a six-night run. The local paper advertised their "new and astounding feats," highlighting Little All Right's marvelousness in the perch pole act with Hamaikari, and illustrating it with a memorable quotation from the *Times*:

> With as much facility as a squirrel ascents the gigantic
> oak in our English forests, so "Little All Right" climbs
> and balances on a bamboo cane, balanced on the shoul-
> ders of the chief without rest of socket, fixing himself in
> any part of it with his feet, stretching out his arms, and
> bowing gracefully to the company.[20]

The Imperials had performed in Bristol before, so the same advertisement billed their appearance as the "Return and Farewell Visit of
Professor Risley's Imperial and Original Japanese Troupe." What the
word "farewell" really meant in this context is unclear, but it seemed to
signify some sort of turning point in Risley's level of involvement with
the Japanese. Tellingly, for the amusement of the juveniles in such a festive season, Professor Risley had also specially engaged another act—that
of Monsieur Henrique and his Celebrated Troupe of Performing Dogs
and Monkeys.

Risley may not have been present for the whole engagement at Bristol. One British paper lists a "Professor Risley" as having embarked on
December 18 for Gibraltar, and Spain, perhaps to secure his long-adver-
tised Spanish troupe.[21] Yet on January 10, 1870, when the Imperials could
be found performing at Southsea, Risley—as logistically difficult as it
might seem—is listed as having joined them. The Imperials then moved
on to Brighton, and by the end of the month they had returned to the
Crystal Palace in London. On March 6, *The Era* reported that they were
on their way to St. Petersburg, Russia, without Risley.[22] But at the end of
April they appeared again in London playbills, back at the Crystal Palace.
After that, mention of them gradually disappears from the British press.

Risley next shows up in April at New York's Tammany Hall, with
his grand Spanish Ballet. He also has a "Great Anglo-European Variety
Show" at a place he started called the Hippotheatron. The acts at the
latter venue included a little bit of everything, even a dog and monkey
show, but the reviews were tepid. Risley's luck seemed to be running
out. By mid-June he was back in his home territory of Philadelphia, the
New York Evening Telegram ominously describing him as "taking Turkish baths and cleaning his skin of the dust of the coulisses in the city of

One of the last Imperial Japanese Troupe announcements that used Professor Risley's name, for performances at the New East London Theatre. Several weeks later, it was announced, Risley would return to America with a different troupe, and the Imperials would go to St. Petersburg. THE ERA, FEBRUARY 6, 1870.

THE LONDON PAVILION.— Important Announcement. The Proprietors of the London Pavilion have much pleasure in intimating that they have succeeded in effecting an Engagement with Professor Risley's Imperial Japanese *Troupe*, including the Renowned Little All-Right. They will make their first appearance on Monday next, Feb 7th ; and as they contemplate shortly returning to Jeddo, the opportunity will soon be lost of witnessing a performance as unique as it is astonishing, and similar to which nothing of the kind has ever been attempted. The whole of their truly wonderful performances will be introduced, and Little All-Right will be found quite "at home" in his peculiar and astounding achievements. Notwithstanding the expense attending the engagement of the above remarkable *Troupe*, and the maintenance of the general bill of fare in its usual attractive form, there will be no alteration in the prices of admission The greatest treat in London.

Brotherly Love. He has nothing in contemplation for which the public will be grateful."[23] Remarkably, he appears in the national census of 1870, on June 22 recorded as living in the 62nd District, 20th Ward of Philadelphia, but not with his wife Rebecca. He is listed as a fifty-six-year-old white male, with one male child over twenty-one, whose occupation is "at home."[24] At the end of January 1871, a benefit was to be held at the Academy of Music in New York for "Prof. Risley, who has not been very fortunate of late in his speculations. . . . ," but it was eventually cancelled because of a storm.[25]

There were still lawsuits for Risley to deal with. On April 21, Risley made the news again when he and Thomas Maguire filed suit against Thomas T. Smith, who several years earlier had managed the Tetsuwari Troupe, Risley's nemesis in San Francisco and later the "left wing" of Maguire & Risley's Imperial Japanese Troupe. It was a complicated lawsuit that referred to convoluted transfers of interest and $15,000 that was supposed to have been paid to Maguire and Risley. In October 1867, it was claimed, Smith had seized proceeds from exhibitions and converted them to his own use. Among other misdeeds, he had also taken the Tetsuwari faction to Cuba without the permission of Maguire and Risley (where he had advertised the troupe as the "Compa. Imperial Japonesa," and his star boy acrobat as "del pequeño All Right"). The judge was apparently convinced. He ordered Smith's arrest. When Smith was unable to post bail to the daunting sum of $10,000, he was hauled off to New York's Ludlow Street jail.[26]

Even when times were bad, Risley was still in motion. He seems not to have been in America when the actual lawsuit was filed, since he is listed as returning from Liverpool on a steamer named the *France*, which docked in New York on May 5, 1871. The passenger manifest, which survives, lists him as a sixty-year-old U.S. citizen whose occupation is a "professional."[27]

Despite his promotion of other acts, Risley remained involved with the Imperials, albeit in a more limited fashion. In the first week of June, they were listed in New York as having been folded into a giant production called John McDonough's TransAtlantic Novelty Troupe, which also included a prodigy violinist, a Viennese ballet, and black-face minstrels. But they were still "Prof. Risley's Imperial Japanese Troupe," with the "Original Little All Right." In this capacity they also appeared on June 10, in the Parshall Opera House, in Titusville, Pennsylvania.[28]

Thereafter, the trail of the Imperials starts to grow faint. There are fewer and fewer mentions of the troupe in the press. Some of the members eventually went back to Japan. As late as 1893, an old Namigorō gave a fascinating interview to a reporter, recalling that he had spent seven years touring in Europe before returning to Japan with his wife, son, and the costumer of the group.[29] Other former members may have stayed in the United States or Europe and melted into local society. Of the individual members, Little All Right was by far the biggest star, with a name recognition that rivaled Risley and became firmly associated with Japan, sometimes to the consternation of the Japanese themselves. In 1871, when the future naval hero of the Russo-Japanese War, Tōgō Heihachirō, studied at Cambridge, he was mistaken by a boy for a Japanese juggler and asked if he knew Little All Right. He had to explain that "jugglers and public entertainers belonged to a different class of society, and that therefore he knew nothing about 'Little All Right' or any of his companions."[30]

Yet after 1870 it becomes hard to distinguish Hamaikari Umekichi—the original All Right—from his legions of similarly-named imitators. A Little All Right—probably the real one—had a starring role in one of the world's first proto-motion pictures, a "Phasmatrope," developed by Henry Renno Heyl and screened in Philadelphia in 1870.[31] In 1871 there was a Little All Right performing with the Satsuma troupe in Australia. In January 1874, in New York, an All Right made the news because he was reported to have enrolled in a grammar school. In 1879, another All Right made the news again when performing at Harry Miner's Theater in New York. Miner was arrested by an officer of the Society for the Prevention of Cruelty to Children, who thought All Right to be too young for such dangerous stunts, but the charges were dropped when it was discovered the boy was sixteen. In reality, if the boy had been the real All Right, by 1879 he would have been twenty-three.[32]

Back in England, in 1874, Risley's former rival, Tannaker Buhicrosan, took out an advertisement in the *Era* that bore uncanny resemblance to Risley's previous one:

> As there are several Persons going round the Provinces using the word Japanese in their Advertisements, and giving a most miserable imitation of one or two minor feats, I CAUTION the Public to beware of such unprincipled Persons, as the only Real Japanese Performers (Natives of Japan) in this country are known by the following titles (Registered):—Tannakers, Little All Right, and Tommy the Wolf.[33]

Yet Tannaker's All Right was reportedly only about five years old. And a year and a half earlier, Tannaker had himself been fined ten pounds for mistreating one of his child performers.[34]

As for Risley, in October 1871, he was busy at the Globe, in New York, trying to manage a group of English acrobats and gymnasts he had brought over, but things were not going well. At the end of the same month, he was also advertising a new talent agency that he had started:

> NOTICE TO THE THEATRICAL PROFESSION OF THE WORLD: PROF. RICHARD R. RISLEY, Well and favorably known in early years, in conjunction with his sons, as the most classical and picturesque performers, having given their exhibitions in all the

Another "Original Little All Right," in a trade card advertisement for Col. T. E. Snelbaker's Majestic Consolidation, a variety troupe active in the 1880s. COURTESY OF DR. ROBERT H. SAYERS.

principal cities of the world with no paralleled success being presented with costly medals by all the crowned heads of Europe, and of late years known as a successful manager and caterer to the public taste, has decided on opening an INTERNATIONAL DRAMATIC AGENCY in his native city, Philadelphia. From his personal and professional acquaintance with artists and managers throughout the world, he flatters himself that he can offer to BOTH inducements to patronize his establishment. . . . Prof. R. Risley. . . .Communications in French, Spanish, Italian and German.[35]

Somewhat mysteriously, on March 13, 1874, a review of a new Risley production also appears in the Harrisburg, Pennsylvania *Patriot*. The previous night, at the local grand opera house, a company of Risley's, called the "Royal Japanese," had performed acrobatic, gymnastic, and posturing feats and been roundly applauded. There is no hint that this troupe had any relation to the Imperials, but the reviewer nonetheless wrote: "Prof. Risley manages an excellent show, one that will recommend itself wherever the troupe appears."[36]

According to one man who saw Risley in Philadelphia around this time in March, he appeared to be fine: "Although he looked his age, and walked as if stiff in the joints, he was well-dressed and had a handsome travelling bag in his hand."[37] A month later, however, at three o'clock in the morning on May 25, 1874, Risley died in the lunatic asylum of the Blockley Almshouse in Philadelphia. He was "broken down in constitution, and reduced from affluence to positive penury," reportedly devastated by what he saw as ingratitude on the part of some of his later acts, especially the English troupe members, who had deserted him. He was probably also distraught over the death a year earlier of his older son, John.

Risley's surviving son, Henry, had finally been forced to commit him to the insane department of Blockley, under the care of a Dr. Richardson, who did everything he could to restore him to good health, to no avail. After a short funeral, held at 35 South Thirteenth Street, and attended only by Henry and a few old friends from the theatre, he was interred at the Mount Moriah Cemetery.[38]

With his death, Risley received his last burst of global fame. Newspapers as far away as Australia ran obituaries for him. Reporters struggled valiantly to summarize his extraordinarily colorful and complicated life in a few paragraphs. The most succinct announcements, like the initial one in Britain's *Era* (which catered to the entertainment business), summed up his life as follows:

> RICHARD RISLEY CARLISLE, known as "Professor Risley," Died in a lunatic asylum in Philadelphia on the 25th of May. He was once an expert and popular gymnast. He brought over to this country the first *troupe* of acrobats from Japan.[39]

Few of the obituaries mentioned that he had introduced Western circus into Japan. And not all the obituaries were kind. A dislike of his usurpation of the word "Professor," a bias against the demimonde of the circus, and a focus on his penniless and lonely end in a lunatic asylum—all these things propelled the *Hartford Daily Courant* to overlook his accomplishments and present his death as a moral lesson:

> Between the truant boy of New Jersey and the insane pauper of Pennsylvania lay the checkered career of the accomplished mountebank, a sort of universal genius of the useless arts, who could do everything that there was no need of doing, and who after all his intermediate triumphs finally went to the bad as thoroughly as anyone could have prophesied from his early run-away, and thus furnished the valuable moral lesson that many, no doubt, will discern as applicable to other persons' wild sons at the present day.[40]

Still, for the remaining years of the nineteenth century, the memory of Risley and what he had done continued to loom large in the public's imagination. One of his panoramas continued to tour California and Australia long after he died. Impresarios tried to emulate his accomplishments with the Japanese, an "Imperial Japanese Troupe" touring Liverpool, England, as late as 1900. Acrobats imitated him, too, juggling others "à la Risley," one pair in Tasmania in 1890 going so far as to call themselves "Professor Risley and son."

All lives end. Risley's life may have ended abruptly on a down note, but he packed far more experience and adventure into his allotted years than most, traveling relentlessly, developing new acts and experimenting fearlessly, and treating the entire world as his audience. He was, above all, a pioneer in global entertainment.

AFTERWORD

In June, 2010, I visited the grave of Takano Hirohachi, the overseer of
the Imperials. He is buried at Taikeiji, a Rinzai Zen temple in Iinomachi, near the northeastern city of Fukushima, in a beautiful but remote
area of rolling green hills. I walked up to the temple on a hot summer day, when the cicadas were still chirping noisily. The abbot of the
temple, Aoki-san, was extremely gracious, despite my having arrived
unannounced. He gladly led me around to a well-tended cemetery in
the back, where cramped family plots with multiple tombstones cover
what, for Japan, is a fairly expansive area. Many of the older tombstones
had inscriptions that have worn faint over the centuries, making them
hard for visitors to identify, but Hirohachi's was then specially marked
with a white-painted wooden post planted in the ground next to it. The
paint on the post had started to peel, but the Japanese writing left on it
identified the tombstone as that of Hirohachi, who "first led a troupe of
Japanese acrobats on a tour of America and Europe" and the author of
a diary that, when finally published, "attracted nationwide attention." I
spent a long time waiting for the sun to move, hoping for the shadow
covering part of the tombstone to move away, but I eventually gave up
and took a photo anyway. While waiting, I had lots of opportunity to
reflect on the significance of both the Imperials, and of Professor Risley,
and the ephemeral nature of fame.

Of the gravesites of former members of the Imperials, Hirohachi's is
arguably the best known and frequented (the others are either unknown,
ignored or, like that of poor Kikujirō, who died in London, difficult

Takano Hirohachi's gravesite in June 2010. © 2012 FREDERIK L. SCHODT.

to access). There was a spike in visitors after his diary was rediscovered and published as a book in 1977 and, especially, a few years later, when popular author Yasuoka Shōtarō wrote his bestseller about the Imperials based on the diary. After I visited in 2010, the wooden grave marker was changed to a stone one by the local historical society. Today, however, visitors are again few and far between, and they are unlikely to return soon in any number. On March 11, 2011, fifty miles away on the coast, a horrific earthquake and tsunami devastated entire towns and caused what, for Japan, was an unprecedented nuclear power plant disaster and radiation leak. Taikeiji temple was spared major physical damage and, unlike a neighboring cemetery, most of its gravestones—including that of Hirohachi's—remained upright. The local residents were also spared a radiation-related permanent evacuation order, but a year later Abbot Aoki was still being careful to limit his intake of local vegetables and the time he spent outdoors.

In 1867, San Francisco's *Daily Morning Call* described Risley as a "famous man," whose "life and varied experiences will form a conspicuous chapter in some history of 'American Showmen,' to be written in the future." Yet nearly 150 years later, in both his homeland and in Europe today, Risley remains largely forgotten outside of a small circle of circus and performing arts aficionados. He is known best, not for bringing Western circus to Japan, or Japanese performers to the West, but for the "Risley act" that he popularized. His story would seem to be great fodder for a novel or a Hollywood movie, but other than an occasional mention in history books, and a tiny cameo role in a little-known 2007 historical novel titled *The Pure Land*, by Alan Spence, no one seems to have yet exploited his fascinating story.

I have never visited Risley's grave, and I'm not sure that I could find it today, even if I tried. Americans tend not to care for graves the same way Japanese do, but Risley's has been particularly neglected. He is interred in Philadelphia's once famous, popular, and sprawling Mount Moriah cemetery. Originally designed along a bucolic pastoral model in 1855 on fifty-four acres of land, in 2004 Mount Moriah was put on Philadelphia's "endangered properties" list. In the spring of 2011 it was officially "closed."

In Japan, it is safe to say, both Risley and the Imperials are better known than in North America. The story of the Imperials, in particular, has recently developed a certain amount of traction beyond the world of academia and performing arts. For one thing, for modern Japanese, recognition of the Imperials—and Japanese troupes that ventured abroad in the second half of the nineteenth century—involves a rediscovery of self.

In the rush to modernize that occurred after 1853, when Japan was forced to interact with the wider world, many indigenous performing arts traditions were forgotten and nearly became extinct. It is true that the aristocratic Noh plays and more popular Kabuki dramas live on, enjoyed by locals and tourists. But traditional *misemono* (spectacles), *kyokugei* and *karuwaza* (acrobatics), and itinerant street performers, came to be seen as old-fashioned and almost embarrassing, perhaps because of their lowly position in an originally feudal society. In 1893, old Namigorō, the butterfly-trick artist, gave a rare interview in which he complained that the Japanese public had come to believe several popular magic tricks were from the West, when in fact they had been taught to

Westerners by Japanese. Today, one of the few vestiges of early Japanese ladder and perch acts can only be seen at New Year, in the acrobatics of the *dezome-shiki*, performed by firemen dressed in traditional garb on ladders. More than anything, the degree to which traditional entertainments have submerged in the popular mind is reflected by the fact that the most commonly used word for "circus" in Japan today is the imported English "*saakasu*." And when young Japanese hear the word *saakasu*, they normally conjure up images not of traditional entertainment but of an older Western variant, with tents, pretty girls in tights taking risks on the trapeze, and mustached ringmasters with black top hats, tails, and a whip.

In this context, Risley and the Imperials received a big publicity boost in 2009 when they appeared in a Japanese comic book. In Japan, *manga*, or comic books, are a full-fledged mass medium enjoyed by the entire population, so stories in them can have enormous public influence. In 2009, noted manga artist Murakami Motoka created *JIN*, which was serialized in a manga magazine, compiled into paperback books, and also turned into a popular television series. In *JIN*, with a plot reminiscent of Mark Twain's *A Connecticut Yankee in King Arthur's Court*, a modern Tokyo brain surgeon finds himself transported back to, and stuck in, mid-1860s Edo, just as the Shogunate starts to crumble. With his knowledge of modern medicine, he survives by curing people's ailments and injuries. Many of his patients are real historical figures. In one episode, he treats none other than the acrobat Hamaikari Sadakichi, who has developed a herniated disk between his L4 and L5 vertebrae. By operating, the doctor makes it possible for Hamaikari to join the Imperial Japanese Troupe that Professor Risley is forming in Yokohama, and to go to America and the Paris Exposition. With remarkable fidelity to history, Murakami weaves the Imperials' story into his fanciful medical tale, and in the process also introduces Risley, Little All Right, and the feats performed by Hamaikari and family before foreigners in Yokohama.

★

Risley and the Imperials, including Little All Right, accept an ovation in Yokohama, as depicted in volume 15 of *JIN*, a serialized manga by Murakami Motoka. SHŪEISHA JUMP COMICS DELUXE. © 2009 MURAKAMI MOTOKA.

In my dreams, I sometimes imagine "Professor" Risley and his Imperial Japanese Troupe in a final act, rising through the fog of history. The music is discordant but mesmerizing. The stage designs are exotic, smoky old-fashioned lamps illuminating a faux Japanese landscape of the mind, perhaps showing a painting of a shrine's *torii*, an absurdly arching bridge, a few pine trees, and Mt. Fuji in the distance. After a florid introduction by Professor Risley, and demonstrations of thrilling and mysterious top-spinning, butterfly tricks, and assorted legerdemain, the Japanese perform impossibly difficult and dangerous acrobatic stunts in the limelight, but always with a special élan, grace, and humor. In the grand finale, Umekichi perches high off the ground on a cantilevered ladder contraption, executing complicated evolutions, teetering precariously but waving his fan ever-so-nonchalantly. Then, as the audience gasps, he shouts "Ayeee!" executes a perfect somersault, and alights on his feet on the stage, where he exclaims "All Right!" sending spasms of pleasure through the spell-bound audience. In the process, Risley and the Imperials once more bridge chasms of cultural differences and, for us, shed new light on the nineteenth-century world of brave global entertainment pioneers, now unnamed and long forgotten.

NOTES

Act 1: Setting the Stage

1   *Daily Alta California*, 19 November 1866.
2   *Daily Alta California*, 22 November 1866.
3   *Daily Alta California*, 1 December 1866; ibid., 5 December 1866.
4   *Daily Evening Bulletin*, 6 December 1866.
5   *Daily Evening Bulletin*, 8 December 1866.
6   *Daily Evening Bulletin*, 11 December 1866.
7   The Hepburn system of romanization, which today is a de facto standard for Japanese, did not become popular until the 1880s. It was first published by the missionary James Curtis Hepburn (to whom all students of Japanese owe a huge debt) in the third edition of his groundbreaking Japanese-English dictionary in 1886.
8   "The Japanese at the Academy of Music," *Daily Morning Call*, 16 December 1866.
9   "The Japanese Larceny of $3,500," *Daily Morning Call*, 5 September 1867 (quoting the *New York Herald*, 12 August 1867); "Dramatic, Musical, Etc.," *Daily Dramatic Chronicle*, 22 December 1866.
10   "The Japanese at the Academy," *Morning Call*, 30 December 1866. The writer's use of the word "Daimos" for the Japanese acrobats is clearly a result of his having seen "daimyo" used in articles about Japan. In Japan's feudal system, *daimyō* (大名) were the supreme lords of each individual domain in Japan.
11   Clarence King, as quoted in the introduction to Mark Twain and Bernard Taper, *Mark Twain's San Francisco* (Santa Clara and Berkeley, CA.: Santa Clara University and Heyday Books, 2003), p. xi.
12   Bret Harte and Edith Goodkind Rosenwald, *San Francisco in 1866: Being Letters to the Springfield Republican* (San Francisco: Book Club of California, 1951), p. 6.
13   *Daily Dramatic Chronicle*, 22 April 1865; "The Need for Instruction in the Chinese and Japanese Languages," *Daily Alta California*, 19 December 1866.
14   James F. Watkins, "San Francisco," *Overland Monthly and Out West magazine*, vol. 4, issue 1, January 1870, pp. 9–23.
15   "To the Public," *Daily Alta California*, 25 March 1851; "Intercourse with Japan,"

Daily Alta California, 26 March 1851.

16   Harte and Rosenwald, *San Francisco in 1866: Being Letters to the Springfield Republican*, p. 71.

17   "By Telegraph to the Union," *Sacramento Daily Union*, 4 January 1867; "Shipping Intelligence," *Daily Alta California*, 1 January 1867.

18   Iinomachi, *Iino chōshi* [A history of Iinomachi], vol. 3 (2) (Iinomachi, Fukushima Prefecture: Iinomachi, 2005), pp. 36–37; Shigeatsu Hayashi, "Nakagawa Namigorō oji no danwa" [A chat with old man Nakagawa Namigorō], *Sokki ihō*, vol. 49, 15 February 1893, pp. 40–44.

19   Iinomachi, *Iino chōshi*, p. 10. Mihara has also suggested that because of his strong Northeastern dialect, to Hirohachi the word "Risley" may have sounded somewhat like "*ijin*," or "foreigner."

20   National Archives and Records Administration (NARA), Washington, D.C., Passport Applications 1795–1905, ARC Identifier 566612 / MLR Number A1 508, NARA Series: M1372, Roll #148; Shigeatsu Hayashi, "Nakagawa Namigorō oji no danwa" [A chat with old man Nakagawa Namigorō], *Sokki ihō*, vol. 52, 30 May 1893, pp. 138–41.

21   *Alta California*, 3 January 1867; *Daily Japan Herald,* 28 November 1866; Hajime Miyoshi, *Nippon saakasu monogatari: umi o koeta karuwaza kyokugeishitachi* (Tokyo: Hakusuisha, 1993), pp. 25–27.

22   *Daily Alta California*, 1 January 1867; ibid., 2 January 1867.

23   *Daily Morning Call*, 3 January 1867.

24   "California Gossip: From Our Own Correspondent," *New York Times,* 10 February 1867.

25   "In Theatrical Record," *Daily Morning Call*, 6 January 1867.

26   Iinomachi, *Iino chōshi,* pp. 37–38.

27   "Amusements, etc.," *Daily Alta California*, 7 January 1867; Iinomachi, *Iino chōshi,* p. 39.

28   "Amusements, etc.," *Daily Alta California*, 8 January 1867.

29   "The Pacific Slope. From our Own Correspondent," *New York Times*, 7 March 1867.

30   "Amusements, Etc., Risley's Japanese Gymnasts—Accident to One of the troupe," *Daily Alta California*, 8 January 1867.

31   "Amusements," *Daily Alta California*, 12 January 1866.

32   "California Gossip . . . From Our Own Correspondent, Friday, Jan. 18, 1867," *New York Times*, 17 February 1867; "Eastward Bound," *Daily Alta California*, 10 January 1867; also, "Tom Maguire, Napoleon of the Stage" pp. 155–56.

33   "Sunday Amusements," *Daily Alta California*, 17 January 1867; "Suit for Services Rendered," *Daily Alta California*, 29 January 1867; *Daily Alta California*, 22 January 1867.

34   *Daily Morning Call*, 16 June 1867. This is in the wake of the visit by the Dragon Troupe.

35   "Professor Richard Risley," *Daily Morning Call*, 20 January 1867.

36   "Passenger Exodus," *Daily Morning Call*, 30 January 1867.

37   "Hunting for Japanese," *Daily Morning Call*, 3 March 1867; "Farewell to Napoleon," *Daily Dramatic Chronicle*, 31 January 1867.

Act 2: The Risley Act

1   "Professor Richard Risley," *Daily Morning Call*, 20 January 1867.

2   Aya Mihara and Stuart Thayer, "Richard Risley Carlisle, Man in Motion," *Bandwagon* 41, no. 1 (1997), pp. 12–14.

3   John Hill Martin, *Chester (and Its Vicinity) Delaware County, in Pennsylvania; with Genealogical Sketches of Some Old Families, by John Hill Martin, Esq.* (Philadelphia [s.n.], 1877), p. 292; Passport Applications, 1795–1905, NARA Microfilm Publication M1372, 694 rolls, General Records Department of State, Record Group 59, National Archives, Washington, D.C.; "Death of a Noted Character," *Daily Patriot*, 28 May 1874. Reprinted from *Philadelphia Evening Telegraph*.

4   Henry Charlton Beck, *Jersey Genesis: The Story of the Mullica River* (New Brunswick, NJ: Rutgers University Press, 1945), pp. 92–101.

5   Email interview with John Kovach, 23 November 2011.

6   Timothy Edward Howard, *A History of St. Joseph County, Indiana* (Chicago: Lewis Pub. Company, 1907), p. 312.

7   John Kovach, "Rizurii 'sensei' shōden (zenpen): butai debyū izen no Richard Carlisle (saakasu gaku tanjō)" [The story of "Professor" Risley (part 1): Richard Carlisle before his theatrical debut (birth of circus studies)], ed. Aya Mihara, *Art Times*, no. 6, July 2010, pp. 4–8; Ancestry.com, *U.S. General Land Office Records, 1796–1907* [database on- line], Provo, UT (Original Data: United States Bureau of Land Management, General Land Office Records, Automated Records Project, *Federal Land Patents, State Volumes, http://www.glorecords.blm.gov/* [Springfield, VA: Bureau of Land Management, Eastern United States, 2007]).

8   Martin, *Chester (and Its Vicinity)*, p. 292.

9   "How Prof. Risley Went in on His Muscle," *Ohio Repository*, 6 March 1861.

10 Ibid.

11 "The Death of a Noted Character," *Daily Patriot*, 23 May 1874.

12 *New York Evening Post*, 25 November 1841; *Baltimore Sun*, 4 January 1838.

13 "The Circus," *Freeman and Messenger*, 4 June 1840.

14 P. T. Barnum and James W. Cook, *The Colossal P. T. Barnum Reader: Nothing Else Like It in the Universe* (Urbana: University of Illinois Press, 2005), p. 46.

15 *Baltimore Sun*, 4 January 1838.

16 *New York Times*, 1 December 1856.

17 "American Enterprize," *Niles National Register* 64 (29 April 1843), p. 144; "American Enterprise," *Brooklyn Eagle*, 11 October 1843; "Circus," *Pittsfield Sun*, 2 May 1844.

18 *American and Commercial Daily*, 4 March 1842; *Sun*, 14 July 1842.

19 William W. Clapp, *A Record of the Boston Stage* (Boston [u.a.]: Munroe, 1853), p. 381.

20 *Pathfinder*, 13 May 1843.

21 *Alton Telegraph and Democratic Review*, 10 June 1843.

22 *Pathfinder*, 13 May 1843.

23 *Argus*, 26 June 1843.

24 *Age*, 24 September 1843.

25 "The Theatre Royal, Dublin, from 1841 to 1845. Part IV," *Dublin University Magazine: A Literary and Political Journal*, vol. 73, no. 434, p. 228; "Chit Chat,"

Age and Argus, 23 December 1843.

26 "Public Amusements for the Week," *Weekly Chronicle*, 21 January 1844.

27 "Haymarket—Professor Risley and His Children," *Age and Argus*, 8 June 1844.

28 Peter Matthews, *The New Guinness Book of Records 1995* (Enfield, Middlesex: Guinness Publishing, 1994), p. 154.

29 Robert M. Sillard, *Barry Sullivan and His Contemporaries: A Histrionic Record* (London: T. F. Unwin, 1901), p. 113.

30 *Age and Argus*, 1 June 1844.

31 Thomas Hughes, *James Fraser Second Bishop of Manchester: A Memoir 1818–1885* (New York and London: Macmillan and Company, 1887), pp. 36–38.

32 "Théatre de la Porte Saint Martin," *Independent*, 20 June 1844.

33 Marian Hannah Winter, "Theatre of Marvels," *Dance Index,* vol. 7 (1948), pp. 22–40.

34 "Theatrical Chit-Chat," *Atlas*, 29 June 1844.

35 "Théatres, Fêtes, et Concerts," *La Presse*, 7 November 1844; "Ambigue-Comique," *La Presse*, 23 December 1844.

36 "Théatres," *La Presse*, 9 June 1845.

37 "Porte-Saint-Martin," *Le Tintamarre*, 3 August 1845.

38 "The Drama," *Bell's Life in London*, 1 February 1846.

39 Gansevoort Melville and Hershel Parker, *1846 London Journal and Letters from England, 1845* (New York: Public Library, 1966), p. 43.

40 "Professor Richard Risley," *Daily Morning Call*, 20 January 1867.

41 William Wells, "Vienna and the Viennese," *The Ladies Repository: A Monthly Periodical, Devoted to Literature, Arts, and Religion*, vol. 11, issue 1, January 1851, p. 20.

42 "Yankee in Naples" (dated 8 January 1847), *New York Sun*, 11 June 1847.

43 "Death of a Noted Character," *Patriot*, 28 May 1874.

44 "Gigantic American Panorama," *Atlas*, 31 March 1849.

45 *Manchester Guardian*, 14 November 1849.

46 Theodore Christian Blegen, "The "Fashionable tour" on the Upper Mississippi," *Minnesota history*, vol. 20 (1939), pp. 382–83.

47 "Incidents in the Life of a Young Equestrian," *Spirit of the Times: A Chronicle of the Turf, Agriculture, Field Sports, Literature and the Stage*, 22 January 1848; ibid., 19 February 1848. "Juan" or "James" Hernandez, as he was known, was actually an Irish-American boy, born "James Shelly." Taken from his family without their permission by an equestrian circus manager named Robinson, he was first given the adopted name of "Jimmy Robinson" and then finally the more-exotic-sounding stage name of "Hernandez."

48 "Professor Risley's Ascent in the Nassau Balloon," *Spirit of the Times*, 15 September 1849.

49 Ibid.

50 "Wanted, A New Government," *Punch, or the London Charivari*, 1846, vol. 10, p. 114; "A Key to the Waterloo Banquet," *Punch*, vol. 10, p. 234.

51 "Sagacity of a Dog," *Spirit of the Times: A Chronicle of the Turf, Agriculture, Field, Sports, Literature*, 27 May 1854, 24, 15, American Peridocial Series Online, p. 172.

Act 3: Going for Gold

1   "Musical-Theatrical," *Daily Alta California*, 19 June 1855; "Arrival of Steamer Uncle Sam, Quickest Trip on Record," *Daily Alta California*, 13 June 1855. In the same issue, Risley is recorded as having signed a special commendation for the ship's captain and crew.

2   "Trotting, Etc., in California," *Spirit of the Times*, 1 September 1855.

3   "Meeting of Physicians at the Metropolitan," *Daily Alta California*, 23 June 1855.

4   "France. General Intelligence," *New York Times*, 1 April 1853.

5   *Daily Alta California*, 23 June 1855; *Times*, 3 July 1852. Louis Soullier was a pioneer in showcasing acts from Asia and, later, in actually traveling there, eventually reaching Japan several years after Risley.

6   "The City: The Performance at the Vatican," *Sacramento Daily Union*, 20 July 1855.

7   *Sacramento Daily Union*, 5, 22, and 27 May 1856 and 17 September 1857.

8   "A Knock Down," *Sacramento Daily Union*, 26 September 1856; "Rain in the Mountains," *Sacramento Daily Union*, 10 October 1856; "Died," *Sacramento Daily Union*, 28 July 1857; "Risley's Ballet Troupe," *Sacramento Daily Union*, 16 May 1856; "Mayor's Court," *Daily Alta California*, 26 October 1855; "Caution to the Public," *Sacramento Daily Union*, 18 December 1855.

9   "Autographs," *Daily Alta California*, 23 June 1855.

10 "Musical-Theatrical: Risley's Vatican," *Daily Alta California*, 16 October 1855.

11 "Great Feat in Ascending an Inclined Rope," *Scientific American*, 23 December 1855, vol. 11, no. 15, p. 120.

12 "Amusements," *Daily Alta California*, 13 May 1856.

13 Albert Dressler, *California's Pioneer Circus* (San Francisco: printed by H. S. Crocker Company, 1926), pp. 19–21.

14 "Resume of San Francisco News," *Sacramento Daily Union*, 4 March 1857; Albert Dressler, *California's Pioneer Circus* (San Francisco: printed by H. S. Crocker Co., 1926), p. 41.

15 Elizabeth Laughlin Lord, *Reminiscences of Eastern Oregon* (Portland, OR: Irwin-Hodson Company, 1903), p. 185.

16 "Later from Oregon," *Daily Alta California*, 11 September 1857.

17 "Marine Journal, Port of Honolulu, H.I.," *Friend*, December 1857.

18 "'Charlie Backus' and the Missionaries," *Friend*, 30 April 1857.

19 "Public Notice," *Friend*, December 1857.

20 "Amusements," *Polynesian*, 21 November 1857.

21 "Risley's Varieties," *Polynesian*, 28 November 1857.

22 "Risley's Varieties," *Polynesian*, 5 December 1857.

23 *Polynesian*, 2 January 1858.

24 *Polynesian*, 2 January 1858.

25 David Burn diary, 1 May 1858 entry, 10 Oct. 1855–15 Sept. 1858, Microfilm–CY 1094, frames 99–338 (B 192: Diary, 1855–1858), State Library New South Wales; *Daily Southern Cross*, 4 May 1858

26 "Professor Risley," *Southern Cross*, 11 May 1858.

27 Parliament New Zealand, Legislative Council and House of Representatives, Maurice Fitzgerald, *Parliamentary Debates, Second Parliament, Legislative Council and*

House of Representatives, 1858 to 1860 (Wellington1886), p. 488.

28   David Burn diary, 15 May 1858 entry; "Notice," *Southern Cross*, 28 May 1858; "Auckland: Extraordinary Haul of Fish," *New Zealander*, 14 August 1858 (quoted in *Australian and New Zealand Gazette*, 4 December 1858).

29   "Back Creek, Amherst (From our own Correspondent) 20th April, 1859," *Star*, 22 April 1859.

30   *Star*, 1 November 1858.

31   *Sydney Morning Herald*, 10 May 1860.

32   John R. Black, *Young Japan. Yokohama and Yedo* (London, Yokohama: Trubner and Company, Kelly and Company, 1880), p. 402.

33   R. S. Smythe, "'Professionals' Abroad," *Cornhill Magazine*, February 1871, pp. 223.

34   "56 Years on the Stage," *Chicago Tribune*, 2 November 1902.

35   "Persons Advertised For," *Sydney Morning Herald*, 20 July 1860; "Kidnapping," *Sydney Morning Herald*, 21 July 1860.

36   "West Maitland," *Sydney Morning Herald*, 1 August 1860.

37   Year *1860*, Census Place: *Philadelphia Ward 10 East District, Philadelphia, Pennsylvania*, Roll *M653_1160*, page *684*, image *25*, Family History Library Film *805160*.

Act 4: Into Asia

1   R. S. Smythe, "'Professionals' Abroad," *Cornhill Magazine*, February 1871, p. 223.

2   Smythe, "'Professionals' Abroad," pp. 223–33.

3   Ibid., pp. 225–26.

4   "Shipping Intelligence," *Bengal Hurkaru and India Gazette*, 20 December 1860; "Amusements in India (From Our Own Correspondent) Mirzapower, 5th April, 1861," *The Era*, 19 May 1861; "Amusements in India (From our Own Correspondent) Calcutta, 20th May, 1861," *The Era*, 7 July 1861.

5   *Bengal Hurkaru and India Gazette*, 8 December 1860; "Indian News: Calcutta: Legerdemain," *Bengal Hurkaru and India Gazette*, 24 December 1860; *Bengal Hurkaru and India Gazette*,1 January 1861; "Amusements in India (From Our Own Correspondent) Calcutta, 20th May, 1861," *Era*, 7 July 1861.

6   *Bengal Hurkaru and India Gazette*, 1 January 1861; *Bengal Hurkaru and India Gazette*, 14 January 1861.

7   "Professor Risley," *Supplement to the Bi-Weekly Hurkaru*, 21 January 1861.

8   "Professor Risley's Soiree Amusante," *Bengal Hurkaru and India Gazette*,12 January 1861; "Risley's Royal Amphitheatre," *Bengal Hurkaru and India Gazette*, 24 January 1861; "Mr. Risley's Royal Amphitheatre," *Bi-Weekly Hurkaru*, 14 February 1861.

9   *Bengal Hurkaru and India Gazette*, 11 February and 10 January 1861.

10 "Risley's Royal Amphitheatre," *Bengal Hurkaru and India Gazette*, 2 May 1861; "Professor Risley's Royal Amphitheatre," *Bengal Hurkaru and India Gazette*, 8 May 1861.

11 "Risley's Royal Amphitheatre," 11 May 1861.

12 *Straits Times*, 8 June and 28 September 1861.

13 "American Loyalty at the Antipodes," *New York Times*, 30 August 1861.

14   *Straits Times*, 13 July 1861.

15   Justus Hurd Taylor, *Joe Taylor, Barnstormer: His Travels, Troubles and Triumphs, During Fifty Years in Footlight Flashes* (New York: William R. Jenkins, 1913), p. 88.

16   *Straits Times*, 3 August 1861.

17   *Straits Times*, 3 and 17 August 1861.

18   *Java-Bode*, 26 October 1861.

19   *Java-Bode*, 18 and 23 September 1861.

20   *Daily Shipping and Commercial News*, 26 September 1862.

21   Taylor, *Joe Taylor, Barnstormer*, p. 119.

22   *Straits Times*, 6 December and 22 and 29 November 1862.

23   *China Mail*, 25 December 1862; "An Old Californian," *Daily Evening Bulletin*, 17 February 1863.

24   *China Mail*, 1 and 8 January 1863.

25   "Manila," *The China Mail*, 19 February 1863.

26   "Manila," *The China Mail*, 16 April 1863.

27   Ibid.

28   "Manila," *Supplement to the China Mail*, 4 June 1863.

29   Taylor, *Joe Taylor, Barnstormer*, p. 88; *Sun*, 1 April 1867.

30   Jonathan D. Spence, *God's Chinese Son: The Taiping Heavenly Kingdom of Hong Xiuquan*, 1st ed. (New York: W. W. Norton, 1996), p. 311.

31   Ibid., pp. 308, 09; J. W. MacLellan, *The Story of Shanghai: From the Opening of the Port to Foreign Trade* (Shanghai: North China Herald, 1889), pp. 80–83.

32   *North China Herald*, 24 October 1863.

33   "An Old Circus Bill," *New York Clipper*, 3 June 1911.

34   Whether this is the same girl referred to by Smythe in his account is unclear. In the mid-nineteenth century, many girl dancers were named La Petite Cerito, after a famous French dancer of that name.

35   *London and China Telegraph*, 4 April and 27 February 1864.

36   Marquis Chisholm, *The Adventures of a Travelling Musician in Australia, China and Japan* (London?: s.n.], 1865), p. 69.

37   "Squaring the Circle in Japan," *North China Herald*, 23 January 1864.

38   Rutherford Alcock, *The Capital of the Tycoon: A Narrative of a Three Years' Residence in Japan*, vol. 2 (London: Longman, Green, Longman, Roberts and Green, 1863), pp. 318–19.

39   *North China Herald*, 20 February 1864.

40   Kashirō Kishi, *Kakuiro: Ikeda Chikugonokami chōhatsu den* (Ihara: Iharashi Kyoiku Iinkai, 1969), pp. 222–25; Chisholm, *Adventures of a Travelling Musician*, pp. 72–73.

41   Chisholm, *Adventures of a Travelling Musician*, p. 69.

Act 5: Yokohama, Japan

1   S. B. Kemish, *The Japanese Empire: Its Physical, Political, and Social Condition and History; With Details of the Late American and British Expeditions* (London: Partridge and Company, 1860), p. 25.

2   Ernest Mason Satow, *A Diplomat in Japan* (London: Seeley, Service and Company limited, 1921), p. 25.

3   *The Japan Punch*, vol. 1 (Tokyo: Yūshōdō Shoten, 1975). pp. 139–40.

4   Black, *Young Japan. Yokohama and Yedo*, pp. 28–29.

5   William Elliot Griffis, *The Mikado's Empire*, new ed. (New York: Harper, 1883), p. 350.

6   "Onward, Press Onward," *Japan Herald,* 19 March 1864.

7   Griffis, *Mikado's Empire*, p. 376.

8   "Onward, Press Onward," *Daily Japan Herald*, 26 March 1864.

9   "Advertisements," *Daily Japan Herald*, 26 March 1864.

10 "Onward, Press Onward," *Daily Japan Herald*, 30 March 1864; "Our Letter from Japan," *Daily Alta California*, 16 May 1864; *The London and China Telegraph*, 28 May 1864.

11 "Onward, Press Onward," *Daily Japan Herald*, 19 and 21 April 1864.

12 "Advertisements,"*Daily Japan Herald*, 21 April 1864.

13 "Mrs. Yeamans's Career," *New York Times*, 8 October 1899.

14 "Fifty-six Years on the Stage," *Chicago Tribune*, 2 November 1902.

15 Annie Yeamans, "Sixty-five Years on the Stage," *The Green Book Album: A Magazine of the Passing Show*, July 1911, p. 221.

16 *Japan Herald*, 5 November 1864; "Ampitheatre," supplement to the *Japan Herald*, 3 December 1864.

17 *Japan Punch*, p. 209; supplement to the *Japan Herald*, 10 June 1865.

18 "City Items: American Enterprise in Japan," *Daily Alta California,* 29 November 1865.

19 Black, *Young Japan. Yokohama and Yedo*, pp. 407–8.

20 Ibid., pp. 403, 404.

21 *Japan Punch*, p. 274.

22 "New Royal Olympic Theater," *Japan Times Daily Advertiser*, 26 September 1865.

23 "Professor Risley's Entertainment," *Japan Times Daily Advertiser*, 3 October 1865.

24 See George Speaight, *A History of the Circus* (London and San Diego: Tantivy Press; A. S. Barnes, 1980).

25 Andrew L. Markus, "The Carnival of Edo: Misemono Spectacles from Contemporary Accounts," *Harvard Journal of Asiatic Studies*, vol. 45, no. 2, p. 504.

26 "Political Tragedies in Japan," *Blackwood's Edinburgh Magazine,* vol. 91, no. 508 (April 1862), p. 424.

27 3 July 1858 letter from Townsend Harris, in Shimoda. Reprinted in "Consul Harris in Japan," *Living Age*, no. 770, 26 February 1859, Third Series, no. 48, pp. 567–71.

28 Sherard Osborn, *A Cruise in Japanese Waters* (Edinburgh and London: Blackwood and Sons, 1859), pp. 191–93.

29 Yū Kawazoe, *Edo no misemono* (Tokyo: Iwanami Shoten, 2000), pp. 92–108.

30 Francis Hall and F. G. Notehelfer, *Japan through American Eyes: The Journal of Francis Hall, 1859–1866* (Boulder, CO.: Westview Press, 2001), p. 199.

31 Ibid., p. 368.

32 Ibid., pp. 574–75.

33 3 July 1858, letter from Townsend Harris, in Shimoda. Reprinted in "Consul Harris in Japan," *Living Age*, p. 571; "Sensation Diplomacy in Japan," *Blackwood's Edinburgh Magazine*, vol. 93, no. 570 (1863), p. 413.

34 "Theatrical News from Shanghai—Bell's Life,"*Launceston Examiner*, 27 December 1866.

35 Mihara Aya, *Nihonjin tōjō: Seiyō gekijō de enjirareta Edo no misemono* [Enter Japanese: a night in Japan at the opera house], 1st ed. (Tokyo: Shōhakusha, 2008), pp. 301–3; "The Japanese Acrobatic Troupe—Something That Is not 'All Right,'" *Daily Alta California*, 8 April 1868; Mihara Aya, "Bakumatsuishinki no gaikōkantachi no yokogao: Nihon no misemonogei wo 'yushutsu' suru,'" [Diplomats Unmasked: Theatre Business of Exporting Japanese Acrobats], *Engeki gakuronsō* [Treatises on Performing Arts], no. 10 (March 2010), pp. 121–53.

36 Mihara, *Nihonjin tōjō*, pp. 301–3.

37 "The Japs," *Brooklyn Daily Eagle*, 20 May 1867

38 Yagishita Hiroko, "Bakumatsu no pasupōto" [Bakumatsu era passports], INFOSTA Forum No. 70, *Journal of Information Science and Technology Association*, vol. 55, no. 2 (2005), p. 103; "Acrobats from Japan," quoted in the *Daily News*, 28 December 1866.

39 Richard Mounteney Jephson and Edward Pennell Elmhirst, eds., *Our Life in Japan with Illustrations from Photographs by Lord Walter Kerr and Signor Beato and Native Japanese Drawings* (London: Chapman, 1869), pp. 81–83.

Act 6: Taking America

1 Olive Logan, *Before the Footlights and Behind the Scenes: A Book about "the Show Business" in All Its Branches: From Puppet Shows to Grand Opera from Mountebanks to Menageries; from Learned Pigs to Lecturers; from Burlesque Blondes to Actors and Actresses: With Some Observations and Reflections (Original and Reflected) on Morality and Immorality in Amusements: Thus Exhibiting the "Show World" as Seen from within, through the Eyes of the Former Actress, as Well as from without, through the Eyes of the Present Lecturer and Author* (Philadelphia: Parmelee and Company, 1870), p.349.

2 Iinomachi, *Iino chōshi*, pp. 40–42; "Cholera in Nicaragua," *Daily Alta California*, 13 January 1867.

3 Iinomachi, *Iino chōshi*, p. 43.

4 "City Affairs," *North American and United States Gazette*, 26 February 1867.

5 Ibid.

6 "Dramatic, Musical & c.," *North American and United States Gazette*, 6 March 1867.

7 "Amusements," *Public Ledger*, 8 March 1867; "The Imperial Japanese Troupe," *Philadelphia Inquirer*, 15 March 1867

8 "The Japanese Acrobats," *North American and United States Gazette*, 2 March 1867.

9 MacElroy, *Philadelphia Directory for . . . containing the names of the inhabitants, their occupations, places of business, and dwelling houses*: [Ab ed. 26 m. d. Tit.]: McElroy's Philadelphia city directory 26 (Philadelphia: Biddle, 1863), p. 638; Michael Bennett Leavitt, *Fifty years in Theatrical Management* (New York: Broadway Publishing Company, 1912), p. 381.

10 Iinomachi, *Iino chōshi*, pp. 43–44.

11 "The Japanese Necromancers," *National Republican*, 8 April 1867; "The Japanese," *National Intelligencer*, 8 April 1867.

12   "The Japanese," *National Intelligencer*, 10 April 1867; "Amusements," *Commercial Advertiser*, 10 April 1867; "Amusements: Wall's Opera House," *National Republican*, 11 April 1867; "Amusements," *National Republican*, 12 April 1867.

13   *Bell's Life in London*, 11 April, 1868.

14   *National Republican*, 11 April 1867.

15   "Visit of the Imperial Japanese Troupe to the President," *Daily National Intelligencer*, 19 April 1867.

16   "Japanese Acrobats at the White House," *New York Herald*, 19 April 1867.

17   Ibid.

18   "President Johnson as a Showman," *Flakes Bulletin*, 8 May 1867.

19   "Private Exhibition to the Japanese at Brady's Gymnasium," *National Intelligencer*, 16 April 1867.

20   "Spicy Talk in the U.S. Senate," *New-York Daily Reformer*, 15 April 1867.

21   Iinomachi, *Iino chōshi*, pp. 45–46.

22   Ibid., pp. 46–47.

23   "Amusements," *New York Times*, 27 April 1867.

24   "Amusements: Academy of Music—The Japanese Jugglers," *New York Times*, 7 May 1867.

25   "An Evening with the Jugglers," from a *New York Post* article quoted in the *Janesville Gazette*, 11 May 1867.

26   "The Drama," *New York Evening Express*, 25 May 1867.

27   "The Japanese Jugglers," *Harper's Weekly: A Journal of Civilization*, June 15 1867, p. 1.

28   "Letter from 'Mark Twain' No. 17 (May 17, 1867)," *Daily Alta California*, 16 June 1867.

29   Iinomachi, *Iino chōshi*, pp. 49–50.

30   Elizabeth Bacon Custer, *Tenting on the Plains; or, General Custer in Kansas and Texas* (New York: Harper and Brothers, 1895), p. 267.

31   "The Japanese in Private Life—A Morning Call Upon Them," *New York Times*, 11 May 1867.

32   "Japanese Cupidity," *The Round Table. A SATURDAY review of politics, Finance, Literature, Society, and art*, vol. 6, no. 130, 20 July 1867, p. 38; *Daily Memphis Avalanche*, 21 February 1868; "Japanese Cupidity," *Round Table*, p. 38.

33   "The 'Japs' in a New Role," *New York Times*, 9 June 1867.

34   Iinomachi, *Iino chōshi*, pp. 49–50; "The Japanese Juggler Robbed," *Boston Herald*, 21 June 1867.

35   "The Japanese Jugglers," *New York Times*, 14 May 1867.

36   "A Terrible Tumble," *New York World*, 14 June 1867.

37   "Town Topics," *New York Times*, 4 August 1867

38   "The Japanese Troupe," *Milwaukee News*, 30 June 1867.

39   "The Japanese Acrobatic Imbroglio," *New York Herald*, 13 August 1867.

40   "The Japanese Imbroglio: 'Little All Right' All Wrong—A Singular Proceeding," *New York Herald*, 27 August 1867.

41   "Trouble in the Japanese Troupe," *New York Evening Post*, 26 August 1867.

42   "Foreign Dramatic and Show News: About Little All Right," letter dated 17 September 1867, in *New York Clipper*, 16 November 1867.

Act 7: At the Exposition

1   Mark Twain, *The innocents abroad, or, The new pilgrims' progress; being some account of the steamship Quaker City's pleasure excursion to Europe and the Holy Land: with descriptions of countries, nations, incidents, and adventures, as they appeared to the author* (San Francisco, CA, and Hartford, CO: H. H. Bancroft and American Publishing Company, 1869), p. 27.

2   Mark Twain, "The Holy Land Excursion," *Daily Alta California*, 5 September 1867.

3   "The Chinese Theatre in the Paris Exposition Park," *Illustrated London News*, 29 June 1867.

4   "The Taicoun and his Tumblers," *Mask*, February 1868, pp. 18–20. According to one Englishman who saw them, in Paris they had some "Japanese bills of the play, which were inimitable, being full of quaint little coloured cuts by native artists of their principal performances."

5   Eiichi Shibusawa, *Shibusawa eiichi taifutsu nikki* (Tokyo: Nihon Shiseki Kyōkai, 1928), pp. 129–36.

6   "Maguire Euchred in Paris," *Daily Dramatic Chronicle*, 7 September 1867; "Maguire Out of Luck Again," *Daily Dramatic Chronicle*, 17 September 1867.

7   "Debuts de la Troupe Japonaise," *Le Figaro*, 22 July 1867.

8   *Le Figaro*, 30 July 1867.

9   Hirohachi Takano and Shidankai Iinomachi, *Hirohachi nikki: Bakumatsu no kyokugeidan kaigai jungyō kiroku* (Iinomachi, Fukushima Prefecture: Iinomachi Shidankai, 1977), pp. 25–26.

10 Ibid., pp. 26–27.

11 Takashi Miyanaga, *Purinsu Akitake no Ōshū kikō: Keio 3-nen Pari Banpaku shisetsu* (Tokyo: Yamakawa Shuppansha, 2000), pp. 8–10.

12 Akitake Tokugawa and Masato Miyachi, *Tokugawa Akitake bakumatsu taiō nikki* (Tokyo: Yamakawa Shuppansha, 1999), pp. 31–33.

13 Shibusawa, *Shibusawa eiichi taifutsu nikki*, pp. 126–28.

14 "Cirque Napoleon: La troupe impériale du Taicoun," *Le Figaro*, 1 August 1867.

15 Takano and Shidankai Iinomachi, *Hirohachi nikki*, pp. 27–28.

16 *L'Indépendance Dramatique*, 24 August 1867.

17 Théophile Gautier, *L'Orient* (Paris: G. Charpentier, 1877), p. 290.

18 Ibid., p. 294.

19 *L'Orchestra*, 30 September 1867.

20 *La Sylphide*, 20 October 1867.

21 Le Panthéon de l'industrie et des arts, 20 October 1867.

22 "Judgment Against Risley," *Daily Dramatic Chronicle*, 24 August 1867.

23 *New York Daily Tribune*, 4 October 1867.

24 *Le Figaro*, 10 September 1867; "Theatricals, etc., in Paris," *New York Clipper*, 26 October 1867;

25 Takano and Shidankai Iinomachi, *Hirohachi nikki*, pp. 31–32.

26 Eugene Rimmel, *Recollections of the Paris Exhibition of 1867* (London: Chapman and Hall, 1868), p. 17.

27 Paul de Saint Victor, "Théatres," *La Press*, 19 August 1867.

28 *L'Independance Dramatique*, 26 October 1867.

29 Takano and Shidankai Iinomachi, *Hirohachi nikki*, pp. 34–35.
30 "All Right," *Daily Alta California*, 17 November 1867.
31 Pivoine, "La Troupe Japonaise du Taicoun," *La Marionnette*, 17 November 1867.

Act 8: The Long Way to London

1   Charles Dickens, "Hard Times," *Household Words*, no. 228 (1854).
2   "Amusements," *Belfast News Letter*, 24 August 1867.
3   "The Japanese Entertainment," *The London and China Telegraph*, 28 February 1867.
4   *The first and only troupe of Japanese conjurors and gymnasts that ever have been allowed to visit Europe: Shanshami-Amingori; or, Marvellous feats of top-spinning ; the butterfly illusion* (London: Nassau Steam Press and W. S. Johnson, 1867), p. 21.
5   "Destruction of Her Majesty's Theatre by Fire," *Lloyd's Weekly London Newspaper*, 8 December 1867.
6   Iinomachi, *Iino chōshi*, pp. 59–60.
7   "Curzon Exhibition Hall," *Birmingham Daily Post*, 25 December 1867.
8   "The Japanese Jugglers," *Birmingham Daily Post*, 27 December 1867.
9   Ibid.
10 "Public Amusements," *Lloyd's Weekly London Newspaper*, 8 December 1867.
11 "The Imperial Japanese Company," *The Era*, 8 December 1867,
12 *Lloyd's Weekly London Newspaper*, 8 and 22 December 1867 and 19 April 1868.
13 "The Theatrical Lounger," *Illustrated Times*, 9 May 1868.
14 "The Japanese Troupe," *Birmingham Daily Post*, 20 January 1868.
15 Ibid.
16 "The Japanese Acrobatic Troupe—Something That is Not 'All Right,'" *New York Herald*, 12 March 1868.
17 Nieu Rotterdamsche Courant, 1 March 1868.
18 "Binnenland. Residentie-Nieuws," *Dagblad van Zuidholland en 's Gavenhage*, 26 March 1868.
19 Iinomachi, *Iino chōshi*, pp. 62–64.
20 "Interieur, Bruxelles," *Le Moniteur Belge*, 5 April 1868.
21 Iinomachi, *Iino chōshi*, pp. 65–66.
22 Ibid.
23 "Death of Hay-yah-ta-kee, in the City of New York," *Frank Leslie's Illustrated Newspaper*, 29 February 1868.
24 "The Japanese Troupe," *Era*, 19 April 1868.
25 "Public Amusements," *Lloyds Weekly London Newspaper*, 29 March 1868.
26 "The Japanese Acrobats at the Lyceum," *Reynold's Newspaper*, 19 April 1868.
27 "The Theatrical Lounger," *The Times*, 25 April, 1868.
28 "The Lyceum Theatre," *Lloyds' Weekly London Newspaper*, 19 April 1868.
29 "The Lyceum," *Examiner*, 18 April 1868.
30 "Lyceum," *Era*, 19 April 1868.
31 "Lyceum," *Penny Illustrated Paper*, 18 April 1868.
32 "Lyceum—The Japanese Troupe," *Daily News*, 13 April 1868.
33 "Lyceum," *Penny Illustrated Paper*, 18 April 1868.
34 "Fire at the Quarters of the Imperial Japanese Troupe," *Lloyd's Weekly Newspaper*,

19 April 1868; Iinomachi, *Iino chōshi*, pp. 66–67.
35   "The Imperial Japanese Troupe," *Daily News*, 1 May 1868.
36   "The Japanese at the Lyceum Theatre," *Era*, 3 May 1868.
37   "Robbing One of the Japanese," *Lloyd's Weekly London Newspaper*, 17 May 1868.
38   Iinomachi, *Iino chōshi*, pp. 68–73.
39   Ibid., pp. 74–75.
40   "The Japanese at the Lyceum," *Era*, 31 May 1868.
41   "Royal Lyceum Theatre," *Lloyd's Weekly London Newspaper*, 14 June 1868.
42   Iinomachi, *Iino chōshi*, pp. 74–75.

Act 9: The Matter of the Contract

1   Mihara, *Nihonjin tōjō*, pp. 301–02.
2   Iinomachi, *Iino chōshi*, pp. 74–76.
3   "Revista de Teatros," *Boletín de Loterías y Toros*, 30 June 1868.
4   "Circo del Principe Alfonso," *Diario Oficial de Avisos de Madrid*, 30 June 1868.
5   Iinomachi, *Iino chōshi*, pp. 75–76.
6   Ryoichi Awamura, "Spain's Japon Clan Has Reunion to Trace Its 17th-century Roots," *Japan Times*, 11 December 2003.
7   Derek Massarella, *A World Elsewhere: Europe's Encounter with Japan in the Sixteenth and Seventeenth Centuries* (New Haven: Yale University Press, 1990), p. 349.
8   "Obramas y Estampas," *La Esperanza*, 1 August 1868.
9   Iinomachi, *Iino chōshi*, p. 76–77.
10   Ibid.
11   "Variedades," Diario Oficial de Avisos de Madrid, 9 July 1868; "Cronica General," *Nueva Iberia*, 8 July 2011.
12   "The Imperial Japanese Troupe," *Daily News*, 13 July 1868; "Professor Risley's Imperial Japanese Troupe," *Era*, 19 July 1868—"Japan is evidently becoming a feature in the English and Continental amusement markets."
13   "Variedades," *Diario Oficial de Avisos de Madrid*, 16 July 1868. Alas, none of trinkets or bromides seem to have survived.
14   "Recortes," *El Imparcial*, 18 July 1868.
15   "Diversiones," *Diario Oficial de Avisos de Madrid*, 30 August 1868; Iinomachi, *Iino chōshi*, pp. 78–79.
16   *El Principado*, no. 256, 17 September 1868, p. 5908. Quoted in Ricard Brú i Turull, *Els origens del Japonisme a Barcelona* [Origins of Japonisme in Barcelona] (Barcelona: Institut Mon Juic, 2011), p. 221.
17   Ricard Bru i Turull, "El Japó Entra En Escena: La Companyia Imperial I Els Primers Acròbates Japonesos a Barcelona," *Assaig de Teatre*, no. 46 (2005), p. 170.
18   Iinomachi, *Iino chōshi*, p. 80.
19   Ibid.
20   Shōtarō Yasuoka, *Daiseikimatsu saakasu* (Tokyo: Asahi Shinbunsha, 1988), pp. 361–64; Iinomachi, *Iino chōshi*, pp. 86, 81.
21   Iinomachi, *Iino chōshi*, pp. 81–82.
22   Ibid., p. 82.
23   Ibid., pp. 82–83.
24   Ibid., p. 83.

25   Mihara, *Nihonjin tōjō*, pp. 301–02.
26   *Daily Alta California*, 19 November 1866.
27   Miyoshi, *Nippon saakasu monogatari*, pp. 25–27.
28   Iinomachi, *Iino chōshi*, p. 83.
29   *Edinburgh Evening Courant*, 14 January 1868; Miyanaga, *Purinsu Akitake no Ōshū kikō: Keio 3-nen Pari Banpaku shisetsu*, Appendix, pp. 4–5.
30   *Le Figaro*, 23 November 1868.
31   Iinomachi, *Iino chōshi*, pp. 86–87.
32   Passenger Lists of Vessels Arriving at New York, New York, 1820–97 (National Archives Microfilm Publication M237, 675 rolls), Records of the U.S. Customs Service, Record Group 36, National Archives, Washington, D.C.
33   Iinomachi, *Iino chōshi*, p. 85.
34   "Amusements," *New York Times*, 22 January 1869.
35   "Amusements," *New York Times*, 23 January 1869.
36   "Amusements," *New York Times*, 25 January 1869.
37   Ibid.
38   Iinomachi, *Iino chōshi*, p. 85.
39   Hayashi, "Nakagawa Namigorō oji no danwa," *Sokki ihō*, vol. 54, 28 October 1893, pp. 242–48.

Act 10: Final Acts

1   "Death of a Noted Character," (reprinted from the *Philadelphia Evening Telegraph*), *The Patriot*, 28 May 1874.
2   Iinomachi, *Iino chōshi*, pp. 88–89.
3   Hirohachi Takano, *Hirohachi nikki: Bakumatsu no kyokugeidan kaigai jungyō kiroku* (Iinomachi, Fukushima-ken: Iinomachi Shidankai, 1982), pp. 95–96; Takashi Miyanaga, *Umi o watatta bakumatsu no kyokugeidan: Takano Hirohachi no Bei-Ō manyuki* [Acrobats who went overseas at the end of the shogunate: Takano Hirohachi's travels in America and Europe] (Tokyo: Chūō Kōron Shinsha, 1999), pp. 201–8.
4   "Amusements," *New York Herald*, 13 June 1869.
5   "General Press Dispatch," *New York Daily Tribune*, 12 April 1869.
6   "Amusements," *New York Daily Tribune*, 19 May 1869.
7   "Public Amusements," *Liverpool Mercury*, 19 June 1869; "The Imperial Japanese Troupe in Liverpool," *Liverpool Mercury*, 24 June 1869.
8   "Theatres, Etc.," *Echo*, 22 July 1869; "Public Amusements," *Lloyds Weekly London Newspaper*, 25 July 1869; "Mr. Glaisher's Experiments in the Car of the Captive Balloon," *Illustrated Times*, 31 July 1869.
9   "Public Amusements," *Lloyd's Weekly London Newspaper*, 15 August 1869.
10   *Era*, 22 August 1869.
11   *Era*, 29 August 1869.
12   *Old Bailey Proceedings Online* (www.oldbaileyonline.org, version 6.0, 29 October 2011), October 1869, trial of Richard Risley (t18691025-903).
13   *Report of the London Committee for the Exposure and Suppression of the Traffic in English Girls for Purposes of Continental Prostitution, 1881* (London: E. Wilson, 1881), p. 13.

14   *Old Bailey Proceedings Online*, October 1869, trial of Richard Risley.

15   Montagu Stephen Williams, Percy Lefroy, and George Henry Lamson, *Leaves of a Life: Being the Reminiscences of Montagu Williams* (London and New York: Macmillan and Company, 1890), pp. 251–52.

16   "The Charge Against Professor Risley," *Illustrated Police News*, 30 October 1869.

17   Ibid.

18   "The Charge Against Professor Risley," *Lloyds Weekly London Newspaper*, 31 October, 1869.

19   *Trewman's Exeter Flying Post*, 1 December 1869.

20   "Pubic Amusements," *Western Mail*, 24 December 1869.

21   "The Mails & Etc.," *Times*, 20 December 1869.

22   "Professor Risley's Great Dramatic and Musical Combination," *Era*, 6 March 1870.

23   "The Stage," *New York Evening Telegram*, 24 June 1870.

24   Year: *1870*, Census Place *Philadelphia Ward 20 District 62, Philadelphia, Pennsylvania*, roll *M593_1406*, page *68B*, image *140*, Family History Library Film *552905*.

25   "Amusements: Prof. Risley's Benefit," *New York Times*, 24 January 1871.

26   "Heavy Suit Concerning the Japanese Troupe—Arrest of the Manager," *New York Times*, 22 April 1871.

27   Year: *1871*, Arrival: *New York, United States*, Microfilm Serial: *M237*, Microfilm Roll: *M237_342*, Line: *10*, List Number: *354* .

28   *New York Clipper*, 3 June 1871; *Titusville Morning Herald*, 10 June 1871.

29   Hayashi, "Nakagawa Namigorō oji no danwa," pp. 242–48.

30   Jonathan Clements, *Admiral Togo: Nelson of the East* (London: Haus Pub., 2010), p. 41.

31   M. J. McCosker, "Philadelphia and the Genesis of the Motion Picture," *Pennsylvania Magazine of History and Biography*, vol. 65, no. 4 (1941), pp. 406–07.

32   "Australian Theatricals," *Era*, 30 April 1871; "Little All Right," *Ohio Farmer*, 24 January 1874; "Trouble About 'Little All Right,'" *New York Times*, 5 March 1879.

33   "General News," *Sun and Central Press*, 18 December 1872; *Era*, 3 May 1874.

34   *Pall Mall Gazette*, 25 February 1875; "Original Correspondence," *Era*, 22 December 1872.

35   *New York Clipper*, 28 October 1871.

36   "Amusements," *Patriot*, 13 March 1874.

37   Martin, *Chester (and Its Vicinity)*, p. 292.

38   "The Late Professor Risley," *Era*, 21 June 1874; "Death of a Noted Character," *Daily Patriot*, 28 May 1874.

39   "The Drama in America," *Era*, 14 June 1874.

40   *Hartford Daily Courant*, 30 May 1874.

SELECT BIBLIOGRAPHY

A wide variety of books, magazines, and newspapers were used to create this book. Databases were particularly helpful, especially those of nineteenth-century newspapers. Some of the most useful databases are listed below, followed by a traditional, select bibliography.

Databases

American Periodicals Series Online, 1740–1900 (http://www.proquest.com/en-US/catalogs/databases/detail/aps.shtml)

Ancestry.com (http://www.ancestry.com)

Biblioteca Nacional de Espana / Hemeroteca Digital (http://www.bne.es/opencms/es/Catalogos/HemerotecaDigital/index.html)

Bibliothèque nationale de France: Gallica: Bibliothèque numèrique (http://gallica.bnf.fr/)

British Library/British Newspapers (1800–1900) (http://newspapers11.bl.uk/blcs/)

California Digital Newspaper Collection (http://cdnc.ucr.edu/cdnc)

Genealogy Bank (http://www.genealogybank.com)

Google Books (http://books.google.com/)

Holland Historische Kranten: Koninklejke Bibliotheek (http://kranten.kb.nl/)

Internet Archive (http://www.archive.org/index.php)

JSTOR (http://www.jstor.org/)

Library of Congress: The Nineteenth Century in Print (http://lcweb2.loc.gov/ammem/ndlpcoop/moahtml/)

Making of America Project (http://digital.library.cornell.edu/m/moa/ and http://quod.lib.umich.edu/m/moagrp/)

National Diet Library of Japan: Digital Resources (http://dl.ndl.go.jp/)

National Library of Australia: Trove (http://trove.nla.gov.au)

National Library of New Zealand: Papers Past (http://paperspast.natlib.govt.nz/)

National Library of Singapore: Singapore Pages (http://newspapers.nl.sg/)

NewspaperArchive.com (http://newspaperarchive.com/)
The Nineteenth Century Index (http://c19index.chadwyck.com)
Old Fulton New York (http://www.fultonhistory.com)

Books and Magazines

Akune, Iwao. *Saakasu no rekishi* [A history of the circus]. 1977.

Alcock, Rutherford. *The Capital of the Tycoon: A Narrative of a Three Years' Residence in Japan.* London: Longman, Green, Longman, Roberts and Green, 1863.

Altick, Richard D. *The Shows of London.* Cambridge, MA: Belknap Press, 1978.

Asakura, Musei. *Misemono kenkyū.* [A study of misemono]. 4th ed. Kyoto: Shibunkaku Shuppan, 1999 (1928).

Assael, Brenda. *The Circus and Victorian Society.* Victorian Literature and Culture Series. Charlottesville: University of Virginia Press, 2005.

Barnum, P. T., and James W. Cook. *The Colossal P. T. Barnum Reader: Nothing Else Like It in the Universe.* Urbana: University of Illinois Press, 2005.

Barr, Pat. *The Coming of the Barbarians: The Opening of Japan to the West, 1853–1870.* 1st ed. New York: Dutton, 1967.

Beck, Henry Charlton. *Jersey Genesis: The Story of the Mullica River.* New Brunswick, NJ: Rutgers University Press, 1945.

Bennett, Terry; Hugh Cortazzi; and James Hoare. *Japan and the Illustrated London News: Complete Record of Reported Events, 1853–1899.* Folkestone, Kent: Global Oriental, 2006.

Black, John R. *Young Japan. Yokohama and Yedo.* London and Yokohama: Trubner and Company, Kelly and Company, 1880.

Blum, Paul C. *Yokohama in 1872: A Rambling Account of the Community in Which the Asiatic Society of Japan Was Founded.* Tokyo: Asiatic Society of Japan, 1963.

Bru i Turull, Ricard. "El Japó Entra En Escena: La Companyia Imperial I Els Primers Acròbates Japonesos a Barcelona." [Japanese appear on the scene: The Imperial Troupe and the first Japanese acrobats in Barcelona]. *Assaig de Teatre,* vol. 46 (2005), pp. 159–74.

———. *Els orígens del Japonisme a Barcelona* [Origins of Japonisme in Barcelona]. Institut Mon Juïc: Barcelona, 2011.

———. "Japanese Influence on Decorative Arts in Barcelona." *Design Discourse Japan,* vol. 4 (2009), pp. 14–19; 49–52.

———. "Les actuacions de la Companyia Imperial Japonesa," *Els orígens del Japonisme a Barcelona* [Performances of the Imperial Japanese Troupe: Origins of Japonisme in Barcelona]. Institut Món Juïc, Ajuntament de Barcelona, Barcelona, 2011, pp. 199–223.

Chisholm, Marquis. *The Adventures of a Travelling Musician in Australia, China and Japan.* London?: s.n.], 1865.

Clapp, William W. *A Record of the Boston Stage.* Boston [u.a.]: Munroe, 1853.

Clements, Jonathan. *Admiral Togo: Nelson of the East.* London: Haus Pub., 2010.

Cortazzi, Hugh. *Dr. Willis in Japan, 1862–1877: British Medical Pioneer.* London and Dover, NH: Athlone Press, 1985.

————. "Yokohama: Frontier Town 1859–1866." *Asian Affairs*, vol. 17, no. 1 (1986), pp. 3–17.

Cortazzi, Hugh, and Sainsbury Institute for the Study of Japanese Arts and Cultures. *Japan in Late Victorian London: The Japanese Native Village in Knightsbridge and the Mikado, 1885*. Norwich: Sainsbury Institute for the Study of Japanese Arts and Cultures, 2009.

DeMetz, Kaye. "Theatrical Dancing in Nineteenth-Century New Orleans." *Louisiana History: The Journal of the Louisiana Historical Association*, vol. 21, no. 1 (Winter 1980), pp.23–42.

Dickens, Charles. "Hard Times." *Household Words*, no. 228 (August 8, 1854), p. 599.

Dressler, Albert. *California's Pioneer Circus*. San Francisco: printed by H. S. Crocker Company, 1926.

Durant, John, and Alice K. Rand Durant. *Pictorial History of the American Circus*. New York: A. S. Barnes, 1957.

Estavan, Lawrence, and United States Works Project Administration. *Introduction to the Series: Monographs: Stephen C. Massett, Singer, Writer, Showman; Joseph A. Rowe, Pioneer Circus Manager*. San Francisco Theatre Research, vol. 1. San Francisco: W.P.A., 1939.

Evans, Mary. "How Risley Lost at Billiards." *Sports Illustrated*, March 29, 1971.

First and Only Troupe of Japanese Conjurors and Gymnasts That Ever Have Been Allowed to Visit Europe, The: Shanshami-Amingori; or, Marvellous Feats of Top-Spinning ; the Butterfly Illusion. London: Nassau Steam Press, W. S. Johnson, 1867.

Gautier, Théophile. *L'orient*. Paris: G. Charpentier, 1877.

Gautier, Théophile, and Ivor Forbes Guest. *Gautier on Dance*. London and Princeton, NJ: Dance Books; distributed in the USA by Princeton Book, 1986.

Griffis, William Elliot. *The Mikado's Empire*. New ed. New York: Harper, 1883.

Groves, Dana. *New Carlisle*. Chicago: Arcadia, 2010.

Hall, Francis, and F. G. Notehelfer. *Japan through American Eyes: The Journal of Francis Hall, 1859–1866*. Boulder, CO: Westview Press, 2001.

Harte, Bret, and Edith Goodkind Rosenwald. *San Francisco in 1866; Being Letters to the Springfield Republican*. San Francisco: Book Club of California, 1951.

Hayashi, Shigeatsu. "Nakagawa Namigorō oji no danwa" [A Chat with Old Man Nakagawa Namigorō]. *Sokki ihō*, vol. 49 (15 February 1893), pp. 138–41; vol. 50 (17 March 1893), pp. 68–73; vol. 52 (30 May1893), pp. 138–41; vol. 53 (31 July 1893), pp.175–79; vol. 54 (28 October 1893, pp. 242–48.

Humbert, Aimé. *Le Japon Illustré. Ouvrage Contenant 476 Vues, Scènes, Types, Monuments Et Paysages*. 2 vols. Paris: L. Hachette, 1870.

Iinomachi, ed. *Iino chōshi* [A history of Iinomachi]. Vol. 3 (2). Iinomachi, Fukushima Prefecture: Iinomachi, 2005.

Illustrated London News. London: William Little, 1842.

Jando, Dominique; Linda Granfield; and Noel Daniel. *The Circus, 1870s–1950s* In English, German and French. New ed. Köln: Taschen, 2010.

Japan Punch, The. Vol. 1 of 10 vols. Tokyo: Yūshōdō Shoten, 1975.

"Japanese Jugglers, The." *Harper's Weekly: A Journal of Civilization*, June 15 1867.

Jephson, Richard Mounteney, and Edward Pennell Elmhirst, eds. *Our Life in Japan with Illustrations from Photographs by Lord Walter Kerr and Signor Beato and Native Japanese Drawings*. London: Chapman, 1869.

Kaempfer, Engelbert; John Gaspar Scheuchzer; Simon Delboe; Hamond Gibben; and William Ramsden. *The History of Japan: Together with a Description of the Kingdom of Siam, 1690–92.* Glasgow: J. MacLehose and Sons, 1906.

Kahn, E. J. *The Merry Partners: The Age and Stage of Harrigan and Hart.* New York: Random House, 1955.

Kawazoe, Yū. *Edo no misemono* [The misemono of Edo]. Tokyo: Iwanami Shoten, 2000.

———. *Misemono tantei ga iku.* [Detective on the trail of misemono]. Tokyo: Shōbunsha, 2003.

Kishi, Kashirō. *Tsuru wa oi wo wasureru: Ikeda Chikugonokami chōhatsuden* [The crane that forgets to age: the story of Ikeda Chikugonokami]. Ihara City, Okayama Prefecture: Ihara-shi Meiji Hyakunen Kankō Iinkai, 1969.

Kitane, Yutaka, and Yuga Suzuki. *Nihon shoki shinbun zenshū: Hennen fukuseiban* [Collection of early Japanese newspapers: chronological reproductions]. . Vol. 57. Tokyo: Perikansha, 1996.

Koon, Helene. *Gold Rush Performers: A Biographical Dictionary of Actors, Singers, Dancers, Musicians, Circus Performers and Minstrel Players in America's Far West, 1848 to 1869.* Jefferson, NC: McFarland, 1994.

Kovach, John. "Rizurii 'sensei' shōden (zenpen): butai debyū izen no Richard Carlisle (Saakasu gaku tanjō)" [The story of "Professor" Risley (part 1): Richard Carlisle before his theatrical debut (birth of circus studies)]. Edited by Aya Mihara. *Art Times,* no. 6 (July 2010), pp. 4–8.

Lemon, Mark; Henry Mayhew; Tom Taylor; Shirley Brooks; F. C. Burnand; and Owen Seaman. "Punch." London: Punch Publications, 1841–70

Leslie, Peter. *A Hard Act to Follow: A Music Hall Review.* New York: Paddington Press: distributed by Grosset and Dunlap, 1978.

Livermore, H. V. *A New History of Portugal.* Cambridge: Cambridge University Press, 1966.

Lockwood, Charles. *Suddenly San Francisco: The Early Years of an Instant City.* 1st ed. San Francisco: San Francisco Examiner Division of the Hearst Corporation, 1978.

Logan, Olive. *Before the Footlights and Behind the Scenes: A Book about "The Show Business" in All Its Branches: From Puppet Shows to Grand Opera from Mountebanks to Menageries ; from Learned Pigs to Lecturers; from Burlesque Blondes to Actors and Actresses: With Some Observations and Reflections (Original and Reflected) on Morality and Immorality in Amusements: Thus Exhibiting the "Show World" as Seen from within, through the Eyes of the Former Actress, as Well as from without, through the Eyes of the Present Lecturer and Author.* Philadelphia: Parmelee and Company, 1870).

Lord, Elizabeth Laughlin. *Reminiscences of Eastern Oregon.* Portland, OR: The Irwin-Hodson Company, 1903.

MacLellan, J. W. *The Story of Shanghai: From the Opening of the Port to Foreign Trade.* Shanghai: North China Herald, 1889.

Markus, Andrew L. "The Carnival of Edo: Misemono Spectacles from Contemporary Accounts." *Harvard Journal of Asiatic Studies.* Vol. 45, no. 2 (1985), pp. 499–541.

Martin, John Hill. *Chester (and Its Vicinity,) Delaware County, in Pennsylvania; with Genealogical Sketches of Some Old Families, by John Hill Martin, Esq.* Philadelphia [s.n.], 1877.

Massarella, Derek. *A World Elsewhere: Europe's Encounter with Japan in the Sixteenth and Seventeenth Centuries.* New Haven: Yale University Press, 1990.

Matsuyama, Mitsunobu. *Jisshō Nihon no tejinashi* [The real history of Japanese magic]. Tokyo: Tokyodo Shuppan, 2010.

McDermott, John Francis. *The Lost Panoramas of the Mississippi.* Chicago: University of Chicago Press, 1958.

Meggendorfer, Lothar. *International Circus: A Reproduction of the Antique Pop-up Book.* London and New York: Kestrel Books and Viking Press, 1979.

Metz, Kaye De. "Dancing Families in New Orleans' Nineteenth-Century English-Language Theatres." *Louisiana History: The Journal of the Louisiana Historical Association.* Vol. 33, no. 4 (1992), pp. 381–97.

Mihara, Aya. "Bakumatsu ishinki no gaikōkantachi no yokogao: Nihon no misemono-gei wo 'yushutsu' suru'" [Diplomats unmasked: theatre business of exporting Japanese acrobats]. *Engeki gakuronsō* [Treatises on performing arts], no. 10 (March, 2010), pp. 121–53.

———. *Nihonjin tōjō: Seiyō gekijō de enjirareta Edo no misemono* [Enter Japanese: a night in Japan at the opera house]. 1st ed. Tokyo: Shōhakusha, 2008.

———. "Professional Entertainers Abroad and Theatrical Portraits in Hand." Nagasaki University Library. http://hdl.handle.net/10069/23366.

———. "Professor Risley and Japanese Acrobats: Selections from the Diary of Hirohachi Takano, a Manager for the Risley Troupe, During the World Tour of 1866–1869." *Nineteenth Century Theatre.* Vol. 18, no. 1/2 (1990), pp. 62–74.

———. "Ritoru Ooru Raito no zushōgaku: Kaigai sakuhin ni egakareta Nihonjin keigyōshi No Baai" [Iconography of Little "All Right": star acrobats of Japanese and various works of art in the West]. *Geinōshi kenkyū [History of the Performing Arts]*, no. 191 (2010), pp. 26–71

———. "Was It Torture or Tune? Japanese Music in Western Popular Theatre." Unpublished paper. Ohtani Women's University, 2006.

———. "Umi o watatta Nihon no misemono: Ritoru Oururai koto Hamaikari Umekichi" [Japanese acts that crossed the ocean: Little All Right, or Hamaikari Umekichi]. *Misemono wa omoshiroi: Bessatsu taiyō; Nihon no kokoro*, vol. 123 (2003), pp. 38–43.

Mihara, Aya, and Stuart Thayer. "Richard Risley Carlisle, Man in Motion." *Bandwagon*, vol.41, no. 1 (1997), pp. 12–14.

Miyanaga, Takashi. *Purinsu Akitake no Ōshū kikō: Keio 3-nen Pari banpaku shisetsu* [The visit of Prince Akitake to Europe; Emissary to the 1867 Paris Exposition]. Tokyo: Yamakawa Shuppansha, 2000.

———. *Umi o watatta bakumatsu no kyokugeidan: Takano Hirohachi no Bei-Ō manyuki* [Acrobats who went overseas at the end of the shogunate: Takano Hirohachi's travels in America and Europe]. Tokyo: Chūō Kōron Shinsha, 1999.

Miyoshi, Hajime. *Nippon saakasu monogatari: umi o koeta karuwaza kyokugeishitachi.* [The story of circus in Japan: acrobats who went abroad]. Tokyo: Hakusuisha, 1993.

Odell, George Clinton Densmore. *Annals of the New York Stage.* New York: Columbia University Press, 1927.

Ōshima, Mikio. *Umi o watatta saakasu geinin: kosumoporitan Sawada Yutaka no shōgai* [Circus performers who went overseas: the life of Cosmopolitan Sawada Yutaka]. 1st ed. Tokyo: Heibonsha, 1993.

Rimmel, Eugene. *Recollections of the Paris Exhibition of 1867*. London: Chapman and Hall, 1868.

Rodecape, Lois Foster. "Tom Maguire, Napoleon of the Stage." *California Historical Society Quarterly*, vol. 20, no. 4 (1941), pp. 289–314; and vol. 21 (1942), nos. 1, pp. 39–74; 2, pp. 141–82 ; and 3, pp. 239–75.

Saito, Ryū. "Yokohama nishiki-e monogatari (7) Yokohama ni kita Risley saakasu" [The story of Yokohama nishiki-e (7) Risley's circus comes to Yokohama]. *Rekishi Dokuhon*, July 2008, pp. 314–17.

Satow, Ernest Mason. *A Diplomat in Japan*. London: Seeley, Service and Company limited, 1921.

"Sensation Diplomacy in Japan." *Blackwood's Edinburgh Magazine*, vol. 93, no. 570 (April 1863), pp. 397–413.

Shibusawa, Eiichi. *Shibusawa Eiichi taifutsu nikki* [Shibusawa Eiichi's diary in Paris]. Tokyo: Nihon Shiseki Kyokai, 1928.

Slout, William L. *Olympians of the Sawdust Circle: A Biographical Dictionary of the Nineteenth Century American Circus*. Clipper Studies in the Theatre. 1st ed. San Bernardino, CA: Borgo Press, 1998.

Smythe, R. S. "'Professionals' Abroad." *Cornhill Magazine*, February 1871, p. 10.

Speaight, George. *A History of the Circus*. London and San Diego: Tantivy Press; A.S. Barnes, 1980.

Spence, Jonathan D. *God's Chinese Son: The Taiping Heavenly Kingdom of Hong Xiuquan*. 1st ed. New York: W. W. Norton, 1996.

St. Leon, Mark. *Circus: The Australian Story*. Melbourne: Melbourne Books, 2011.

Suzuki Shūichi. "'Hirohachi nikki' to nihonreki-seireki gappi taishyō hyō" [A comparison of dates in «Hirohachi Nikki» with those on the lunar and the solar calendars], *Jinbungaku kenkyūshohō*, vol. 42, March 2009, pp. 51–80.

Takano, Hirohachi. *Hirohachi nikki: Bakumatsu no kyokugeidan kaigai jungyō kiroku*. [The Hirohachi diary: a record of acrobats touring abroad at the end of the shogunate]. Iinomachi, Fukushima Prefecture: Iinomachi Shidankai, 1982.

Takano, Hirohachi, and Shidankai Iinomachi. *Hirohachi Nikki: Bakumatsu no kyokugeidan kaigai jungyō kiroku*. Iinomachi, Fukushima Prefeture): Iinomachi Shidankai, 1977.

Taylor, Bayard, and William Elliot Griffis. *Japan in Our Day*. Illustrated Library of Travel. New York: Scribner, 1892.

Taylor, Justus Hurd. *Joe Taylor, Barnstormer: His Travels, Troubles and Triumphs, During Fifty Years in Footlight Flashes*. New York: William R. Jenkins Company, 1913.

Thayer, Stuart. "Man in Motion: Richard Risley." *Bandwagon*, vol. 41, no. 1 (January–February 1997).

Tokugawa, Akitake, and Masato Miyachi. *Tokugawa Akitake bakumatsu taiō nikki*. [Tokugawa Akitake's diary while in Europe at the end of the shogunate]. Tokyo: Yamakawa Shuppansha, 1999.

Twain, Mark, and Bernard Taper. *Mark Twain's San Francisco*. Santa Clara and Berkeley, CA: Santa Clara University and Heyday Books, 2003.

United States Works Project Administration. *Tom Maguire; Dr. David G. (Yankee) Robinson; M. B. Leavitt*. San Francisco: W.P.A., 1938.

Wallett, W. F., and John Luntley. *The Public Life of W. F. Wallett, the Queen's Jester;*

an *Autobiography of Forty Years' Professional Experience and Travels in the United Kingdom, the United States of America (Including California,) Canada, South America, Mexico, the West Indies, &C.* London [etc.]: Bemrose and Sons [etc.], 1870.

Watkins, James F. "San Francisco." *Overland Monthly and Out West magazine,* 1870.

Watt, Marguerite McCord, and Kathlyn V. Wade. *New Carlisle, The Story of Our Town, 1835–1955.* Laporte, IN: 1956.

Williams, Montagu Stephen; Percy Lefroy; and George Henry Lamson. *Leaves of a Life: Being the Reminiscences of Montagu Williams.* London and New York: Macmillan and Company, 1890.

Winter, Marian Hannah. *The Theatre of Marvels.* American ed. New York: B. Blom, 1964.

———. "Theatre of Marvels." [In]. *Dance Index* 7 (1948), pp. 22–38.

Wirgman, Charles. *The Japan Punch.* 10 vols. Tokyo: Yushodo Booksellers Ltd., 1975.

Wittmann, Matthew W. "Empire of Culture: U.S. Entertainers and the Making of the Pacific Circuit, 1850–1890." University of Michigan, 2010.

Yagishita, Hiroko. "Bakumatsu no pasupōto" [Bakumatsu era passports]. Infosta Forum No.70. *The Journal of Information Science and Technology Association,* vol. 55, no. 2 (2 February 2005), p. 103.

Yasuoka, Shōtarō. *Daiseikimatsu saakasu.* [The circus at the end of the millennium]. Tokyo: Asahi Shinbunsha, 1988.

Yeamans, Annie. "Sixty-Five Years on the Stage." *The Green Book Album: A Magazine of the Passing Show* (July 1911).

Yokohama Kaikō Shiryōkan. *Yokohama mono no hajime kō* [An Introduction to Yokohama]. 3rd ed. Yokohama City: Yokohama Kaikō Shiryō Fukyū Kyōkai, 2010.

INDEX